Online
Information
Retrieval

Concepts, Principles, and Techniques

This is a volume in
LIBRARY AND INFORMATION SCIENCE
A Series of Monographs and Textbooks
Consulting Editors: HAROLD BORKO and ELAINE SVENONIUS,
University of California, Los Angeles

The complete listing of books in this series is available from the Publisher upon request.

Online
Information
Retrieval

Concepts, Principles, and Techniques

Stephen P. Harter
School of Library and Information Science
Indiana University
Bloomington, Indiana

ACADEMIC PRESS, INC.
Harcourt Brace Jovanovich, Publishers
San Diego New York Boston
London Sydney Tokyo Toronto

ACADEMIC PRESS, INC.
1250 Sixth Avenue, San Diego, California 92101

United Kingdom Edition published by
ACADEMIC PRESS INC. (LONDON) LTD.
24–28 Oval Road, London NW1 7DX

Library of Congress Cataloging in Publication Data

Harter, Stephen P.
    Online information retrieval.

    (Library and information science)
    Includes index.
    1. On-line data processing.   2. Information
retrieval.   I. Title.   II. Series.
QA76.55.H37   1986   025.5'24   85-26714
ISBN 0–12–328455–4 (hardcover) (alk. paper)
ISBN 0–12–328456–2 (paperback) (alk. paper)

Printed in the United States of America
91   92   93   94   9 8 7 6 5 4 3 2

Contents

v

Chapter 4

REFERENCE DATABASES

Chapter 5

THE PROCESS OF ONLINE SEARCHING

Chapter 6

EFFECTIVE COMMUNICATION

Chapter 7

SEARCH STRATEGIES AND HEURISTICS

Chapter 8

SOURCE DATABASES

Chapter 9

TRENDS, PROBLEMS, AND ISSUES

Preface

Online searching has been an important tool of library and information science for some years. During this time, several excellent books have been written that introduce the reader to various technical aspects of online searching, such as how to select a terminal, establish costs and charging policies, manage an online search service, identify important databases, and obtain training. Other books have been written that concentrate on the command language of one or more systems. Still others are directories of databases or search services. With perhaps one or two exceptions, these books devote relatively little space to concepts and principles related to the preparation, conduct, or interpretation of an online search. The purpose of the present book is to concentrate on these fundamentals.

A considerable literature devoted to online searching has appeared in specialized journals such as *Online, Online Review,* and *Database Magazine*; more general journals such as *Special Libraries* and *Journal of the American Society for Information Science*; the proceedings of various online conferences; and books. Curiously, online searching and its literature seem to have developed almost independently of the discipline of information storage and retrieval and its own literature, in spite of their many close conceptual relationships. The present book relates central concepts, principles, and techniques of information storage and retrieval to the practice of online searching, with the ultimate goal of helping the reader learn *how to think about* online information retrieval. Thus the book can be very roughly viewed as the Boolean intersection of the two fields.

I believe that online information retrieval is a problem-solving activity of a high order, requiring knowledge and understanding for consistently good results. Not all searches are difficult enough to deserve this characterization. But to satisfy a complex information need efficiently and effectively, understanding of basic concepts and principles is required. This book concentrates on an elucidation of these concepts and principles. It does not attempt to duplicate material in books that emphasize other aspects of online searching.

Chapter 1 introduces the reader to the book's organization and to the overall search process. Online information retrieval is viewed as a communication process between an information seeker and an information store, with a professional intermediary as a possible third party. Chapter 2 examines the nature of languages as they affect this communication process. Natural languages, controlled vocabularies, system command languages, and citation indexing "languages" are explored, compared, and contrasted. Chapter 3 examines concepts of database structure, file structure, sort sequence, and parsing rules, and how these are related to the search process. Boolean logic, field searching, word proximity searching, and truncation are also discussed in terms of this conceptual framework.

Chapter 4 discusses characteristics of reference databases, with special emphasis on principles for evaluation and selection. Chapter 5 examines the online searching process as an intellectual activity, and reviews research that has studied this process. Chapter 6, "Effective Communication," treats the evaluation of search output from several perspectives: that of the end-user, the searcher, and the search system. The reference interview is also discussed in depth in this chapter, and the concepts of relevance and pertinence are introduced.

Overall strategies or approaches to online information retrieval are discussed in Chapter 7, including major facet strategies, cited reference strategies, and approaches to non-subject, fact, and multiple database searching. The chapter concludes with an extended treatment of the most important heuristics, or tactics, for modifying a search online in order to achieve specific outcomes. Chapter 8 introduces source databases, again with an emphasis on evaluation. The book concludes with a discussion of important trends, problems, and issues in online information retrieval, including, among others, using a microcomputer, gateway systems, end-user search systems, legal issues, and a consideration of the responsibilities of professional search specialists.

A theme running continuously throughout this book is the notion of evaluation. The need for critical analysis and review—of databases, command languages, system responses, relevance and pertinence of retrieval results to an information need, and perhaps especially of oneself, as a communicator, planner, and searcher—is in one sense the central message of this book. If the book helps to make the reader more sensitive to these concerns and provides a conceptual foundation on which evaluation can take place, then its goals have been met.

The overall perspective of this book is that of the system user—the searcher—rather than the designer of online systems. It is intended to be read by students, practicing librarians, and information specialists who want to add to their knowledge and understanding of the process of online information retrieval and of issues related to this process. It should be suitable as a textbook to support classes in schools of library and information science, and in draft form it has been so used, in the School of Library and Information Science at Indiana University. Finally, end-users who are willing to devote the time and effort required to master the material should also find the book helpful to their understanding, although as noted, the primary orientation of the text is toward information professionals.

DIALOGs Version 2, and other command languages are occasionally used to illustrate concepts and principles of file structures, parsing rules, system defaults, syntax rules, sort orders, and the like. But it should be stressed that the book does not attempt to teach DIALOG or another command language, nor is prior knowledge of a command language required to read it. However, the book has been organized so that it can be used effectively with the simultaneous study of one or more command languages, using system manuals or other sources, if the reader wishes.

The book includes many examples illustrating the material presented, and each chapter concludes with a "Problems" section, intended to stimulate further thought and understanding. An extended glossary of technical terms is also provided.

I am grateful to my former students at Indiana University and the University of South Florida, who directly and indirectly encouraged me to write this book.

Chapter 1

Introduction to Online
Information Retrieval

1.1 THE INFORMATION RETRIEVAL PROBLEM

The graphic record of humanity, as represented by its accumulated data, information, knowledge, and wisdom, numbers in the billions of pieces. Although interesting and useful distinctions between data, information, knowledge, and wisdom have been suggested [1], the differences between them is not central to the main thrust of this book and we shall not deal with them. The word 'information' will be used generically, to refer to raw data, facts, knowledge as it is reflected in a technical or scholarly literature, numerical projections or analyses, and even wisdom. An important criterion is that it should be *recorded*—as ink on paper, images on film, sequences of punches on paper tape, digital signals stored in a computer's memory, or in many other forms.

Assume that a person who is working on a practical, scholarly, or scientific project has a need for a particular piece of information. How can this data be found, from among the billions of other bits of the accumulated human record that do not relate to the problem at hand? This is the *information retrieval problem*—a problem that must be nearly as old as the discovery of writing itself.

For simplicity, suppose that the total available stock of human records that might conceivably apply to an information problem is available for examination in a central collection. A solution to the information retrieval problem is then easy to conceptualize. It is simply this: to examine the items in the collection, one by one, accepting some items but rejecting most, until each item has been examined. Through the application of this procedure,

1

all those materials, and only those materials, that relate to the problem of interest will have been selected.

Any objections that may be raised to this scheme are practical rather than theoretical. Clearly a perfect theoretical solution to the information retrieval problem has been presented; we have located all and only the items in the collection that are helpful to the user. However, it is equally clear that for any but the smallest of collections the time required to carry out the procedure will be unacceptably great. This leads to the need for developing information retrieval systems.

An *information retrieval system* is a device interposed between a potential user of information and the information collection itself. For a given information problem, the purpose of the system is to capture wanted items and to filter out unwanted items. This goal is pragmatic: to make acceptable the time required to satisfy the information need, or to conclude that it cannot be satisfied. In a town's public library, for example, the card catalog or online catalog is an information retrieval system applied to a local collection of books and other materials. The indexing and abstracting journal *Psychological Abstracts* that is found in many university libraries can be regarded as an information retrieval system that assists a user with a "collection" of published materials relating to the discipline of psychology. However, as we intend the term to be understood, information retrieval is a concept that applies to systems and functions outside as well as within the framework of traditional libraries. According to this broader view, the human brain itself can be viewed as an enormously powerful information retrieval system. More directly, various products of the mind are designed with the information retrieval function in mind: a card file of recipes, an envelope stuffed with income tax receipts, a set of personnel records stored in metal drawers, and an electronic computer [2].

It should be observed in passing that because of the ambiguity of language and because of the translation between natural, human languages and the artificial languages required by most information retrieval processes, such systems necessarily will be imperfect. Indeed, a central, recurring theme of this book deals with the nature of these imperfections and how the user can best deal with them. Once the ideal solution of examining every item in a collection for relevancy has been discarded, it will normally be necessary to accept less than perfect retrieval results. This idea will be explored more fully in subsequent chapters.

1.2 ONLINE SEARCHING

We now move from general considerations to the type of system that is the focus of this book. An *online* information retrieval system is a computer and associated hardware—terminals, communication lines and links, modems and disk drives—as well as complex software packages that carry out storage and retrieval functions on databases. Databases are collections of information that exist in machine-readable form, that is, in a digital form in which they can be processed by computers and other data processing equipment. In an online interactive mode of computer use the system user is in direct and continuous communication with the host computer, and is able to react to and interact with the system. In other words, the computer and the user together sustain a human/computer dialog.

Some of the earliest examples of online information retrieval systems were designed by commercial airlines to store and retrieve reservation data. Because of the volume of transactions and the number of terminals required, large-scale applications such as these require super minicomputers or mainframe computers. Smaller scale storage and retrieval applications such as business inventory control, small document files constructed and maintained with database management systems, or a circulation or serials control system for a library can be carried out on minicomputers or microcomputers.

This book takes an even more restricted view of information retrieval. We limit ourselves principally to consideration of publicly accessible online information retrieval systems—called *vendors* or *search services*—available through dial-up computer and communications facilities. The phrase *online information retrieval*, or *online searching*, will be used to refer to a process in which a human being uses a computer terminal to interact with a search service, in an attempt to satisfy an information need. Note that the searcher may or may not personally possess the information need motivating the search. In the former case the searcher is also the *end-user* of the information retrieved; in the latter the searcher functions as an intermediary—a librarian or other information specialist. In either case the result of the process is the retrieval of needed data or information from *databases*.

A *database* is a file of individual records in machine-readable form. Records in the database might comprise facts or figures, bibliographic citations or abstracts, or even the full texts of encyclopedia articles, scholarly papers or research reports. The concept of record is a function of the type of database being considered, and will be examined more fully in later chapters.

There might be many purposes for wanting to carry out an online search. One might be looking for specific pieces of data or facts: e.g., the correct bibliographic information associated with a book or research report, properties of a given chemical substance, the population of Afghanistan in 1960, or the telephone number and address of all Asian firms exporting toys for U.S. consumption. Perhaps the information need deals exclusively with numeric data, and requires the retrieval of data and the computation of descriptive or inferential statistics or projections based on the data. Or, one may be interested in knowledge—in a literature associated with a specific topic within a discipline or with a scientific or scholarly research question. This last class of search problems is more amorphous and ambiguous than the others; it is by no means always clear what one's information need really is, how to best express the information need in words if one does clearly recognize it, or how to tell when it has been satisfied.

Figure 1.1 shows the relationship between searcher and search service. The searcher, motivated by an information need, sits in office or home at a computer terminal, or personal computer that is functioning as a terminal, and accesses the computer of the search service. Communication between the terminal and the host computer is carried out through public telephone systems and usually through so-called *packet-switching* telecommunication networks such as Tymnet, Telenet, and Uninet [3].

The search system typically resides on a remote mainframe computer or large minicomputer, with databases stored on magnetic disk systems that permit a computer reasonably rapid access to files (normally a few seconds). The searcher communicates with the system using a *command language*, or by selecting items from a *menu* of choices. Digital signals are produced by the searcher on the keyboard of a remote terminal, converted to analog signals by a *modem*, and are sent along communications lines to the host computer, where they are converted back to digital signals. The system software then interprets the signals as commands, performs the commands, and provides feedback to the searcher. In this way indexes to the databases may be examined, sample records printed or displayed, and various techniques and approaches for retrieving the wanted information explored. Thus a dialog can take place between the searcher and the information retrieval system. Eventually, one hopes, this dialog will lead to the retrieval of data, information, or a source of knowledge that will satisfy the information need motivating the search.

Our fundamental interest in this book is on the act of online information retrieval and on factors directly affecting the search process. Several excellent introductions to online searching have been published that explore matters introduced only in a general way in the remainder of this chapter [4]. The reader is referred to one of these texts or other sources for more detailed discussions of such topics as telecommunications, costs and charging policies, how to select terminal equipment or log onto search systems, details of the command languages of particular vendors, and how to set up and manage an online reference service in a library or information center. While there will necessarily be occasional reference in this book to these topics, they will be discussed only insofar as they directly affect the search process—the planning of strategies and tactics, particular characteristics of databases and search systems that affect searching, the execution of searches online, the analytical process demanded of the search specialist, and the interactive behaviors and responses characterizing the dialog between searcher and machine.

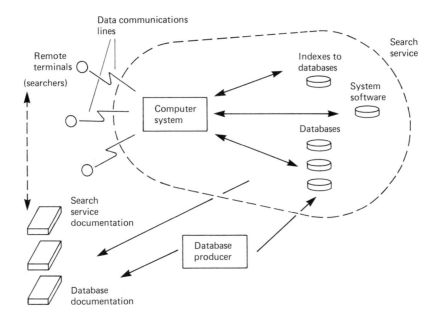

Figure 1.1   Online information retrieval.

1.3   DATABASES

There are several directories of databases and search services that can be consulted to obtain current information regarding the content and characteristics of databases and services available to the general public for online searching. Among these are the *Directory of Online Information Resources*, the *Datapro Directory of Online Services, Computer-Readable Data Bases: A Directory and Data Sourcebook,* and the *Directory of Online Databases* [5]. The growth in the number of databases has been remarkable. Martha Williams reported that in 1965 there were fewer than 20 databases publicly available for information retrieval purposes, and that in 1975 this figure had increased to more than 300 [6]. Nine years later, the *Directory of Online Databases* reported no fewer than 2453 databases generated by 1189 database producers, and accessed by 362 online search services [7]. The criteria for inclusion in the *Directory* were that the database must be accessible online, must be *publicly* available, and must be searchable through a telecommunications link to an online search service or network.

We will adopt the taxonomy developed by Cuadra Associates to distinguish among several types of databases. These are listed and briefly defined in Table 1.1. *Reference Databases*, including *bibliographic* and *referral* databases as subclasses, contain representations or surrogates of existing sources of data, information, or knowledge; they refer the searcher to other, more complete, sources. Records in bibliographic databases contain clues concerning the intellectual content and physical characteristics of pieces of the graphic or printed record of humanity—journal articles, research reports, patents, books, etc. Referral databases lead one to sources other than print materials—persons, organizations, research projects, forms of non-print media, etc.

Reference databases attempt to distill the essential characteristics of primary sources, using conceptual and analytical skills and techniques of cataloging, classification, and indexing from the library and information science professions. The result of these efforts is a shorter, much more succinct surrogate of the original. Unfortunately, a loss of information and distortion of meaning of the original inevitably accompanies the conceptual analysis process, a problem that must be treated most carefully in the search process.

Source databases are primary sources of data or information, composed of the full or complete texts of the information in question, and including materials prepared specifically for distribution by electronic means. There is no distillation or loss of information in a source database, and a searcher has access to the entire available record, whether that be an encyclopedia or newspaper article, properties of certain chemicals, or particular demographic data for citizens of the State of Indiana from 1940 to the present. Source databases can be classified into three subclasses: *numeric, textual-numeric*, and *full text* databases. Table 1.1 discusses and provides examples of each of these types. There are now many more publicly available source databases than reference databases, although this is a relatively new phenomenon. Table 1.2 reports the results of a random sample drawn from the *Directory of Online Databases* [8]. More than 55% of the databases in the sample were source databases, while only 34% were reference databases. The inclusion of computer software in the category of source databases will swell this large class even further in future editions of the *Directory*.

Some databases have hard-copy (print) counterparts that can be found in many public, academic, and special libraries and information centers. Indeed, many databases have found their way into machine-readable form as a necessary by-product of modern printing technologies that are increasingly computerized. Thus printed indexing and abstracting journals such as *Psychological Abstracts* or *Current Index to Journals in Education* historically were available in machine-readable form only because the computer was used in the typesetting process. As online information retrieval continues

TABLE 1.1
Taxonomy of Machine-Readable Databases*

REFERENCE DATABASES—representations of and references to primary sources. May include abstracts or summaries. Subclasses include:

BIBLIOGRAPHIC DATABASES—the primary sources are published or unpublished documents (print format). May include abstracts. Examples are:

BIOSIS PREVIEWS. Producer: BioSciences Information Service. Contains more than three million references to published works in life science subjects. 1969 to present.

MEDLINE. Producer: U.S. National Library of Medicine. Contains more than four million references to published works in the broad field of biomedicine. 1964 to present.

SOCIAL SCISEARCH. Producer: Institute for Scientific Information. Contains more than one million references to articles published in 1500 journals in the social sciences and selected articles from the natural, physical, and biomedical sciences. 1972 to present.

ERIC. Producer: National Institute of Education. Contains more than 500,000 references to the journal and fugitive literature in the field of education. 1966 to present.

CA SEARCH. Producer: Chemical Abstracts Service. Contains more than five million references to the literature of chemistry and its applications. 1967 to present.

REFERRAL DATABASES—the primary sources are persons, organizations, pieces of research in progess, audiovisual materials, etc. Examples are:

ELECTRONIC YELLOW PAGES. Producer: Market Data Retrieval, Inc. In several files, these databases are the machine- readable versions of yellow page entries from 4800 U.S. telephone books. Current directories only.

TRADE OPPORTUNITIES. Producer: U.S. Department of Commerce. Contains approximately 70,000 records of live purchase requests by the international market for U.S. goods and services. 1977 to present.

DEVELOP. Producer: Control Data Corp. Contains over 15000 descriptions of products, services, and assistance available to developing countries. 1979 to date.

SOURCE DATABASES—primary sources of data or information, containing the full or complete text found in the original source. Also includes materials prepared specifically for electronic distribution. Subclasses include:

NUMERIC DATABASES—original numeric or statistical data, such as financial or census data, results of a research study, etc. Often in the form of time series. Examples are:

DEFENSE DATA BANK. Producer: Data Resources, Inc. Contains 5000 time series relating to U.S. Department of Defense spending and costs.

U.S. AGRICULTURE. Producer: Chase Econometrics/Interactive Data. Contains 1100 weekly, monthly, quarterly, and annual time series supplied by the U.S. Department of Agriculture. Includes prices received and paid by farmers, farm income, consumer and wholesale prices, feed grain prices, etc. 1950 to date.

PTS TIME SERIES. Producer: Predicasts, Inc. Coverage includes production, consumption, price, and usage statistics for agriculture, mining, manufacturing, service industries, and general economic and demographic data, both U.S. and international. Years vary, but earliest date is 1957.

TEXTUAL–NUMERIC DATABASES—containing fields of mixed textual and numeric data. Includes dictionary or handbook data. Examples are:

CHEMSEARCH. Producer: DIALOG Information Retrieval Service, using data provided by Chemical Abstracts Service. Includes all chemical substances cited in the most recent six issues of *Chemical Abstracts.*

DISCLOSURE II. Producer: Disclosure, Inc. Information extracted from reports filed with the U.S. Securities and Exchange Commission by approximately 9000 publicly owned companies. Current.

(continues)

TABLE 1.1 (*continued*)

U.S. EXPORTS. Producer: DIALOG Information Retrieval Service, using data provided by the U.S. Bureau of the Census. Time series of statistics collected on exports of merchandise from the United States to other countries. 1978 to present.

FULL TEXT DATABASES—original textual material belonging to primary source items, such as encyclopedia, court decision, newspaper, or journal articles. Examples are:

ACADEMIC AMERICAL ENCYCLOPEDIA. Producer: Grolier Electronic Publishing, Inc. Contains 32,000 general encyclopedia articles aimed at high school and college students and interested adults. 1980 to present.

HARVARD BUSINESS REVIEW. Producer: John Wiley & Sons, Inc. under an agreement with the Harvard Business Review. Contains all articles published in the *Harvard Business Review* since 1971.

CHRONOLOG NEWSLETTER. Producer: DIALOG Information Retrieval Service. The online version of the monthly news publication of DIALOG. 1981 to present.

---

*The classification is from Cuadra Associates' *Directory of Online Databases* 5(1) (Fall 1983).

to increase in volume, we can expect machine-readable versions of databases, to have more and more value in their own right, and even for databases to exist solely in electronic form. For the present, valuable insights concerning online databases can often be gained by study of the print version of the database prior to a search. Table 1.3 lists several examples of machine-readable databases and their print counterparts.

This brief introduction to databases available for online searching should be adequate to provide an initial background. Important characteristics, search problems, and evaluative criteria associated with each major class of databases will be discussed in separate chapters later in the book.

TABLE 1.2
Relative Proportions of Databases*

Type of database	Percentage of total
Source databases	
full text	16.0%
numeric	29.8
textual/numeric	9.0
software	0.5
(total)	55.3%
Reference databases	
referral	11.2%
bibliographic	23.4
(total)	34.6%
Mixed types (more than one)	10.1%

*Percentages were computed on the basis of a random sample of 188 databases drawn from the listings in Cuadra Associates, Inc. *Directory of Online Databases* 6 (No. 1) (Fall 1984).

TABLE 1.3
Selected Databases and Their Print Counterparts*

Database	Print Counterpart
AGRICOLA	Bibliography of Agriculture
BIOSIS (PREVIEWS)	Biological Abstracts
	Biological Abstracts/RRM
BOOKS IN PRINT	Books in Print
CA SEARCH	Chemical Abstracts
CIS INDEX	Index to the Publications of the United States Congress
COMPENDEX	Engineering Index
ERIC	Current Index to Journals in Education
	Resources in Education
FEDERAL REGISTER	Federal Register
HISTORICAL ABSTRACTS	Historical Abstracts
INSPEC	Physics Abstracts
	Electrical and Electronic Abstracts
	Computer and Control Abstracts
MEDLINE	Abridged Index Medicus
PSYCINFO	Psychological Abstracts
SCISEARCH	Science Citation Index

*A machine-readable database may not exactly coincide with its print counterpart. In order to address differences in organization, content, or accessibility for a particular database as it is possible to search *through a given vendor*, the detailed description of that database, as it is described in the appropriate vendor documentation, should be consulted.

1.4 SEARCH SERVICES

A search service or vendor of online search services is an organization that provides clients or information specialists with online access to databases in machine-readable form. The search service acquires, or in some cases, produces, databases that it believes will be used by its clientele. It writes and maintains software systems that permit the searching of these databases. It leases or purchases and maintains large computers and auxiliary equipment, and writes documentation describing how its databases can most efficiently and effectively be searched using its system.

Most vendors are commercial organizations. All charge for the services provided. Normally a major portion of this charge is for the time taken to carry out a given search, usually measured in fractions of *connect hours*, that is, by the amount of time the searcher's terminal has been directly connected to the host computer. For example, the ERIC database on the DIALOG search service costs $25 per connect hour at the standard rate.

Readers from academic or commercials environments who are perhaps used to charges for computer use being based on the actual time expended by the host computer's central processing unit (sometimes called CPU time) should carefully note this difference. Charging by connect hours penalizes a searcher for wasting time—or simply thinking—online. This fact has important implications for how efficient online information retrieval must be conducted. It suggests that, insofar as is possible, searchers should plan their work as completely as possible before connecting to the search service computer. It also suggests that actions taken by online searchers should be swift and decisive, responsive to system feedback, and as likely to achieve the desired results as is possible.

Although applications of online systems to information retrieval were demonstrated and tested experimentally in the 1950's and 1960's, it was not until the early 1970's that the availability and cost of appropriate technologies, i.e., computer time-sharing, remote terminal equipment, and communications capability, made large scale information retrieval feasible [9]. Among the earliest systems were Lockheed's DIALOG, the System Development Corporation's ORBIT, and the National Library of Medicine's MED-LINE. A listing of a few major search services as well as a characterization of the type of databases to which they provide access and the clientele they serve is given in Table 1.4. The *Directory of Online Databases* listed a total of 362 vendors of online services in Fall, 1984, but the great majority of these have a somewhat narrow focus and are not widely used compared to those appearing in Table 1.4 [10].

The distinction between search services and database producers should be noted. Although sometimes a database producer is also a search service (as with Lexis and Westlaw, the National Library of Medicine, and OCLC Inc.), the majority of search services do not produce most of the databases to which they provide access. Rather, motivated by economic factors, the commercial search services acquire the databases from which they believe they can make an eventual profit. Some databases can be accessed through several search services, as is the case with ERIC, Medline, the Academic American Encyclopedia, and BIOSIS. Other databases may have an exclusive relationship with a single search service. Still others, such as databases produced by the Institute for Scientific Information and The National Library of Medicine, may be offered through a search service operated by the database producer but may also be accessed through other search services such as BRS and SDC.

1.5   SEARCH SPECIALISTS AND CLIENTS

The focus taken in this book is on factors affecting the online information retrieval process. Often this process involves both *search specialists* and *end-users*. It has been noted that the searcher may in fact also be an end-user—that is, the individual with the information need. End-user searching

TABLE 1.4
Some Major Search Services*

Search Service	Nature of Services Offered
Bibliographic Retrieval Services (BRS)	Offers access to more than 80 databases, principally referral and bibliographic. Searched mainly by academic and information specialists; end-users.
Compuserve Information Corporation	More than 200 databases provide access to popular reference and source information such as advertising, advice, columnists, news, business information, sports, weather, shopping, travel advisory, and numerous other consumer and executive services. End-users.
Control Data Corp./ Business Information Services	More than 20 source databases in business and economics. Special librarians and other information specialists.
DIALOG Information Services, Inc.	More than 170 databases, mainly referral and bibliographic. Academic and special librarians and other information specialists; end-users.
Dow Jones & Co., Inc.	More than 15 reference and source databases providing factual data on news, current market quotations, financial statistics. Special librarians and other information specialists; end-users.
Mead Data Central	More than 30 reference and source databases related to legal research. Law librarians; end-users.
National Library of Medicine (NLM)	More than 20 databases dealing with medical research and practice. Searched in medical schools, hospitals, and other medical facilities by medical librarians; end-users.
The Source	More than 40 databases provide access to reference and source information such as advertising, advice, columnists, news, sports, weather, as well as other services. End-users.
System Development Corporation (SDC Information Service)	More than 60 databases, mainly referral and bibliographic. Academic and special librarians and other search specialists; end-users.
I.P. Sharp Associates, Ltd.	More than 170 source databases related to business and economics. Special librarians and other information specialists.

*Data are drawn from Cuadra Associates, Inc. *Directory of Online Databases* 6 (No. 1) (Fall 1984).

is increasing as search services such as Compuserve and the Source vie for an audience interested in sources of popular data and information.

Moreover, established vendors of scientific and scholarly information and data, such as DIALOG and BRS, have expanded their services to appeal to direct searching by a mass popular audience. DIALOG's "Knowledge Index" and "BRS After Dark," both introduced in early 1983, represent direct attempts to market online search services to a growing population of personal computer owners, although neither system includes the powerful and sophisticated search features available in the parent system used by search specialists. *Gateway systems*—microcomputer interfaces between host search systems and the microcomputer/terminal of the end-user—are also increasing the extent of end-user searching. These ideas are discussed more fully in Chapter 9.

However, despite an inevitable increase in end-user searching, it is likely that most online information retrieval will continue to be carried out by intermediaries, at least for complex, difficult information needs, for the same reasons that most of us leave other specialized and complex tasks to the experts in our society. There may come a time when knowledge-based expert systems—computer programs functioning as search specialists—will be able to handle most simple searches well. However, search intermediaries promise to play an important role in online information retrieval for the foreseeable future.

Search specialists can be found in libraries of all kinds, but are located especially in college and university libraries and in the information centers and other special libraries associated with business and industrial organizations, law firms, and medical establishments. Some search specialists are freelance entrepreneurs, in business for themselves and actively marketing their services to special user populations. Clients of online information retrieval search specialists include undergraduate and graduate students and faculty in academic libraries, and scientists, engineers, businessmen, doctors, lawyers, and many others using special libraries and information centers to help satisfy their information needs.

A complex and powerful tool is most efficiently wielded by one who not only possesses an aptitude for and interest in the work, but also has been educated in the concepts and principles underlying the design of the tool and who frequently practices and hones the skills required in its use. Specialists in online information retrieval are no exception to this generalization. As intermediaries between end-users and search systems, they play an important role in the solution of the information problems of their clients.

Unfortunately, there is an obvious difficulty with the client/intermediary relationship that arises from the necessity for the information problem to be accurately communicated to and understood by the search specialist, if good results are to be achieved. If the search problem is conceptually complex, or if communication problems occur at one or more levels, a significant loss or distortion of information can occur. This could result, in the worst case, in the solution of a different information problem than that initially posed. The question of communication between searcher, system, and end-user is explored more fully later in the chapter.

1.6 INTRODUCTION TO THE SEARCH PROCESS

Given an online information retrieval system and a searcher, who may or may not be the end-user, the search process can be broken into discrete components, to be carried out roughly in the order given. These are

1. Understand the information need
2. Formulate search objectives
3. Select one or more databases and search systems
4. Identify major concepts and their interrelationships
5. Select an overall approach or strategy for attacking the information problem
6. Identify a variety of ways to express the concepts in words, phrases, symbols, etc.
7. Identify the fields of the records that will be searched in the databases selected
8. Translate decisions made in steps (2)–(7) into formal statements expressed in the command language of the search system
9. For each of the steps (2)–(7), consider and plan alternatives in case initial attempts do not meet search objectives
10. Logon to the search system of choice and enter the initial search statement formulated in (8)
11. Evaluate the intermediate results against the search objectives
12. Iterate. That is, on the basis of the results of the evaluation obtained in (11), and considering the alternatives planned in step (9), as well as new ideas obtained while online, on the basis of system feedback, decide whether to print the results and stop, or go on. One might return to any of the steps, perhaps even to step (1). The process continues until satisfactory results are obtained.

These steps will be discussed more completely in subsequent chapters. For now, it should be observed that, although the sequence of steps presented is roughly descriptive of most searches, they are closely related to one another in non-obvious ways. For example, although one's selection of a database certainly must precede the selection of vocabulary elements and fields to be searched in this database, considerations relating to vocabulary and search-able fields may themselves affect one's initial choice of database. To take another example, even one's search objectives (step (2)) should be affected by what is possible to achieve in a given database and search system. Thus the steps (1)–(12) should not be regarded in a linear, algorithmic manner. Even though it suits a pedagogical purpose to list the "steps" in this partic-ular order, we suggest that for best results, a more holistic approach is needed.

Central to several of the steps in the search process is the concept of com-munication, whether this be binary communication between host computer and user terminal or verbal communication between end-user and search spe-cialist. We turn now to a detailed consideration of this assertion.

1.7 COMMUNICATION AND INFORMATION RETRIEVAL

It has been stated that communication is not only the essence of what we mean by human; it is a property of life itself in its many manifestations [11]. Certainly communication is central to effective information retrieval.

Figure 1.2 illustrates a simplified view of information retrieval through an intermediary—a search specialist. The intermediary, normally using an interactive, conversational approach, seeks to understand the information need of the client. Satisfied that the search problem is understood, the searcher prepares an approach—a strategy, or plan—for seeking the information in one or more databases. The database selection process itself may be diffi-cult. Criteria for database evaluation and selection are discussed in depth in Chapters 4 and 8. As part of the database evaluation, selection, and search planning processes, search system and database documentation may need to be extensively consulted. Eventually, satisfied with the preparation, the searcher enters the system, and interactively queries one or more databases, roughly following the steps discussed in the previous section of this chapter. Following the completion of the search, the results, consisting of printed cita-tions, abstracts, full texts, numerical data, statistics, etc., are given to the client, who evaluates the results. Usually, at this point, the process is complete.

Figure 1.2 actually describes two communication processes, the first between a person with an information need and a search specialist and the second between the search specialist and an information retrieval system. Warren Weaver, generalizing from Claude Shannon's concept of informa-tion theory, distinguished between three levels of communication: *technical, semantic,* and *effective* [12]. In the context of online information retrieval, technical communication refers to *data*, semantic communication to the *mean-ing* of these data, and effective communication to the *behavior* of the search

Figure 1.2   Simplified view of information retrieval through an intermediary.

specialist and how well it addresses the true information need of the client. We will adopt the Shannon and Weaver model to our discussion of client/intermediary communication as well as searcher/system communication. Both processes will be examined more closely, beginning with the dialog between the searcher and the system.

The communication process between a search specialist and an end-user or client is illustrated in Figure 1.3. It is assumed that the client has an underlying need and wishes to search an information retrieval system, through an intermediary, for data or information that will partially or completely satisfy that need. This need and the actions finally taken by the searcher to satisfy it, are at the pragmatic, or effective level of communication. At this final step, one is concerned with whether or how well the information need has been satisfied by the actions of the searcher. But before effective communication can take place, a foundation must be laid with accurate semantic and technical communication.

Technical communication deals with the communication of data. Accurate

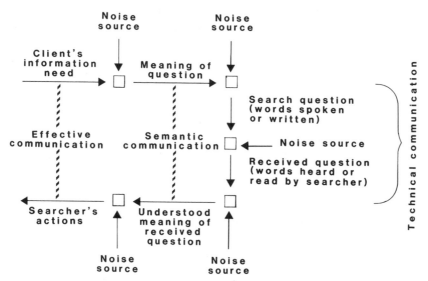

Figure 1.3   Communication between client and search intermediary (following Shannon and Weaver).

technical communication between a client and a search specialist takes place when the searcher receives the exact verbal or written data that was communicated by the client. These data take the form of sensory impressions received by the eye or ear of the searcher and subsequently processed. For written search requests, communication failures can take place through sloppy or smeared handwriting. More often, the search negotiation process is a verbal dialog, in which technical communication failures are speech data not transmitted accurately to the ear of the searcher. Causes of such failure might include background noise, an unfamiliar accent, or slurring of words. If important words spoken or written by a client are not perceived accurately by the search specialist, semantic and effective communication cannot occur, except by accident.

Assuming that technical communication between search specialist and client has taken place accurately, that is, that the words transmitted were the words received (and perceived), another hurdle must be cleared. The searcher must, through careful questioning and good interpersonal communication skills, accurately identify the meaning of the words used, as intended by the client. Unless searcher and client share a common meaning for the data transmitted, the searcher's attempts to express concepts in alternative ways will be frustrated. Since a computer searches for *words* and not *concepts*, one must express important concepts in as many ways as possible, especially for comprehensive searches. The searcher who does not understand a concept of interest will be unable to do an effective job of finding or evaluating alternative ways of expressing that concept in words.

Finally, communication between searcher and client may fail even if accurate technical and semantic communication have occurred. Every reference librarian knows that library patrons who ask for help do not always ask for what they need or even want. People with information needs will often try to restate the need in the way that they perceive the information retrieval system will be able to best handle it.

For example, a student's request for information about Florida animals might reflect an actual information need concerning the mating habits of alligators or environmental concerns related to water birds of the Everglades. The student has restated the need under the mistaken impression that this will help the retrieval process. In fact, if an effective *reference interview*, or *question negotiation session* is not carried out between client and patron, the actions of the librarian may fail to even approximately satisfy the information need, even though technical and semantic communication have taken place without error.

The tendency to restate an information need to meet one's preconceived notion of how the system (or librarian) might best be able to handle it is not uncommon, even among sophisticated library users. It is a problem that

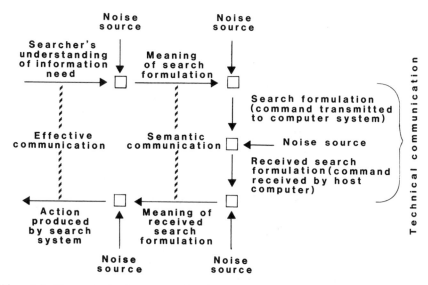

Figure 1.4 Communication between search and search system (following Shannon and Weaver).

must be dealt with carefully for truly effective communication in the information retrieval process, as in library reference work more generally.

The online searcher must not only be able to communicate effectively with the client, he or she also must communicate effectively with the search system. Figure 1.4 illustrates the communication process that takes place between searcher and online IR system.

Technical communication between searcher and search system refers to the transmission of binary data, most usually in the EBCDIC or ASCII character code. The ASCII code and other binary coding systems represent characters (that is, letters, numerals, punctuation marks, blank characters, etc.) by strings of binary digits, or *bits*. The ASCII representations of the characters '#,' 'Q,' and 'q' are 0100011, 1010001, and 1110001, respectively. Messages to a search service are composed of characters represented by these binary digits. These bits are converted to electrical signals by a *modem*, acoustically or electrically connected to the searcher's terminal, and in that form are transmitted over communications lines, to be converted back to binary digits by another modem for processing by the host computer operated by the search service.

Noise refers to distortions of the signal, changes to the signal as it was originally produced. Electrical disturbances in the atmosphere, poor acoustical connections, or "bad" lines are sources of electrical noise. Any change in the transmitted signal will produce a change in the data represented. Changing the fifth bit in 0011011 from a '0' to a '1,' for example, changes the ASCII character represented from a '3' to an 's.' A failure in technical communication, even a change in a single bit, can produce an erroneous command to a search system and lead to unexpected results. The failure to transmit data accurately can obviously cause major problems, since if a system command is garbled, the system response has little chance of being what it was intended to be, that is, the response to the command typed at the keyboard. The transmission of binary data was explicitly dealt with by Claude Shannon in his mathematical theory of communication, or *information theory*, as it has come to be called [13].

Technical communication errors can take place in another way as well. If the searcher has misspelled a command or search term, the system will act on the erroneous command, rather than the command intended, again producing aberrant results.

Semantic communication between searcher and search system deals with the meaning of the words and symbols used in the search formulation and whether these words and symbols have the same meaning to the search system as they do to the searcher. There are two aspects to this. First, the meaning of the commands permitted by the search system—the *effect* that each command will produce—must be understood by the searcher. This is by no means trivial. The command languages of the major search systems are reasonably complex, and it has been conjectured that some commands may be conceptually difficult for many searchers, even professionals [14]. Although the few most important commands of search systems like BRS appear simple and indeed, can apparently be learned easily, there may be many ramifications of using a given command in particular circumstances. Also, many commands have subfeatures. And the more complex systems have many less-used, but potentially very powerful commands in addition to the basic ones. The effect of certain kinds of commands on retrieval, especially as determined by system design features such as file loading practices, defaults, and alphabetizing practices will be discussed in detail in Chapter 3.

Semantic communication between searcher and system is also important at the vocabulary level. Even if system commands are used correctly, retrieval is not likely to be successful if the meaning of the search terms used to describe the search problem (the *problem description language*) does not agree with the meaning of the same terms as they are used in the database being searched. Characteristics of natural languages as well as indexing, cataloging, and classification languages used to describe documents are called *document description language*. These will be discussed in Chapter 2.

Finally, at the effective level, a searcher who fails to interpret system feedback accurately and modify search behavior accordingly may well obtain a literal answer to a search question but not address, even moderately well, the true information need of the client. Knowing when to stop, when not to stop, and how to best modify one's actions according to system feedback are not technical or even semantic skills. They comprise both the art and the science of online information retrieval. We will attempt to address some of the most useful of these approaches—principles, techniques, strategies, heuristics, tactics—in subsequent chapters, culminating in Chapter 7. Personal characteristics of the searcher are also important. Chapter 5 examines information retrieval as a problem solving process, not unlike the process of scientific inquiry.

Online information retrieval is a complex process, involving several levels of communication, both between the searcher and the search system and, if the searcher is an intermediary, between the searcher and a client. Communication may fail in either of these processes at the technical, semantic, or effective levels. It may fail because of an inadequate understanding of an information need, or because of misspellings or typographical errors or data transmission errors. Or, it may fail because of inadequate understanding of system characteristics such as file loading practices or alphabetizing conventions. It may fail because inadequate attention has been paid to the representation of a search problem in a problem description language, or because inappropriate languages or search terms were selected. Finally, it may fail because the searcher was not willing or not able to interpret and react appropriately to system feedback by modifying, polishing, and improving search results. These communication problems will be addressed throughout the remainder of this book, with Chapter 2 focusing on problems of semantic communication.

PROBLEMS

1. Find and discuss two examples of information retrieval systems not discussed in Chapter 1. Show how in each case the system can be viewed as a "filter" that separates wanted information from that which is not wanted.

2. A perfect information retreival system is one that, in response to requests for information, always retrieves what is wanted and never retrieves anything that is not wanted. Can you think of an example of such a system? State any assumptions you make explicitly.

3. Suppose that an information problem exists and that we wish to search a "library" for information to solve the problem. Discuss the assertion that one should be prepared to accept less than perfect retrieval results once the ideal solution of examining every item in the library for relevancy to the problem has been rejected. Are there exceptions to this generalization?

4. Examine an indexing or abstracting journal such as *Reader's Guide* or *Psychological Abstracts*. List all of the access points provided to the records in the print version of the database. That is, identify all the ways in which a particular journal article might be found through the indexes provided.

5. Provide hypothetical examples of communication failures between a client with an information problem and an information specialist, where the communication failure took place:

   a. at the technical level
   b. at the semantic level
   c. at the effective level

6. Examine one or more of the directories to machine-readable databases listed in reference
[5]. On the basis of subject content, coverage, size, and your knowledge of corresponding print
tools, try to identify several of the most important databases for scientific and scholarly work
in the sciences; social sciences; humanities.

7. Examine one or more of the directories to machine-readable databases listed in reference [5].
On the basis of subject content, coverage, size, and your knowledge of corresponding print tools,
try to identify several of the most important databases for answering "popular" information
needs. Discuss.

NOTES AND REFERENCES

1. For example, see Taylor, Robert S. "Value-added processes in the information life cycle."
Journal of the American Society for Information Science 33 (Sept. 1982) 341–346; Boorstin, Daniel
J. *Gresham's Law: Knowledge or Information?* Remarks at the White House Conference on Library
and Information Services, Washington, D.C., Nov. 19, 1979 (Washington, D.C.: Library of
Congress, 1980); Belkin, Nicholas J. "Information concepts for information science." *Journal
of Documentation* 34(1) (March 1978) 55–85; Ingwersen, Peter. "A cognitive view of three selected
online search facilities." *Online Review* 8(5) (1984) 465–491.

2. For a cogent early discussion of the information retrieval problem and possible approaches
to its solution using the electronic computer, see Swanson, Don R., "The Formulation of the
Retrieval Problem." In Garvin, Paul L., *Natural Language and the Computer.* (New York: McGraw-
Hill Book Company, Inc., 1963). pp. 255–267.

3. See "Transmission of Information: An Overview," by George R. Thoma, *Journal of the
American Society for Information Science* 32 (March 1981): 131–140, for an introduction to telecommunications technologies. An older, though still excellent source is Martin, James. *Introduction
to Teleprocessing.* (Englewood Cliffs, NJ: Prentice-Hall, 1972).

4. Among these are Fenichel, Carol H., and Hogan, Thomas H. *Online Searching: A Primer.*
Second edition. (Marlton, New Jersey: Learned Information, 1984); Meadow, Charles T. and
Pauline Cochrane. *Basics of Online Searching.* (New York: Wiley, 1981); Chen, Ching-chih and
Susanna Schweizer. *Online Bibliographic Searching: A Learning Manual.* (New York: Neal-Schuman,
1981); Balnaves, John, et al. *A Workbook in Information Retrieval.* Fifth edition. (Canaberra,
Australia: Canberra College of Advanced Education, 1980); Borgman, Christine L., et. al. *Effective
Online Searching: a basic text.* (New York: Marcel Dekker, Inc., 1984.); Maloney, James J. *Online
searching technique and management.* (Chicago: ALA, 1983); Maloney, James J., ed. Online search-
ing technique and management (Chicago: American Library Association, 1983); Gilreath, Charles
L. *Computerized literature searching: research strategies and databases.* (Boulder, Colorado: Westview
Press, 1984); Palmer, Roger C. *Online reference and information retrieval.* (Littleton, Colorado:
Libraries Unlimited, 1983).

5. Cuadra Associates, Inc., *Directory of Online Databases; Guide to Online Databases.* (Boca
Raton, FL: Newsletter Management Corporation, 1983); Williams, Martha E., ed. *Computer-
Readable Databases: A Directory and Data Sourcebook.* (Washington, D.C.: Knowledge Industry
Publications, Inc., 1982); Hall, James L. and Marjorie J. Brown. *Online Bibliographic Databases:
An International Directory.* Third edition. (London: Aslib, 1983).

6. Williams, Martha. "Data Bases—A history of developments and trends from 1966 through 1975." *Journal of the American Society for Information Science* 28 (March 1977) 71-78.

7. *Directory of Online Databases* 6(1) (Fall 1984).

8. *Directory of Online Databases* 6(1) (Fall 1984).

9. For historical treatments of the early online information retrieval industry, see Bourne, Charles P. "On-Line Systems: History, Technology, and Economics". *Journal of the American Society for Information Science* 31 (May 1980): 155-160; Cuadra, Carlos A., "Commercially Funded On-Line Retrieval Services—Past, Present, and Future." *Aslib Proceedings* (January 1978) 2-15; Cuadra, Carlos A. "Online Systems: Promises and Pitfalls." *Journal of the American Society for Information Science* 22 (March April 1971) 107-114; McCarn, Davis B. and Joseph Leiter, "On-Line Services in Medicine and Beyond." *Science* 181 (July 27 1973) 318-324.

10. Cuadra Associates, Inc., *Directory of Online Databases* 6 (No. 1) (Fall 1984).

11. Pierce, John R. "Communication." *Scientific American* 227 (No. 3) (Sept. 1972) 31-41.

12. Shannon, Claude E. and Warren Weaver. *The Mathematical Theory of Communication.* (Urbana, Illinois: The University of Illinois Press, 1964).

13. Shannon and Weaver.

14. Fenichel, Carol H., "Online Searching: Measures that Discriminate Among Users with Different Types of Experience." *Journal of the American Society for Information Science* 32 (1) (1981) 23-32; Vigil, Peter J., "The Psychology of Online Searching." *Journal of the American Society for Information Science* 34(4) (1981) 281-287.

Chapter 2

Languages for Information Retrieval

2.1 SOME CHARACTERISTCS OF LANGUAGE

Chapter 1 introduced the idea of an information retrieval system as a human artifact in which technical, semantic, and pragmatic communication are important components. Using an information retrieval system as a filter, end-users search collections of data, either directly or through an intermediary, to try to satisfy their information problems. Online searching is information retrieval in which data are stored in machine-readable (binary) form, and in which computer and communications technologies are tools utilized in the search.

As a communication process, online searching relies on *languages* to carry out three major functions. First, languages are used to represent the content of documents, data, and other forms of information. Second, the information problems of users are represented in terms of language. Finally, languages are used to instruct the computer to carry out search and retrieval functions. This chapter explores each of these important classes of information retrieval languages.

Every language, whether natural or artificial, is characterized by its vocabulary, its syntax, its logical structure, and its domain. The *vocabulary* of a language consists of those words—strings of contiguous characters—that are allowed to be used in the language. Vocabulary elements constitute the building blocks from which more elaborate constructions can be formed. The *syntax* of a language consists of those rules governing how elements of the vocabulary can be combined to form legitimate expressions and sentences in the language.

For example, the character strings 'we', 'recognize', 'the', and 'truth' are words in the English language, and the character string 'we recognize the truth' is a syntactically correct way of combining these words into an English sentence. On the other hand, 'glypff' is not an English word, nor is 'we truth recognize the' expressed in correct English syntax, even though it is composed entirely of English words. Similar observations can be made for formal or artificial languages such as mathematics, information and problem description languages for information retrieval, and search system command languages.

The logical structure or taxonomy of a language refers to the nature of the relationships between vocabulary elements in the language. This is a particularly important characteristic of formal languages, and will be discussed more fully later in the chapter.

Besides vocabulary, syntax, and logical structure, languages can be discussed in terms of their domains—the concepts in the real world or in a theoretical, formal world they are meant to describe. It is important to distinguish between *concepts* and the *symbols* that represent them. A concept is an abstract idea, and human beings use symbols to stand for, or represent, concepts. The concept represented by a symbol is called its *meaning*. Semantic communication is concerned with this meaning.

In the formal language of arithmetic, for example, numerals, arithmetic operators, and relational operators are among the symbols human beings use to express ideas concerning the concept of number. These symbols are elements of the vocabulary of arithmetic. The character string "2 + 2 = 4" combines a few such vocabulary words into a statement that happens to be written in correct syntax (for ordinary arithmetic), whereas the string " + 2 = 4 -" is not. Note that the numbers (concepts) two and four are represented in these expressions by the Arabic symbols '2' and '4,' but they could have been equally well been represented by II and IV, or 49/24.5 and 4*1, or // and //// or in any of infinitely many other ways. The concepts they represent, that is, the meaning of the ideas of two and four, remain unchanged from representation to representation.

It should be observed that a sentence can be syntactically correct and yet false in a given domain (that is, in a particular context or interpretation). Another way of putting this is to say that the relationship between the idea expressed in the sentence and the subset of the world it describes may be assigned the truth value "false." In mathematics, the sentence "1 + 1 = 10" is syntactically correct. When interpreted in the decimal numeration system, the sentence is false, but in the context of a binary numeration system, the sentence is true. The "truth" of a mathematical sentence is a function of the context in which the sentence is interpreted. This is no less true for natural languages.

Just as ideas of number are represented with the language of arithmetic, so are the concepts and ideas of our everyday life represented in symbols called words. And just as mathematical notions can be expressed in a variety of ways, so can ideas concerning commerce and science and love. Whether a language is natural or artificial, then, the elements of its vocabulary should be recognized as symbols representing underlying ideas. And frequently human beings use a variety of ways to represent a given concept. For effective information retrieval, it is crucial to recognize this fact clearly, *because computers deal with symbols, not concepts.* When requests are put to an information retrieval system as character strings, these strings are matched against other character strings that have been used to describe the information in a database. Thus it is the matching of symbols, not concepts, that effects retrieval. It follows that careful consideration of the vocabulary used to represent a search problem or topic is crucial for effective retrieval.

Consideration of the problem context is also important. For if the "truth" of a given statement depends on its context, one must go beyond the terms used to formulate a search request and beyond even the syntax used to combine these terms, to fully understand the meaning underlying the request. The same formal request put forth by two different individuals might dictate very different information seeking responses, depending on the contexts in which the information seekers have posed the question. It follows that if an intermediary is to perform a search for a client, an understanding must be gained, not only of the meaning of the formal request, but also of the context in which the request takes place. In traditional librarianship, this understanding is gained in the *reference interview*, or the *question negotiation session*, as it is sometimes called. This important process will be examined more closely in Chapter 6.

Beyond information description languages and problem description languages, both natural and artificial, another type of language is important for information retrieval. The *command language* of a search system is, like mathematics and programming languages such as BASIC, Pascal, and PL/1, a formal language with its own syntax and vocabulary elements (or keywords), logical structure, and semantics. The next section of this chapter introduces a set of generic commands for online information retrieval. The remainder of the chapter will examine major classes of information and problem description languages.

2.2 COMMAND LANGUAGES OR INFORMATION RETRIEVAL

Operational online information retrieval systems are one of three types: *command-driven, menu-driven,* and *mixed mode.* In menu-driven systems, the user is constantly forced to make a selection of actions from among several choices offered by the system. For example, in BRS/After Dark, after a retrieved item has been printed, the system responds:

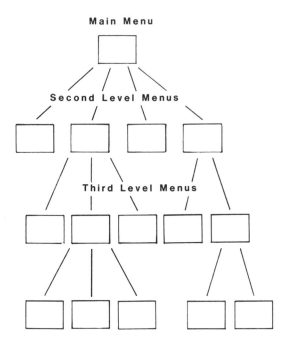

Figure 2.1   Tree structure of menu-driven information retrieval system.

END OF ITEM. HIT ENTER KEY TO SEE NEXT ITEM, S TO CON-
TINUE SEARCHING, M TO RETURN TO DATABASE MENU, OR O
TO SIGN OFF__:
The searcher is given four choices; no other option is evidently possible.

A menu-driven system often has a hierarchical, or tree structure design
(see Figure 2.1). The searcher selects an option from the first, or *main menu*,
determining which of the major paths of the hierarchy is to be followed.
A new menu is then displayed, outlining the major categories of that path,
and the user again makes a selection. Continuing in this way, the user proceeds in a step-wise fashion through the menu structure to the level wanted.

The main menu of the Compuserve Consumer Information Service is given
in Table 2.1. Suppose that one wanted to carry out a search in Grolier's *Academic American* encyclopedia on Compuserve. The *Academic American* is
classified under menu choice #1, home services. The user selects choice #1,
obtaining a second menu (see Table 2.2). If the user selects choice #2 from
this menu, a new menu of choices is presented, from which the particular
service wanted may be selected (see Table 2.3).

Actually, both BRS/After Dark and Compuserve are examples of mixed
mode systems. For example, a Compuserve user can proceed directly to the
third level menu in Table 2.3 by typing, *at any time*, the command: GO
HOM-20. HOM-20 is the *address* of this particular menu. It is possible to
go directly to any menu, if one knows its address, using the GO command.

TABLE 2.1
Compuserve Information Service
Main Menu

Compuserve   Page CIS-1
Compuserve Information Service
  1 Home Services
  2 Business & Financial
  3 Personal Computing
  4 Services for Professionals
  5 User Information
  6 Index

Compuserve publishes an index that provides these addresses directly. The Academic American Encyclopedia is at location AAE of the menu structure, and the command GO AAE will take the user directly to this location. Note the mnemonic features of the menu names that make remembering addresses somewhat easier for system users.

Menu-driven systems have the advantage that they can be comparatively easy for a novice to use. This can be somewhat deceiving, however. If one makes a wrong choice at any level, it can be time consuming and frustrating to retrace the steps in the menu structure. Also, it is by no means always obvious what the logical choice in a menu might be. Why should a user expect to find the *Academic American* under 'home services'? Might not this service equally well be classified under 'personal computing,' or perhaps even 'services for professionals'? Other examples of potential ambiguity in menu-driven systems can easily be found.

TABLE 2.2
Compuserve Second-Level Menu

Compuserve   Page HOM-1
HOME SERVICES
  1 News/Weather/Sports
  2 Reference Library
  3 Communications
  4 Home Shopping/Banking
  5 Discussion Forums
  6 Games
  7 Education
  8 Home Management
  9 Travel
 10 Entertainment

TABLE 2.3
Compuserve Third-Level Menu

Compuserve   Page HOM-20
REFERENCE LIBRARY
  1 Academic American Encyclopedia
  2 Information on Demand
  3 U.S. Government Publications
  4 Bibliographic Services
  5 Family   6 Fashion
  7 Gardening   8 Golf
  9 Development 10 Science
 11 Satire   12 Sexuality
 13 Wine

Another disadvantage of menu-driven systems is that power and flexibility are sacrificed by forcing user options into a menu structure with only a limited number of choices. *Command languages* can provide much more flexibility, and at the same time relieve experienced users of the frustrating and tedious task of proceeding through a familiar, yet unescapable menu structure.

The major disadvantage of a command-driven system for online information retrieval is that the user must be quite familiar with the command language of the system to use it effectively. A *prompt* is a special character or group of characters used by the system to indicate its readiness to carry out a command. On DIALOG, for example, the prompt is a question mark (?). When a prompt is transmitted to a user's terminal by an information retrieval system, it means that the user is able to type a command on the terminal keyboard and send it to the host system. More exactly, it means that the search system is ready to *receive* such a command. Regardless of the type of language that is employed, an online information retrieval system uses commands that fall into several general classes.

Table 2.4 displays a broad classification and introduction to generic commands found in information retrieval languages used with systems such as DIALOG, ORBIT, and BRS. This typology does not apply to numeric databases and search systems, in which many additional capabilities than those listed may be present (see Chapter 8). Also, functions other than searching that might be available on a system, such as document ordering, electronic mail, and word processing, are not included in the classification.

Another, broader classification, consisting of only four classes of commands, is suggested in [1]. Negus has provided a detailed study of the possible standardization of retrieval system commands [2]. And in a cogent analysis, Gebhardt and Stellmacher have identified a set of basic principles for the design of man/machine languages for information retrieval [3]. A useful exercise is to apply the principles suggested by Gebhardt and Stellmacher to the evaluation of the command languages of commercial information retrieval systems.

In a particular search system, each of the classes of commands listed in Table 2.4 may be represented by several commands and subcommands. Each of these has its own syntax, special vocabulary, logical structure, and meaning. If a syntax rule is followed improperly by a searcher, the system may respond with an error message. For example, the TYPE command in DIALOG is an *output* command, with the syntax:

TYPE m/n/p, or
T m/n/p,

where m is a valid set number, n is one of several possible print formats,

TABLE 2.4
Broad Classes of Search System Commands

1. *Starting up and shutting down.* Connecting to and disconnecting from the search system; rules and protocols for logging onto and logging off from the system; changing system defaults such as line width; changing passwords.

2. *Selecting databases for searching.* Choosing an initial file to search; changing files. Obtaining information regarding which files are likely to contain keywords of interest.

3. *Creating and erasing sets.* Building sets of retrieved information; deleting sets; examining alphabetically or conceptually related terms online and creating sets from these lists; truncating search terms; methods of specifying that two search terms be present in the same piece of text; range searching.

4. *Combining two or more sets into new sets.* Search logic: Boolean operations AND, OR, NOT.

5. *Obtaining tutorial or status information.* Summarizing syntax of commands, characteristics of databases, news. Summarizing search logic and history; checking elapsed time/cost.

6. *Output.* Printing selected data from retrieved records at the terminal in specified formats; sorting records; causing records to be printed offline and mailed; interrupting output; erasing characters or commands.

7. *Restricting output of retrieval sets.* Limiting or making more specific already existing sets or all subsequent output according to specified criteria (e.g., by restricting output to articles written in certain languages, published during certain dates, etc.)

8. *Saving searches.* Storing, displaying, and executing previously created searches or parts of searches; modifying stored searches; selective dissemination of information.

and p is a valid document number or range of valid document numbers, e.g., 1-20. There are some shorter forms of this command as well, in which not all information is given and the system makes certain assumptions about what is intended by the searcher.

Example 2.1. Suppose a searcher had created a set labeled #1 that contained wanted information. (How sets are created and what they contain are not important to this discussion; these topics will be discussed in Chapter 3. Here we are interested only in the syntax of system commands and how the system responds to user errors. Nor is the fact that the example is given in the DIALOG language important. Other examples could easily be given for other command languages.) If the searcher were mistakenly to enter the command

TUPE 1/7/3

DIALOG would respond with an error message:

SET-NUMBER SYNTAX ERROR

This ambiguous and likely to be misleading message is caused by the misspelling of the keyword "TYPE." The system examined the command string, noted that the first character was a T, and then correctly assumed that the command was a TYPE statement. The next character in the command, however, was not a Y, as expected. It then assumed that the abbreviated form of the TYPE command—the single letter T—was intended. The letter T may be used to abbreviate the word 'TYPE,' but, according to the syntax rule for this command, the character following the type command (T or TYPE) must be a valid set number. Instead, the searcher typed a "U." This is not a valid set number, and hence the technically correct but confusing error message, SET-NUMBER SYNTAX ERROR is the result.

Example 2.2. Suppose the searcher typed the command

TYPE 1/11/1-7

DIALOG would respond "INVALID FORMAT CODE," meaning that there *is* no print format 11 in DIALOG databases. This message, too, is somewhat ambiguous to a novice, although somewhat less so than the message in Example 2.1. Neither is particularly "user-friendly."

In Version 2, a major revision of DIALOG introduced in early 1985, the typographical error of Example 2.1 results in the message:

> > > Item list not allowed with accession number.

If a request is made to print records in a nonexistent document format, as in Example 2.2, Version 2 does not produce an error message. The system simply types the record requested in a format that *does* exist. In experiments done with this command in ERIC, the format selected was the full bibliographic record.

Presumably both of these changes were attempts to make Version 2 more user friendly than its predecessor. Neither is an improvement over the old DIALOG, in the view of this writer. The issue of how to design user friendly systems is highly complex, and has been addressed primarily in the literature relating to online public access catalogs (OPACS) in libraries. A book by Hildreth [4] addresses these questions in depth, and is a good place to begin study of the problem.

The observation that syntax errors sometimes result in ambiguous error messages should not be construed as a criticism of the system designers. Indeed, having observed that a particular command has incorrect syntax, the system cannot be certain in its diagnosis of what action was intended by the user. Usually the system must make an assumption regarding the probable intention of the searcher. However, this assumption can be incorrect, leading to a confusing error message, as in the examples. The system user needs to be prepared for this possibility.

Not all language usage errors result in system error messages, however. Indeed, logical errors, or typographical errors resulting in a system action that is different than the one intended by the user, but with no accompanying error message, are more subtle and much more difficult to detect than syntax errors.

Example 2.3. A DIALOG searcher wanting to type the 4th item of set #5 in format 3 should enter:

TYPE 5/3/4.

Interchanging the 5 and 3 in this formulation would in most databases result in a syntactically acceptable command: "type the fourth record of set 3 in format 5." Since the command is syntactically correct (if the named set exists), no error message would result. The system would simply print the wrong record.

The last example demonstrates a difficult and pervasive problem in online information retrieval: how to recognize and react appropriately to subtle logical or semantic command language errors. This problem will be treated more extensively in Chapter 3.

The reader is urged to explore the syntax of BRS, ORBIT, DIALOG, or other search system of interest by carefully reviewing the system documentation. Unless the nuances of a command language are well understood, effective retrieval will often be impossible. Although mastering the command language of a search system is mainly a technical skill, it is clearly a prerequisite to efficient and effective retrieval. This book will not attempt to describe or explain in detail the command language of any particular search system, although as has been stated, DIALOG will be used from time to time for illustrative examples. The reader will want to explore the command language of some system (but not necessarily DIALOG) in depth.

There have been several published studies comparing the command languages of online information retrieval systems [5]. However, since the languages of existing systems are continually evolving, the results of these studies are of interest mainly for the questions they ask and the approaches they take. In a thoughtful analysis of languages for information retrieval, Charles Meadow asserts his view that the differences among the major languages are superficial, and that these were apparently designed for use by professional intermediaries, not end-users. Meadow argues that there is no single language best suited to all information retrieval functions, and makes a strong case for the desirability of diversity in retrieval languages [6].

There are several major types of information- and problem-description languages for information retrieval—languages for indexing and classification. These languages possess quite different characteristics. The remainder of this chapter introduces several main classes of these languages and discusses their implications for online information retrieval.

2.3   NATURAL LANGUAGES

We begin by looking at some of the characteristics of living languages such as English and Russian. Some human languages, Latin, for example, are no longer used and are thus no longer dynamic and changing. Such languages tend to become codified and formalized, much like the command and programming languages of computers. Because of their static structure and vocabulary, these languages do not present the same problems for information or problem representation as do languages in active use by a community of human beings. To distinguish between dead human languages or formal languages and languages like English, the term *natural language* is used in this book to refer to living human languages.

If two different words can be used to represent the same (or nearly the same) idea, they are called synonyms. 'Bashful' and 'shy,' 'emancipate' and 'free,' and 'victory' and 'conquest' are examples of pairs of synonyms or near-synonyms. If natural language is used as an information retrieval language, the existence of synonyms and near-synonyms will increase the difficulty of online information retrieval, because, as was noted earlier, computers do information retrieval by matching symbols, not the concepts represented by these symbols. Information retrieval systems do not now, and almost certainly never will, permit the effective searching of concepts or ideas directly. To communicate effectively with an information file or database, the searcher must formulate abstract ideas using symbols—words, phrases, and codes— just as in communication with another human being.

Suppose that a particular concept is the object of an information retrieval search, and that natural language is the language of expression. If a search formulation is constructed that fails to include all relevant synonyms for the concept, then some information items may not be retrieved. That is, the words and phrases used in the formulation will not match some of the words and phrases that describe the concept in the database, and the retrieval results will suffer from missed information. In natural languages, there are often many ways to express a given idea. To find as many items as possible that discuss a given topic when searching a database consisting of natural language texts, then, the searcher must try to anticipate all possible words and phrases that might have been used to express the concept of interest.

Example 2.4. Suppose that a requester is interested in the idea of using

TABLE 2.5
Some Phrases that Represent Aspects of the Concept "intelligent interfaces between naive users and search systems"

user-friendly interfaces	intermediary search systems
user-interface systems	intelligent interfaces
knowledge-based systems	computer interfaces
intelligent terminals	search systems for naive users
expert systems	computer intermediaries
end-user operations	natural language interfaces
search intermediaries	intelligent front-ends
gateway systems	

a computer as an intelligent interface between a naive online searcher and an information retrieval system, and wants to carry out a literature search on this topic. This is a relatively new concept, and one in which much research and commentary is currently taking place. The literature on this subject suggests that certain aspects of the concept might be expressed using any of the words and phrases listed in Table 2.5. Variant word forms such as the singular form of nouns might also be used, and other phrases may occur to the reader as well. In addition, names of specific experimental or commercial systems such as IIDA, CONIT, Search Helper, Data Transfer System, USERKIT, SCIMATE, FRED, PRIMATE, and OL' SAM might also be introduced into the search formulation. (The subject of computer interfaces between users and search systems is discussed in Chapter 9.)

If the requester of Example 2.4 wants all, or nearly all the citations in the information science literature to papers discussing this concept, then as many of these natural language terms must be anticipated and used as is affordable. However, there is another, more difficult problem. Some of the terms listed are "better" than others in the sense that they bear more directly on the topic wanted. Some of the phrases are much broader or more ambiguous than others. It follows that the terms listed are not really synonymous and probably cannot be usefully treated as such in an online search. Although the phrases listed in Table 2.5 are closely related to one another and to the information need of the requester, the relationship is more complex than simply synonymity. For good results, this problem will have to be faced by the searcher as well.

Semantic ambiguity is another problem arising from the "words not concepts" characteristic of online searching. English and other natural languages include many instances of two words that are identical in spelling (and therefore identical to a computer) but refer to entirely different concepts. Examples of such homographs are 'play,' meaning a theatrical production as well as certain activities of children, 'red,' meaning both a communist and a color, and 'salt,' a series of arms limitation talks, a chemical compound, a sailor, or the act of artificially enriching, as in a mine. Meadow gives the example of 'He covered the field' as an example of an English full sentence homograph [7].

English and other natural languages contain many examples of ambiguity due to homographs. Ordinarily the context of a potentially ambiguous word, phrase, or sentence within a paragraph or larger unit of text, as well as a cultural context shared by writer and reader, makes its meaning clear (or disambiguates the homograph). However, dealing with cultural and textual contexts in this way is beyond the capability of online information retrieval systems, except in the most rudimentary way. Consequently, comprehension of meaning in a particular context is the responsibility of the online searcher, who must use language in the search formulation that is not only adequate to represent the information need, but also appropriate for the databases being searched. A sophisticated information retrieval system might suggest likely words and phrases to a searcher, but the decision regarding appropriateness must be the responsibility of a human being.

The ambiguity problem caused by homographs is probably the fundamental reason that mechanical translation of natural languages, an ongoing research interest of linguists since the late 1940's, has failed utterly to achieve its apparent early promise. An amusing, probably apocryphal machine translation of the aphorism 'The spirit is willing but the flesh is weak'' from English to Russian and back to English clearly reveals the difficulty of word for word translations that ignore context and somehow avoid meaning virtually altogether. The translated and re-translated quotation was: ''The vodka is good but the meat is rotten.''

A useful contemporary summary of early work in mechanical translation is provided by Victor H. Yngve [8], and a comprehensive review of the literature through 1977 is given by Hutchins [9]. The close connections between mechanical translation and linguistics more generally with information storage and retrieval are made explicit by Sparck Jones [10], Fishman [11], and Montgomery [12].

Ambiguity in natural language is a lesser problem in a homogeneous, highly specialized, technical literature such as a subset of particle physics, because in a narrow field a given word or phrase tends to be used to refer to approximately the same concept whenever it is used. But in less technical disciplines such as education and in heterogeneous literatures (for example, in such multidisciplinary databases as *Comprehensive Dissertation Abstracts* and *Magazine Index*), the multiple meaning problem in natural language can be a substantial challenge to overcome.

The word ''hard'' has been used to characterize disciplines that possess

TABLE 2.6
Selected Disciplines Arranged from "Hard"
to "Soft "*

---

mathematics (hardest)
chemistry
physics
computer science
geology
French
agronomy
library science
office administration
economics
management
history
music
speech
art and architecture
dance
education
psychology
sociology
fine arts (softest)

---

*Extracted from a table in McGrath, William. "Relationship between hard/soft, pure/applied, and life/nonlife disciplines and subject book use in a university library." *Information Processing and Management* 14 (1978) p. 22.

a firm conceptual, research-based foundation and which have a relatively well-defined structure. These are compared to "soft" disciplines. William McGrath [13] has related the hard/soft concept to the idea of paradigm development as outlined by Thomas Kuhn in *Structure of Scientific Revolutions* [14]. In some disciplines, fundamental beliefs, values, assumptions, attitudes, and methodologies relating to the structure and identity of the important problems of the discipline are shared by the community of scholars and scientists working in the discipline. This shared understanding is the *paradigm* of the field, governing the characteristics of research in that discipline. In general, paradigmatic disciplines are the hard sciences, while the social sciences and humanities are soft. Table 2.6 lists several disciplines in rank order, from hard to soft, as identified by McGrath [15].

Many disciplines in the soft sciences and humanities are in a non-paradigmatic stage, where community consensus does not and may never exist. One might expect that in such disciplines, words may be used in many different ways. This question was investigated by Wiberley, who analyzed the precision of meaning of entry terms in leading encyclopedias and dictionaries in the humanities [16]. The study found that approximately 60% of the terms in the sample examined were singular proper names, posing a simple problem for retrieval, according to the author. On the other hand, Wiberley confirmed that much of the humanist's vocabulary is imprecise, using such terms as 'Methodists,' 'Realism,' 'apperception,' and 'magic' as examples of words that have many different referents in the disciplines belonging to the humanities.

Buckland has observed that hardness and softness are intellectual properties of disciplines, stemming from the extent to which concepts are *definable*. Areas of study such as the physical sciences tend to treat definable concepts while softer areas such as welfare economics deal with human behavior and values, in which concepts are not very definable [17]. Probably what Buckland means by this is *measurable*, and moreover, measurable in such a way that the scholars in the discipline generally agree with the paradigm within which the measurements are carried out. Love and magic are certainly definable concepts; the problem is that there is no general agreement even on what the dictionary definitions of these concepts ought to be, and certainly not on how to measure them. To take a specific example, it is probably not possible to provide an operational definition for love that would be acceptable generally by a community of philosophers as externally valid.

The implications of these observations for online information retrieval are clear. In soft disciplines—the social sciences and humanities—search problems posed in natural language will generally be more difficult to express in words than will problems in, say, solid state physics. That is, there is a semantic ambiguity inherent *in the discipline itself* that can be expected to impede the search process. Linguistic approaches and computer matching devices cannot substitute for conceptual fuzziness. The social science concepts of *paradigm, hard,* and *soft* are themselves excellent examples of terms that are soft in meaning. A search for these concepts in a database such as *Sociological Abstracts* or *Philosophers Index* would probably encounter serious problems of ambiguity caused by homographs. The question of how the precision of the terminology of various disciplines affects information retrieval in that discipline has only begun to be studied, and is a rich area for further exploration.

There is another kind of ambiguity other than that caused by homography that deserves discussion. *Contextual ambiguity* results from the capability of information retrieval systems to identify occurrences of two or more character strings (words, phrases, or other search strings) in the same piece of text—that is, together in the same sentence, paragraph, full record, etc.

Example 2.5. Suppose that a search on the topic of information theory is to be conducted. The searcher decides to retrieve all citations containing the words 'information' and 'theory' together (somewhere) in the same sentence.

Some thought will reveal that the action described in Example 2.5 will not guarantee that retrieved articles treat the subject of 'information theory.'' For, although present in the same piece of text, 'information' and 'theory' need have no particular semantic relationship to each other. Consider a document containing the following sentence: ''The general public needs more information regarding the underlying theory supporting alternative devices and techniques for solid waste removal, as well as their effects on the environment.'' The search described would retrieve this document, erroneously. The assumption underlying the use of this search technique is that words that are contextually related must be semantically related. While sometimes correct, this assumption is also often false, resulting in so-called *false drops*, or *false coordinations.*

Some information retrieval systems permit the false drop problem to be made less severe by allowing the searcher to reduce the size of the text that two or more words are required to appear in simultaneously. The assumption that underlies this capability is that the smaller the piece of text, the more likely contextual proximity will imply a semantic relationship. In the most restrictive case, if the search system will permit the requirement that the two words 'information' and 'theory' be not only in the same sentence but also adjacent to one another (that is, occurring as a two word phrase), the probability is high that the two words will be related semantically. Of course the semantic ambiguity problem may still exist if the phrase 'information theory' is used in more than one way in the database that is searched.

A final problem with using natural language for information retrieval lies in its inability to handle with any grace the hierarchical relationships that often exist between concepts. Generic searches—searches on a general class of concepts—are impossible to conduct in natural language without a great deal of effort, as the following example shows.

Example 2.6. A faculty member in a department of physical education wants to conduct a comprehensive literature search on the impact of ideas from the field of sports medicine on training practices in collegiate athletic programs. To represent the *athletics concept*, searching on the term 'athletics' and its near synonym 'sports' as well as variant word forms will retrieve many useful items. But if natural language is the language of expression, neither of these terms comes even close to being sufficient for comprehensive retrieval. Indeed, an article discussing sports medicine practices in training for baseball probably will be more likely to use the specific term 'baseball' rather than the more general terms 'athletics' or 'sports.' The same observation may be made for the other sports: archery, golf, lacrosse, orienteering, tennis, waterskiing, and wrestling, to name just a few.

For a comprehensive search on this information problem, the searcher will have to name every specific sport and generic terms for general classes of sports as well as any subclasses that may exist. *Track and field*, for example, is a subclass of sports that includes many individual sports: javelin, broad jump, and the like. In natural language, there is no substitute for naming every subclass and specific members of a more general class, if a comprehensive search on the general class is what is wanted. The lack of ability to make generic searches is one of the most difficult problems in using natural language for information retrieval.

Several problems with the use of natural languages for information retrieval have been discussed. These include synonymity, semantic ambiguity caused by homographs, semantic ambiguity inherent in "soft" disciplines, contextual ambiguity resulting in false drops, and the lack of ability to perform generic searches. Search devices for tackling these problems with natural language will be introduced in a later chapter. A systems approach toward their solution is examined in the next section of the chapter: the development and use of controlled vocabularies.

2.4 SUBJECT INDEXING

Chapter 1 distinguished between source databases, containing undistilled texts of numeric or textual information, and reference databases, containing summaries or surrogates of primary sources of information. In particular, bibliographic databases are reference databases containing surrogates of bibliographic materials such as journal articles, books, and newspaper articles. In traditional librarianship, *cataloging* is the name of the intellectual process of preparing a surrogate record representing a bibliographic item. In information storage and retrieval this process is called *indexing*. Although the perspective and the examples provided in this chapter relate primarily to bibliographic databases, the concepts are fundamental and generally apply to all reference databases. The perspective is that of access to information through subject indexing with an artificial, or *controlled* vocabulary.

The information retrieval process should be closely tied to the indexing process. Indeed, the sole purpose of indexing is for the storage and subsequent retrieval of the document surrogates, or records, which can then lead the searcher to the documents themselves, and to the information and knowledge contained therein. In bibliographic databases, an index is intended to act as a substitute for the documents themselves, so that, given a request for information, those documents in the database not helpful to the request are eliminated from consideration and those that are likely to be helpful are displayed. Indexing is not done as an end in itself. Rather, it is one of several approaches to the information retrieval problem.

An *index record* for a document is a concise representation, or surrogate, of the document from a particular point of view. This 'point of view'' is what ties the indexing process to the retrieval process. Although it can be argued that there exists an objective reality to a document (or more generally, to any collection of information) that has nothing to do with a particular point of view, a more modern characterization of the indexing process stresses the subjectivity of such assessments. Indeed, if objective descriptions of documents can in fact be provided, they are not likely to be as useful to a potential population of human beings as a description of the document tailored to the particular perspective of that population.

For example, Mother Goose rhymes are important to the research of specialists from the perspectives of fairy tales, myths, English literature, English history, and psychoanalysis. For effective information retrieval, the indexing given particular rhymes would (or should) reflect this orientation. To take a second example, descriptive material concerning a river might be looked at from the point of view of transportation, alternative energy sources, biological organisms, recreation, or industrial waste. The decision concerning which concepts are ''indexable'' in a given document is a function of perspective. Other examples can easily be given.

Assuming the point of view of the user population has been established, the indexing process consists of two basic steps. First, a decision must be made regarding what the document is *about*, from the perspective taken. And second, the concepts must be expressed in the vocabulary of a document description language. The language selected might be natural language, some modified form of natural language, or terms selected from a controlled vocabulary.

Figure 2.2 illustrates the parallels between the indexing and retrieval processes. In each case there is a ''problem'' requiring intellectual analysis. For subject indexing, the problem is a document or other piece of primary source material for which the major concepts are to be identified, from the point of view of the potential user population. For information retrieval, the problem is to analyze the information need of a human being into its constituent concepts or facets, from the particular point of view of that user. In each case, the language used to express the summary statement—the surrogate—is natural language, the language of the information seeker or author.

When the problem has been analyzed into its constituent parts, a second

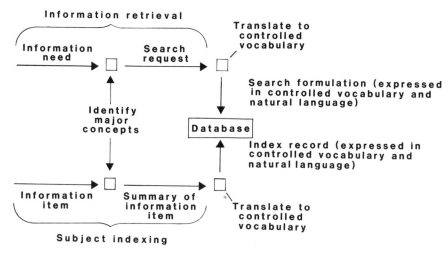

Figure 2.2   Parallel processes: subject indexing and information retrieval.

step must be taken. In subject indexing, the summary of the information item must be translated from natural language into the controlled vocabulary of the indexing language. For bibliographic material, the resulting index record is called a *bibliographic record*. Taken together, a set of bibliographic records constitutes a bibliographic database.

Similarly, the information retrieval specialist must translate the search request into the controlled vocabulary of the indexing language. During the online information retrieval process, this search formulation is matched against the set of bibliographic records in an online mode, and records meeting the search conditions are retrieved. Acting interactively, the searcher may modify the formulation to improve the results as necessary.

The indexing process invariably results in the loss of information, regardless of whether an artificial language or natural language has been employed. The more ambiguous the concepts being represented, the more information is lost through the surrogate. Representing persons by their social security numbers involves little loss of information in one sense, as the relationship is, at least roughly, a one-to-one relationship. Representing machine parts by part numbers, states by two letter codes, and journals by their CODENs might be expected to work well in most instances. But certainly the essence of what is meant by a human being is not captured well by a number, nor are the functional specifications of machine parts or the subjects of the articles appearing in journals.

It is useful to distinguish between relatively hard, unambiguous information or data such as the name of the author of a journal article or the language in which the article was written and soft or fuzzy information such

TABLE 2.7
**Some Characteristics of a Journal Article That Might Be of Interest for Storage
and Future Retrieval**

Relatively "hard" data
    author(s) and affiliation(s)
    laboratory in which work was carried out
    whether animal or human subjects were used
    year of publication
    document type
    name of journal
Relatively "soft" subject data
    Information expressed in natural language
    title
    brief summary of the article (abstract)
    key terms (keywords and proper names) extracted from the text
    full text of the article
    Terms assigned from controlled vocabularies
    classification categories
    broad subject headings
    terms from a subject thesaurus representing major concepts of the article

---

as the subjects or major concepts treated in that article. Conducting a search for hard information—straightforward facts—usually involves little more than learning the syntax rules for the representation of the data of interest. Subject searching for soft information—ideas and concepts—is much more delicate and complex. Similar observations hold for the indexing process.

Example 2.7. Suppose that a piece of research is reported in an article in the journal *Science*, and we want to represent the essence of the information in a shorter form for storage and future retrieval. What might be considered important characteristics of the article to include in a surrogate (that is, to index for storage and future retrieval)? Table 2.7 lists a few characteristics that might be considered useful.

The first class of characteristics listed in Table 2.7, including such characteristics of the article as author's name, year of publication, name of journal, and language, are hard in the sense that there is usually little ambiguity associated with them. However, there can be significant problems even with this type of data.

The second class of characteristics are related to the problems studied in the research, and are fuzzier in nature. The title of the article is written by its author. In scientific journals, these are usually fairly descriptive, but this is often not true for softer disciplines. An *abstract* of a piece of text is an abbreviated representation of the contents of the text, usually preceding the text itself in the journal. It permits readers to quickly decide the pertinence of the article to their own information needs, and to decide whether to read further. Authors of journal articles are sometimes asked to write their own abstracts by journal editors. Guidelines for preparing abstracts have been published [18].

Editors or authors may also extract key terms (either proper names or natural language keywords) from the text itself. The extraction of key terms and proper names from the body of the journal article, sometimes referred to as uncontrolled indexing, does not involve the use of an artificial language. Words used by the author are simply removed from the text and used as access points for subsequent retrieval. Finally, the full text of the article itself can be viewed as a "characteristic" of the article, as a special limiting case.

In each of the classes of data described in the second category listed in Table 2.7, there is considerable loss of information. This is true even for full text of the article, in which a completed research project is described in an abbreviated form in a written report. In each of these data classes, the research project is represented by a brief surrogate of the original research. And in each case, the problems associated with the use of natural language described in the previous section of this chapter are present and troublesome.

The third class of data listed in Table 2.7 also results in a loss of information. In addition, these approaches attempt to index the subject content of the article using an artificial language—a controlled vocabulary. Controlled vocabularies take several forms, including subject heading lists, special thesauri for narrow subject areas, hierarchical classification systems, and others. No attempt is made to study all possible forms in this book. However, some representative examples will be briefly examined in the remainder of this chapter.

2.5 CONTROLLED VOCABULARIES

There are several reasons for considering the use of an artificial language to represent information. As discussed earlier in this chapter, there are many problems with the use of natural languages for information retrieval, including synonymity, semantic ambiguity resulting from the existence of homographs, the semantic ambiguity inherent in "soft" disciplines, false drops caused by contextual ambiguity, and the difficulty of performing generic searches. The use of controlled vocabularies—artificial languages for the

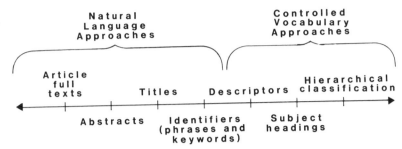

Figure 2.3   Information description languages, aranged by degree of departure from natural language.

representation of information—can to a large degree solve these problems. However, controlled vocabularies have their own problems. They are not panaceas. The characteristics, advantages and disadvantages of subject indexing using controlled vocabularies will be explored in the pages that follow.

Figure 2.3 lists some major classes of information description languages, arranged along a continuum, by the degree to which each approach departs from natural language prose. On the left half of the continuum are represented the natural language approaches to information representation, including the full text of the article, abstract, and title. A fourth class, here called *identifier*, refers to keywords that are extracted from the original text by indexers. Discussion of identifiers will be deferred until later.

The first and simplest form of vocabulary control is the use of *descriptors*, as listed and described in a *thesaurus*. A thesaurus is a controlled vocabulary, usually derived from a dynamic, growing document collection, in which the elements of the vocabulary have certain logical relationships with one another. The functions of a thesaurus are to define and list valid and invalid elements of the vocabulary, and to exhibit the relationships among the valid terms. Many of the problems observed earlier with natural language—homographs, synonyms, generic searches, and even false coordinations—are dealt with in the structure of the thesaurus. An example of one segment of a thesaurus of concepts related to privacy is provided in Table 2.8.

The basic relationships between elements of the vocabulary in a thesaurus are:

BT	broader term
NT	narrower term
USE	use
UF	used for
RT	related term
SN	scope note

USE and UF point toward and away from valid vocabulary elements, respectively. If 'operations research' were selected by the thesaurus makers as the preferred term (that is, to become a valid element of the vocabulary, to be

TABLE 2.8
Portion of Harter, Stephen P. *Thesaurus of Privacy Descriptors; Interdisciplinary Concepts and Relationships**

PHYSICAL SECURITY
    BT   security
    RT   access controls
           administrative security
           communications security
           data security
           encryption

POLYGRAPHS
    UF   lie detectors
    BT   electronic eavesdropping
    RT   employment testing
           invasion of privacy
           personality measurement
           psychophysiology

PRIVACY
    RT   autonomy
           civil liberties
           common law, privacy
           confidentiality
           constitutional right of privacy
           dignity
           freedom
           freedom of information
           individualism
           information policy
           public interest
           respect
           security
           social behavior
           social processes

PRIVACY ACT OF 1974
    BT   privacy legislation, U.S.
    RT   data processing technologies
           dissemination of personal information
           obsolescence of personal information
           personal information systems, public sector
           social security number

PRIVACY LEGISLATION, INTERNATIONAL
    RT   data processing technologies
           information utility
           personal information systems, international
           privacy legislation, U.S.

PRIVACY LEGISLATION, U.S.
    NT   Buckley Amendment

(continues)

TABLE 2.8 (*continued*)

      Fair Credit Reporting Act
      Privacy Act of 1974
  RT civil liberties
      common law, privacy
      constitutional right of privacy
      credit records
      educational records
      freedom of information
      freedom of the press
      privacy legislation, international
      social impact of technology

privacy transformations
  USE ENCRYPTION
PRIVACY INVESTIGATIONS
  RT counter surveillance
      snooping
      surveillance
PRIVILEGED COMMUNICATION
  RT confidentiality
      medical records
      medical research
      professional ethics
      research records
      welfare records
PROFESSIONAL ETHICS
  UF ethical behavior
  RT computer crime
      confidentiality
      individualism
      information gathering methods
      medical records
      medical research
      privileged communication
      research records
      security

property
  USE PERSONAL PROPERTY
PSYCHOLOGICAL TESTING
  UF educational testing
  BT information gathering methods
  NT achievement testing
      employment testing
      intelligence testing
      personality measurement
      vocational aptitude testing

(continues)

TABLE 2.8 (*continued*)

RT   behavior modification
       behavioral research
       brainwashing
       dissemination of personal information
       drugs
       educational records
       espionage
       invasion of privacy
       medical research
       personal information
       personal records
       personnel records
       psychophysiology
       social research
       subaudible information
       subliminal information

*Unpublished manuscript, Bloomington, Indiana, 1981.

used instead of 'operations analysis' and other near-synonyms) then the thesaurus entry reflecting this decision would be:

OPERATIONS RESEARCH
UF   operations analysis

The thesaurus would also contain a parallel entry for operations analysis, directing the user who consults it toward the preferred term. In this way, thesauri control the synonym problem of natural language. If natural language contains several terms that might be used to represent the same, or nearly the same, concept, the thesaurus would guide the choice of vocabulary toward the single valid term. Note that the selection of a preferred term from among several candidates may be arbitrary.

The guidance provided by USE and UF references is particularly helpful to the information retrieval specialist, who now (theoretically, at least) need not think of all possible ways of representing a given concept, if the database being searched is one that has been indexed using a thesaurus. The preferred term can be used for the search, just as it was used in the indexing process, to represent all occurrences of the concept in the database.

The *scope note* is used to distinguish between potential homographs. If there is more than one potential use of a particular word or phrase in a database, then the scope note is used to clarify the intended meaning. Sometimes parenthetical expressions that modify the term are also used to distinguish between two different concepts represented by the same word or phrase.

Example 2.8. In the 1980 edition of the *Thesaurus of ERIC Descriptors*, the following entries can be found (see Figure 2.4):

RELAXATION TRAINING *Mar. 1980*
CIJE: 188   RIE: 96   GC: 230
SN Training that emphasizes the acquisition of skills and techniques for managing and reducing stress, anxiety, and tension
UF Progressive Relaxation (1967-1980)
BT Psychotherapy
RT Anxiety
    Biofeedback
    Desensitization
    Hypertension
    Hypnosis
    Physiology
    Stress Management
    Transcendental Meditation

RELEASED TIME *Jul. 1966*
CIJE: 44   RIE: 92   GC: 630
SN Time granted to students, employees, or institutionalized persons to pursue special activities
UF Day Release
    Study Release Programs
    Work Release
RT Correctional Education
    Employer Employee Relationship
    Flexible Working Hours
    Industrial Training
    Leaves Of Absence
    Off The Job Training
    Personnel Policy
    Religious Education
    Sabbatical Leaves
    School Schedules
    Scope Of Bargaining

RELEVANCE (EDUCATION) *Jul. 1969*
CIJE: 3,217   RIE: 1,811   GC: 330
SN Applicability of what is taught by schools to the needs and interests of students and society

RELIABILITY *Jul. 1966*
CIJE: 576   RIE: 456   GC: 820
SN Extent to which something is consistent, dependable, and stable over repeated trials (note if applicable use the more specific terms "test reliability" and/or "interrater reliability")
UF Consistency
    Dependability
NT Interrater Reliability
    Test Reliability
BT Evaluation Criteria
RT Correlation
    Error Of Measurement
    Error Patterns
    Expectation
    Generalizability Theory
    Performance
    Prediction
    Probability
    Quality Control
    Relevance (Information Retrieval)
    Risk
    Sample Size
    Statistical Analysis
    Statistical Data
    Statistical Distributions
    True Scores
    Validity
    Weighted Scores

Relief Teachers
USE SUBSTITUTE TEACHERS

RELIGION *Jul. 1966*
CIJE: 578   RIE: 628   GC: 430
NT Buddhism
    Christianity
    Confucianism
    Judaism
    Taoism
RT Beliefs
    Biblical Literature

RELIGIOUS CULTURAL GROUPS *Jul. 1966*
CIJE: 182   RIE: 167   GC: 560
UF Religious Groups
NT Catholics
    Jews
    Protestants
BT Groups
    Buddhism
RT Caste
    Christianity
    Clergy
    Confucianism
    Culture
    Ethnic Groups
    Ethnic Relations
    Interfaith Relations
    Judaism
    Minority Groups
    Nuns
    Priests
    Religion
    Religious Conflict
    Religious Organizations
    Taoism

RELIGIOUS DIFFERENCES *Jul. 1966*
CIJE: 75   RIE: 66   GC: 510
BT Differences
RT Individual Differences
    Interfaith Relations
    Intermarriage
    Religion
    Religious Factors

RELIGIOUS DISCRIMINATION *Jul. 1966*
CIJE: 54   RIE: 57   GC: 540
BT Social Discrimination
RT Affirmative Action
    Anti Semitism
    Ethnic Discrimination
    Interfaith Relations

RELIGIOUS ORGANIZATIONS *Jul. 1966*
CIJE: 96   RIE: 137   GC: 520
UF Religious Agencies (1966 1980)
    Organizations (Groups)
BT Churches
RT Church Related Colleges
    Clergy
    Institutions
    Nonprofit Organizations
    Religion
    Religious Cultural Groups
    Voluntary Agencies

RELOCATABLE FACILITIES *Dec. 1972*
CIJE: 22   RIE: 20   GC: 920
UF Portable Facilities
    Temporary Facilities
    Facilities
BT Air Structures
RT Building Innovation
    Encapsulated Facilities
    Facility Expansion
    Facility Planning
    Flexible Facilities
    Mobile Classrooms
    Mobile Clinics
    Mobile Laboratories
    Prefabrication

RELOCATION *Jul. 1966*
CIJE: 137   RIE: 257   GC: 550
SN The voluntary or forced removal of an individual or group and establishment in a new place
NT Rural Resettlement
BT Migration
RT American Indian History
    American Indians
    Area Studies
    Family Mobility
    Geographic Location
    Labor Problems

UF Curriculum Relevance
   Educational Relevance
RT Accountability
   Career Education
   Core Curriculum
   Curriculum Development
   Curriculum Evaluation
   Educational Improvement
   Educational Needs
   Educational Objectives
   Educational Responsibility
   Education Work Relationship
   Experimental Colleges
   Experimental Schools
   Free Schools
   Futures (Of Society)
   Living Learning Centers
   Nontraditional Education
   Student Educational Objectives
   Student Interests
   Student Needs
   Student School Relationship
   Vocational Education

RELEVANCE (INFORMATION RETRIEVAL)   *Jun. 1969*
   CIJE: 229   RIE: 131   GC: 710
SN The number of retrieved documents judged relevant in proportion to the number of documents returned in response to a query
UF Precision Ratio
   Recall Ratio
BT Ratios (Mathematics)
RT Bibliographic Coupling
   Evaluation Methods
   Information Retrieval
   Performance
   Reliability
   Search Strategies
   Systems Analysis
   User Satisfaction (Information)

Churches
Church Programs
Church Role
Church Workers
Clergy
Creationism
Cultural Activities
Humanities
Hymns
Interfaith Relations
Islamic Culture
Meditation
Modernism
Mysticism
Naturalism
Nuns
Philosophy
Priests
Religious Conflict
Religious Cultural Groups
Religious Differences
Religious Discrimination
Religious Education
Religious Factors
Religious Organizations
State Church Separation
Theological Education
Traditionalism

Religious Agencies (1966 1980)   *Jul. 1966*
USE RELIGIOUS ORGANIZATIONS

RELIGIOUS CONFLICT   *Jul. 1966*
   CIJE: 73   RIE: 43   GC: 540
BT Conflict
RT Culture Conflict
   Ethnicity
   Interfaith Relations
   Religion
   Religious Cultural Groups
   Religious Discrimination
   Religious Factors

Religion
Religious Conflict
Religious Factors
Reverse Discrimination
Social Bias

RELIGIOUS EDUCATION   *Jul. 1966*
   CIJE: 482   RIE: 360   GC: 400
SN Instruction in religion at any level not leading to a degree in theology (note: prior to mar80, this term was not restricted by a scope note -- for formal education for careers in religion, including the clergy, use "theological education")
BT Education
RT Catholic Educators
   Catholic Schools
   Church Programs
   Church Related Colleges
   Church Workers
   Clergy
   Ethical Instruction
   Ethics
   Lay Teachers
   Parochial Schools
   Released Time
   Religion
   Theological Education

RELIGIOUS FACTORS   *Jul. 1966*
   CIJE: 502   RIE: 329   GC: 520
BT Influences
RT Creationism
   Cultural Influences
   Religion
   Religious Conflict
   Religious Differences
   Religious Discrimination

Religious Groups
USE RELIGIOUS CULTURAL GROUPS

Labor Turnover
Labor Utilization
Land Settlement
Migrants
Migration
Migration Patterns
Nonreservation American Indians
Occupational Mobility
Place Of Residence
Population Distribution
Population Trends
Refugees
Residential Patterns
Rural To Urban Migration
Transfer Policy
Transfer Programs
Urban To Rural Migration
Urban To Suburban Migration

REMARRIAGE   *Oct. 1982*
   CIJE: 34   RIE: 7   GC: 520
SN The act or state of marriage following widow(er)hood or divorce
BT Marriage
RT Divorce
   Kinship
   Stepfamily
   Widowed

Remedial Arithmetic (1966 1980)
USE ARITHMETIC; REMEDIAL MATHEMATICS

Remedial Courses (1966 1980)
USE REMEDIAL INSTRUCTION

Remedial Education
USE REMEDIAL INSTRUCTION

Remedial Education Programs
USE REMEDIAL PROGRAMS

Figure 2.4   Page from *Thesaurus of ERIC Descriptors.*

RELEVANCE (EDUCATION)
SN Applicability of what is taught by schools to the needs and interests
of students and society
:
:

RELEVANCE (INFORMATION RETRIEVAL)
SN The number of retrieved documents judged relevant in proportion
to the number of documents returned in response to a query
:
:

Thus there are two meanings for the descriptor RELEVANCE represented
in the *Thesaurus*, and the parenthetic qualifiers are used to disambiguate
them.

BT and NT indicate broader terms and narrower terms, respectively, and
are used to suggest hierarchical relationships. The following might be an entry
in a particular thesaurus:

DOGS
BT   MAMMALS
NT   BEAGLES
        SCHNAUZERS
        COLLIES

The related term relationship (RT) suggests that two concepts are in *some*
relationship to one another. However, the relationship should neither be hierarchical (BT,NT) nor one of synonymity (USE,UF). RT relationships are
more subtle than either of these, and the list of terms listed as being related
to a given term in a thesaurus is likely to contain fairly heterogeneous terms.
These terms should *not* be regarded as synonymous. They are meant only
to suggest some interesting conceptual relationships that may (and may not)
be useful to an indexer or a searcher in representing a given information
problem.

Finally, we should note how the problem of false drops or false coordinations is handled by a thesaurus. If a phrase like 'information theory' is in
common use in a discipline, then it may become a descriptor in its multi-
word form, rather than as two separate words. In this way the two concepts
of information and theory are said to be *pre-coordinated* in the controlled
vocabulary. A pre-coordinate system is a controlled vocabulary in which
specific, complex subjects involving the intersection of two or more simpler
concepts are themselves elements in the indexing language. In ERIC, for
example, a searcher interested in the concept of information theory can search
on the descriptor 'information theory' instead of the separate terms 'infor-

mation' and 'theory.' This obviates the false drop problem caused by *post-coordination*, that is, by combining the natural language terms at the time of the search.

Identifiers are natural language words and phrases that are intended to serve as additional entry points to an information source—access points that would not otherwise be possible because the concepts cannot be represented using thesaurus terms. The Educational Resources Information Center (ERIC) describes the concept of an identifier in the following way:

> "Identifiers" are key words or "indexable" concepts intended to add depth to subject indexing that is not always possible with Descriptors alone. Identifiers are not found in the *Thesaurus*, since they are generally: (1) proper names, or (2) concepts not yet represented by approved Descriptors [19].

Proper names offer the potential to specify such information as a geographic location, the name of an educational test, or a piece of legislation. Their potential retrieval value for this purpose is obvious. In the second case, words or phrases may be used as identifiers if they seem to be representing a concept that, for whatever reason, has no counterpart in the controlled vocabulary—in this case the *Thesaurus of ERIC Descriptors*. In this latter category might be found new concepts—ideas on the cutting edge of research. Or, they might simply be too specific or too rarely used by scholars or scientists writing in the literature of the discipline to be included as descriptors in the thesaurus, in the judgment of the thesaurus builders. Hence such terms as 'probabilistic indexing,' 'queuing theory,' and 'online searching' did not appear in the 1984 edition of the *Thesaurus of ERIC Descriptors* although all are in common use in library and information science. However, an ERIC indexer might assign an article discussing aspects of online searching the identifier 'online searching.'

Example 2.9. In the 1980 edition of the *Thesaurus of ERIC Descriptors*, the term 'operations research' is a descriptor. The following terms are listed as narrower than or related to operations research: game theory, action research, cost effectiveness, critical path method, information theory, linear programming, long range planning, management systems, mathematical models, models, planning, quality control, and search strategies. However, the following concepts of operations research do *not* appear in the *Thesaurus*: queuing theory, dynamic programming, exponential growth and decay, Bradford's law, Lotka's law, Poisson distribution, and many others.

Consequently, a searcher interested in finding material in the ERIC database on the concept of exponential growth would have to look for this phrase either as an identifier or in natural language passages—full texts, abstracts, or titles. Moreover, searching under the term 'operations research' will *not* retrieve all items discussing concepts of operations research. Just as in natural language, each of these descriptors must be entered separately if a search on the general subject of operations research is what is wanted.

Lists of controlled subject headings are related to subject thesauri. These are perhaps best exemplified by the subject heading lists used in most traditional libraries in the United States: *Sears List of Subject Headings*, used in most public libraries and *Library of Congress Subject Headings*, used in most university libraries [20]. Figure 2.5 shows a portion of this latter work. Note that USE and UF are replaced by "see" and "see from" (x).

Subject heading lists tend to use terminology that is much broader than that found in thesauri. Moreover, far fewer related terms are typically suggested, through the "see also" (sa) and "see also from" (xx) links. "See also" links do not distinguish between hierarchical relationships and related terms, unlike the thesaurus, which uses BT, NT, and RT to make these distinctions.

There is an important philosophical difference as well between thesauri and subject headings. Subject heading lists are often *a priori* attempts to represent the whole of the structure of the universe (or at least a subset thereof) and are not based on specific document collections. In contrast, thesauri are usually derived from existing, living and growing collections of books, journals, etc. in a subject discipline. The vocabulary in a thesaurus is meant to address problems of synonymity and semantic ambiguity in these collections. There is a pragmatic aspect to the construction of thesauri that is not present in the philosophical work of subject heading makers or classificationists. We will return to this point later in the chapter.

A final type of artificial language for document representation is the classification scheme. The most familiar of these is probably the Dewey Decimal Classification (DDC). Used in the United States primarily to classify books, the Dewey Decimal Classification (DDC) is an *a priori* representation of all human knowledge in a great hierarchy. Melvil Dewey began with ten classes of knowledge, and used the decimal numeration system to represent these classes. As each class was divided into subclasses, and those into sub-subclasses, the decimal system provided a natural means of representing the hierarchical relationships between concepts. However, there is no good way of introducing new knowledge that does not logically fit into the scheme. Charles Meadow [21] discusses in detail the example of "artificial earth satellite" that in the DDC is assigned the number 629.138 82. This is broken down as follows:

600	Technology (applied science)
620	Engineering
629	Other branches of engineering
629.13	Aeronautics
629.138	Uses of aircraft
629.138 8	Space flight

Artificial earth satellites and space flight both appear under 'uses of aircraft,'' which is the only place that they can logically occur in DDC, and yet where clearly they do not belong. Meadow's lengthy and cogent analysis of this example is well worth reading to show both the strengths and the weaknesses of traditional classification systems.

There is not sufficient space in this book to deal with any depth the principles and issues of thesaurus, index, and classification construction and use. This short introduction has only scratched the surface, and the interested reader is encouraged to pursue these subjects further [22].

Much time has been spent in this chapter discussing issues relating to one's choice of problem and document description languages. This is a crucial subject because the online searcher will typically have numerous problem-representation languages that might be used in a given database. In most databases, natural language searching in titles, abstracts, identifiers, and even full texts is often possible. Depending on the database, descriptors, subject headings, and classification codes may also be available for use.

Thus the searcher is faced with an embarrassment of riches. Which of the several options or mixtures of options is best for a particular search problem? What are advantages and disadvantages associated with each approach? Under what conditions will searching natural language passages be useful? Descriptors? Classification codes? Although it will not be possible to provide definitive answers that apply to every search problem and database to these and related questions, an attempt will be made in the next section of this chapter to address these concerns.

2.6 CONTROLLED VOCABULARIES
AND NATURAL LANGUAGES: A COMPARISON

Controlled vocabularies and natural language each have advantages and disadvantages for information indexing and online information retrieval. For example, where one is rigid, inflexible, but precise, the other is highly expressive, flexible, but potentially ambiguous. Table 2.9 summarizes these general

Poets, Spanish
— 17th century
Poets, Women
See Women poets
Poets as teachers
sa Poetry-in-the-Schools Program
xx Authors as teachers
Teachers
Poets-in-the-Schools Program
See Poetry-in-the-Schools Program
Poets laureate (PR505)
x Laureates
Poets' monuments (Indirect)
xx Monuments
Sepulchral monuments
Poggio a Caiano. Villa
x Lorenzo de Medici Villa, Poggio a Caiano
xx Architecture, Domestic—Italy
Poggio-Marinaccio, Corsica. Torra di Zenninchi (DC801.P)
x Torra di Zenninchi; Poggio-Marinaccio, Corsica
Zenninchi Tower, Poggio-Marinaccio, Corsica
xx Towers—France
POGO (Computer program)
xx Computer graphics
Pogonophryne (QL638.N6)
xx Nototheniidae
Pogoro (Bantu tribe) (DT443)
x Wapogoro (Bantu tribe)
xx Ethnology—Tanganyika
Pogoro language (PL8601)
xx Bantu languages
Pogórze Dynowskie, Poland
See Dynów Upland, Poland
Pogórze Przemyskie, Poland
See Przemyśl Upland, Poland
Pohai, Gulf of
See Po Hai, China

xx World War, 1939-1945—Campaigns—Libya
Point Batman, Australia
See Batman Point, Australia
Point defects (QD921)
sa Color centers
Flux pinning
Impurity centers
x Defects, Point
xx Crystals—Defects
Dislocations in crystals
Impurity centers
Point Ellice Bridge, Victoria, B.C.
See Victoria, B.C.—Bridges—Point Ellice Bridge
Point estimation
See Fix-point estimation
Point four program
See Technical assistance, American
Point mappings (Mathematics)
x Equations. Recurrent
Mappings, Point (Mathematics)
Recurrence relations in functional differential equations
Recurrent equations
xx Differentiable dynamical systems
Functional differential equations
Mappings (Mathematics)
Point-of-purchase advertising
See Advertising, Point-of-sale
Point-of-sale advertising
See Advertising, Point-of-sale
Point-of-sale industry
See Point-of-sale systems industry
Point-of-sale systems industry (Indirect) (HD9999.B9)
sa Cash registers
Credit cards
x Point-of-sale industry
Point-of-sale terminals industry
xx Office equipment and supplies

Pointillism
See Neo-impressionism (Art)
Points, Projectile
See Projectile points
Points of contact (Conflict of laws) (Indirect)
sa Citizenship as point of contact (Conflict of laws)
Domicile as point of contact (Conflict of laws)
Locus regit actum
x Connecting factors (Conflict of laws)
Test factors (Conflict of laws)
xx Conflict of laws
Points of the compass
See Cardinal points
Poison-ash
See Poison-sumac
Poison bottles (Indirect)
x Bottles
Poison control centers (Indirect)
sa Poisoning. Accidental
xx Emergency medical services
Health facilities
Poisoning, Accidental
Toxicology
Poison-dogwood
See Poison-sumac
Poison-elder
See Poison-sumac
Poison gas
See Gases, Asphyxiating and poisonous
Poison-ivy (SB618.P6)
x Poison oak
Example under Poisonous plants
— Control (Indirect) (SB618.P6)
xx Weed control
Poison oak
See Poison-ivy
Poison pen letters
See Anonymous letters
Poison spider

Pohansko site, Czechoslovakia
  xx Czechoslovakia—Antiquities
Pohjanmaa, Finland
  x Etelä-Pohjanmaa, Finland
    Keski-Pohjanmaa, Finland
    Österbotten, Finland
    Ostrobothnia, Finland
    Pohjois-Pohjanmaa, Finland
Pohjois-Pohjanmaa, Finland
  See Pohjanmaa, Finland
Pohjois-Suomen malmitiedostoprojekti
  x Ore Data File Project for Northern
    Finland
  xx Information storage and retrieval
    systems—Mines and mineral
    resources
    Ore-deposits—Finland
Poi (TX360.H3)
Poidevain family
  See Le Poittevain family
Poikilotherms
  x Cold-blooded animals
    Ectotherms
    Heterotherms
  xx Animal heat
    Body temperature
    Zoology
Poilly family
  x Depoilly family
Poincaré series
  x Series, Poincaré
Poinsettias (Culture, SB413.P63)
Point, Critical
  See Critical point
Point, Transition
  See Transition temperature
Point 175, Battle of, 1941 (D766.93)
  x Sunday of the Dead, Battle of, 1941
    Totensonntag Battle, 1941

Point-of-sale terminals industry
  See Point-of-sale systems industry
Point of view (Literature) (PN3383.P)
  sa First person narrative
  x Fiction—Technique
    Narration (Rhetoric)
Point Omega
  See Omega Point
Point Pleasant, Battle of, 1774 (E83.77)
  xx United States—History—Revolution,
    1775-1783—Campaigns and battles
    Virginia—History—Colonial period, ca.
    1600-1775
Point processes (QA274.42)
  sa Poisson processes
  x Processes, Point
  xx Stochastic processes
Point Roberts, Wash.
Point-to-point horses
  See Hunters (Horses)
Point-to-point racing (Indirect) (SF359.4)
  sa Steeplechasing
  xx Horse-racing
    Horse-shows
    Steeplechasing
  — England
    sa Lady Dudley Challenge Cup
Pointe-aux-Buissons site, Québec
  xx Indians of North America—Québec
    (Province)—Antiquities
    Iroquois Indians—Antiquities
    Québec (Province)—Antiquities
Pointe de Grave, France
  See Grave Point, France
Pointe du Raz, France
  See Raz Point, France
Pointers (Dogs) (SF429.P7)
  sa German short-haired pointers
    German wirehaired pointers
  xx Bird dogs

  See Black widow spider
Poison-sumac (SB618.P)
  x Dogwood, Poison
    Poison-ash
    Poison-dogwood
    Poison-elder
    Swamp-dogwood
    Swamp-sumac
  Example under Poisonous plants
Poisoners (Indirect)
  xx Poisoning
Poisoning (Indirect)
  sa Poisoners
    Self-poisoning
    Trials (Poisoning)
  xx Assault and battery
    Criminal law
    Forensic toxicology
    Homicide
    Murder
Poisoning, Accidental (Indirect)
  sa Poison control centers
  xx Accidents
    Poison control centers
    Poisons
    Toxicology
  — Prevention
    See Poisons—Safety measures
Poisoning of catalysts
  See Catalyst poisoning
Poisoning of fish
  See Piscicides
Poisonous animals (Indirect) (QP941)
  sa Arthropoda, Poisonous
    Poisonous fishes
    Poisonous shellfish
    Poisonous snakes
    Toxins
    Venom
  x Animals, Poisonous

Figure 2.5 Page from *Library of Congress Subject Headings*.

TABLE 2.9
General Attributes of Natural Language and Controlled Vocabularies

Natural language	Controlled Vocabularies
highly expressive	not very expressive
very difficult to make generic searches	relatively easy to make generic searches
permits a variety of access points	permits only a few access points
problem with synonyms	controlled for synonyms
problem with homographs	controlled for homographs
problem with false drops	pre-coordinated for false drops
highly flexible	highly inflexible
highly representative of reality	not very representative of reality
represents (any) many points of view	represents a single point of view
requires no training to use	requires training
easy to represent new concepts	difficult or impossible to represent new concepts
easy to represent complex concepts	difficult or impossible to represent complex concepts
ambiguous, fuzzy, soft	unambiguous, precise, hard
unstandardized	standardized
freedom of expression	highly restricted freedom of expression
not very compact	highly compact
no indexing necessary	problems with inconsistent indexing
user must think of own search terms, synonyms, etc.	additional terms are suggested by cross reference structure
high degree of exhaustivity	low degree of exhaustivity

attributes. It should be noted that the attributes listed as characteristic of controlled vocabularies do not describe all controlled vocabularies equally well. They are listed as generalizations that, while generally characteristic of many controlled vocabularies, may fail to be true for particular examples.

The advantages of controlled vocabularies for the problems of semantic and contextual ambiguity (homographs and false drops) and synonym control have already been discussed. However, a price must be paid for this control. Specifically, the vocabulary in any controlled language is limited, inflexible, and rigid. One's freedom of expression is greatly curtailed with a controlled vocabulary, and it may be difficult or impossible to represent new or complex concepts.

In addition to these problems, the number of concepts indexed in a given document using controlled vocabularies is relatively small compared to the number of entry points to a document offered by natural language approaches. Typically, only a few terms from a controlled vocabulary are assigned to represent a document. This number is called the depth or *exhaustivity* of the indexing. However, even highly exhaustive indexing, such as that provided by the National Library of Medicine for its databases, cannot begin to approach the exhaustivity provided by natural language, especially that offered by the full text of the document. Because a given document is assigned only a few terms from the controlled vocabulary (the actual number depending on the indexing policy of the database producer) there are only a few terms that one can select from the vocabulary that would succeed in retrieving that document, compared to many times this number of possibilities using natural language approaches.

However, the apparent advantages of natural language can also be seen as disadvantages. The flexibility and expressiveness possible in natural languages are made possible by the ambiguity inherent in the language. If unambiguous expression is what is wanted, natural language may be a disaster. Inflexibility may be regarded as an advantage, depending on the application.

A few of the characteristics listed in Table 2.9 deserve further comment. The observation that controlled vocabularies do not represent reality is directed more to hierarchical classification systems than to thesauri. In a revolt against classification that began in the 1950's, Taube, Shera, Jones, and others objected to the artificiality of controlled vocabularies and hierarchical classification in particular. As Jesse Shera put it, classical Aristotelian logic and the "unyielding scaffold of the hierarchy" fail "to take into account the interconnectedness of real things" [23].

This is the problem of *mutual exclusivity* implicit in every hierarchical classification scheme. The division of the universe into genus, species, subspecies, etc. has as its fundamental assumption that, excepting classes that are related at the generic/specific level, none of the classes at any given level of the hierarchy have anything in common with any of the other classes at that level, or any other level. But, it can be argued, the real world is not this way. In the real world, everything is interconnected. This point was made cogently by Jones, who carefully examined several pairs of classes commonly thought of as mutually exclusive: life and death, man and woman, beach and sea. For each, Jones showed that the distinction is a myth, a convenient device of language and thought, but not representative of reality [24].

The second difficulty with hierarchical classification systems is true of controlled vocabularies as a class. That is the problem of "point of view." All perception requires a point of view, but in the real world, these are in a state of constant revision and change. Moreover, the perspective of one human being is likely to be different from that of another. While classification (or conceptualization) at the individual level is necessary for thought, it is not obvious that a single artificial language is particularly useful for the species as a whole. To invent a language is to freeze a single point of view in time and to require everyone to adhere to it:

Classification is the crystallization or formalization of inferential thinking, born of sensory perception, conditioned by the operation of the human brain, and shaped by human experience. It lies at the foundation of all thought, but it is pragmatic and it is instrumental. It is at once permanent and ephemeral. Permanent because without it cognition is impossible; ephemeral because it can be rejected when its utility is exhausted [25].

The artificiality and subjectivity inherent in attempts to apply a hierarchical classification system to the representation of knowledge is summed up nicely in a statement that has been attributed to William E. Batten: "Only God can classify" [26].

We suggested earlier that the point of view problem is one common to all controlled vocabularies, not simply classification systems. Catalogers, indexers, and classificationists are individuals, and no matter how much training is provided them to control or destroy this individuality for the sake of standardization and uniformity, they will remain individuals with differing perspectives. Different indexers are, therefore, likely to assign different index terms to the same documents. There has been a substantial amount of research verifying this hypothesis, many of which are cited in Cooper's paper, "Is Interindexer Consistency a Hobgoblin?" [27]. Although in this paper Cooper demonstrated that consistency in indexing will not *necessarily* lead to improvements in retrieval effectiveness, one is left with a sense of unease regarding sole reliance on a tool which has been shown again and again to be constructed in a most inconsistent manner.

The implications of these attributes of natural language and controlled vocabularies for online information retrieval are not obvious. It would be a mistake to conclude, as some have done, that one or the other approach should be condemned to disuse. Rather, there are occasions in which the use of thesauri, subject headings, or classification systems offer an excellent approach to a literature. For other search problems, natural language searching of full texts, abstracts, titles, or identifiers offers the most hope for success. For still other problems, a mixture of approaches would seem most useful.

Since the 1950's, a body of research in information storage and retrieval has confirmed a general finding that automatic indexing based on statistical, syntactic, and semantic analysis of natural language text produces results at least as acceptable as those achievable with controlled vocabularies. Seminal early work was done by Swanson [28] and Cleverdon and Keen, at Cranfield, England [29]. Gerard Salton has, in his many experiments with the SMART system, been the most consistently productive researcher in automatic indexing for the past two decades [30], and in a recent book, Salton and Michael McGill provide an excellent introduction to this body of research [31].

Despite much evidence supporting the efficacy of natural language, sometimes supplemented by automatic techniques, it should be noted that, to date, little comparative research has been carried out with the very large databases currently available for searching in libraries and information centers using commercial search services. Moreover, most research has been done with hard engineering or scientific databases. In short, it is by no means clear, from current research findings, that controlled vocabularies can or should be discarded in favor of natural language.

The research question posed in much early work in information storage and retrieval was: what is the "best," or "ideal" problem and document description language for information retrieval? This is now recognized as not being a useful question. Most researchers now believe that the "best" approach, if indeed one exists, depends on the information problem and its context as well as the search systems and databases to be used. For the present at least, online information retrieval will be conducted most effectively with a mixture of controlled vocabularies and natural language.

When should natural language or controlled vocabularies be used in online information retrieval? The following cautious generalizations can be made. One should consider searching using natural language if:

1. Subtle nuances of meaning are important to the information seeker, requiring the specificity and expressiveness of natural language to represent a concept. This would be most likely to occur if the concept is new or has been discussed in the literature using a variety of words and phrases.

2. Appropriate terms with which to represent a concept do not exist in a controlled vocabulary.

3. The information seeker wants to carry out a comprehensive search on a topic or problem, including the retrieval of peripheral materials. In such a case it is often useful to supplement terms in a controlled vocabulary to increase the number of items retrieved in the search.

4. The literature to be searched is poorly defined, belonging to a "soft" discipline.

One should consider searching using a controlled vocabulary if:

1. Accurate, precise, unambiguous representation of concepts of the information need can be accomplished using the controlled vocabulary.

2. The information seeker wants to carry out a limited search that retrieves a few, highly useful items, and excludes the retrieval of peripheral materials.

3. The subject matter to be searched is well-defined, belonging to a "hard" discipline.

4. Generic searches are possible in the controlled vocabulary.

In practice, most searchers probably use a combination of approaches for most problems. Most bibliographic databases can be searched using any combination of the following: abstracts, titles, identifiers, descriptors or subject headings, and classification codes. In addition, full texts of journal articles are available for searching on increasingly many databases. Because of the wealth of possibilities presented to the searcher, there is a need for new vocabulary aids for the online searcher. Several interesting suggestions for such tools have been made by Piternick [32]. These include enhanced thesauri and lists of subject headings, term listings, synonym listings, and merged vocabularies.

The choice of vocabulary terms to represent the concepts of a search problem is not a trivial decision. There are no easy rules. This issue will be addressed continuously throughout the remainder of the book.

2.7 CITATION INDEXING

This chapter concludes with a brief introduction to citation indexing. Strictly speaking, citation indexing is less a *language* than it is a methodology for dealing with certain artifacts of the writing process: cited references appearing in published scientific and scholarly papers. Citation approaches to online information retrieval are based neither on natural language nor controlled indexing languages. They are based on an assumption that is as powerful as it is simple: that an author's act of citing a work of another author means that there is a semantic relationship between the citing and cited works.

There may be many reasons for one paper citing another. An author may wish to pay homage to a true pioneer. An idea or method may be borrowed from the cited paper. The author of the cited paper may be described as the source of a laboratory technique, as representing a different but related line of inquiry, as a collaborator on derivative work, as the source of an idea that is to be pursued in the present work, as the author of a particularly well-stated passage, as useful background reading, or even as the precursor of the present research. As a byproduct of the derivative nature of the scientific enterprise, citations form a vital link between the present work and what has come before.

There are of course other reasons for citing a paper. One might cite a particularly unproductive line of investigation, or methodology that is wanting in one or more respects, or an incorrect assumption, or outright errors that the present paper will in due time set straight. Self citation also presents some problems of interpretation. Even in these cases, however, there is usually a semantic link between the cited and citing papers. The nature of the link may require additional investigation to understand, but it is usually there.

The idea behind citation indexing is simple. Suppose that one knows of a published work that meets one's information need, wholly or in part. Further, suppose that other papers have cited this work. Now we have assumed that there is a semantic relationship between the cited and citing papers. It follows that there is likely to be a semantic link *between the citing paper and the information need*. A link has been established, forward in time, between the original work and papers that have cited the work, and by so doing, new papers can be discovered that relate to the present information need.

The use of citation indexes for literature searching and online information storage and retrieval was initiated by Eugene Garfield, who established the Institute for Scientific Information (ISI) to carry out his ideas. Garfield was inspired by *Shepard's Citations*, long used as a tool by the legal profession. The historical development of ISI's *Science Citation Index*, followed by *Social Sciences Citation Index*, and *Arts & Humanities Citation Index*, is described by Garfield in [33].

In its printed forms, *Science Citation Index* and its companion publications are citation indexes. Their major feature is that they list, for cited references in the sciences, social sciences, and arts and humanities, all those papers published in the journals indexed that have cited those references. Online, these can all be retrieved at once. Using the printed indexes, several volumes will need to be examined. The reader who has not examined and used the print versions of these tools is urged to do so.

Our primary interest in this book is in the machine-readable versions of these tools, available as databases for online searching on several search systems. The major advantages of citation approaches to subject searching are:

1. One need not be concerned with the natural language/controlled vocabulary problems outlined in the remainder of this chapter. If a paper can be found that meets the information need and has been cited in the published literature, semantic links from this seed to other papers can be established with no additional information. If desired, searches can be cycled by using as additional seeds the newly discovered documents that meet the information need.

2. The approach lends itself to interdisciplinary problem areas. Most controlled vocabulary approaches to literature searching are based on rather narrow definitions of a discipline (education, sociology, psychology, etc.), operationally defined by the list of journals indexed by the database producer. In contrast, citation approaches will reveal a pertinent article even if it has been published in a journal in another discipline. It would be extremely difficult to find such a paper either through a natural language or a controlled vocabulary approach, without an enormous amount of effort.

3. Citation indexes can be used to go forward in time, in contrast to the use of published bibliographies, which lead one backwards in time. Taken together, these two approaches can be extremely useful and complementary search devices.

Currently, citation approaches are probably underutilized as tools for

online information retrieval. Later in the book several approaches using citation indexing will be suggested. As supplements to natural language and controlled vocabulary approaches to information retrieval, or even as the primary
tool of investigation, citation indexes can be extremely valuable tools of
inquiry.

PROBLEMS

1. Obtain the documentation describing the command language of an operational information
retrieval system, such as ORBIT or MEDLINE. Study the vocabulary and rules of syntax for
the system, and answer the following questions:

a. What is the prompt for the system? Is it possible to type characters *before* receiving the
prompt from the system? If so, can you tell how the system will treat the typed characters?

b. Try to classify each command in the language into one of the eight command classes identified in this chapter.

c. Apply the Gebhardt and Stellmacher principles discussed in reference [3] to the analysis
of the command language. What are the strengths and weaknesses of the language based on
these principles?

d. In some command languages for information retrieval, there are several ways of requiring
that, in order for retrieval to take place, two words must be present in the same piece of text
(that is, in the same bibliographic record, or sentence, or paragraph, etc.). Identify and discuss
each approach that is possible in the language you have selected. Which approaches are most
likely to result in false drops? Which are least likely? Why?

e. An old example of a false drop is the retrieval of information on blind Venetians when
what is wanted is material on Venetian blinds. Can the command language you have selected
distinguish between these two cases? How?

2. Discuss syntax errors in the context of communication between an information retrieval system and a searcher. Are such errors best regarded as failures in technical, semantic, or pragmatic
communication?

3. Invent several examples of semantic ambiguity, contextual ambiguity, the specific/generic problem, the viewpoint/context problem, and synonymity in natural language. Try to select all examples from a homogeneous subject area (e.g., mathematics, education, agronomy, or anthropology).

4. From the definitions given for identifier and descriptor, explain if the same term can appear
both as an identifier and a descriptor in the same database. What implications does this have
for online information retrieval?

5. Select a thesaurus in a discipline with which you are familiar. Examine the RT references listed
under a given term, and try to explain the relationship indicated between each of the pairs of
concepts listed.

6. An interesting class exercise demonstrating the different points of view that might be brought
to the indexing of a document is to have each student in the class index the same interdisciplinary article. Not only will dozens of different words, phrases, and word forms result, but also
several distinct points of view will emerge, reflecting the *a priori* background and orientation
of each student. Two papers that work well with this exercise are: Rosenberg, Victor, "The
Scientific Premises of Information Science." *Journal of the American Society for Information
Science* 25 (4) (July August 1974) 263–269; and Cawkell, Anthony E. "Search Strategy, Construction and Use of Citation Networks, with a Socio-Scientific Example: "Amorphous Semi-
Conductors and S.R. Ovshinsky." *Journal of the American Society for Information Science* 25
(March April 1974) 123–130.

7. Set up a hierarchical classification system to represent the class of all automobiles, so that any given automobile can be placed into its "pigeonhole" in the hierarchy. Factors that should be considered in your classification are make, style, color, and cost. Discuss advantages and disadvantages of your classification in terms of information retrieval and suggest alternative ways to represent the same information.

8. Examine the print version of *Social Science Citation Index*. Look up a "classic" paper on some subject, such as Vannevar Bush's "As We May Think," published in the *Atlantic Monthly* in 1945. How often was it cited during the past five years by journals in the social sciences indexed by SSCI? From what disciplines did the citations come? By studying this example, try to identify some potential strengths and problems with citation indexing.

9. What are some of the most important general differences between searching in natural language fields as compared to controlled vocabulary fields? Under what conditions would you choose one approach over the other? Frame your answer in the context of a bibliographic database of your choice. Give examples.

10. Conduct a manual literature search in *Library Literature* on the subject of "user-friendly" online computer systems by finding one or more articles and reading it to identify additional search terms. Then try looking up these terms, and continue the process. What terms did you find that appear to be used to represent aspects of this concept? (Try to find several.) How many of these terms were successful in retrieving relevant documents from *Library Literature*? Now examine the *Thesaurus of ERIC Descriptors*. Which of the terms you found are descriptors? Explain which fields and vocabulary elements you would search, if you were to conduct this search online, using ERIC.

NOTES AND REFERENCES

1. Cochrane, Pauline A., "Can a Standard for an Online Common Command Language be Developed." *Online* 7 (January 1983) 36–37.

2. Negus, A.E., *EURONET Guidelines: Standard Commands for Retrieval Systems*. Final Report on a Study Carried Out for the Commission of the European Communities, DGXII. London: The Institution of Electrical Engineers, 1977, 66 pp.

3. Gebhardt, Friedrich and Imant Stellmacher. "Design Criteria for Documentation Retrieval Languages." *Journal of the American Society for Information Science* 29 (No. 4)(July 1978) 191–199.

4. Hildreth, Charles R. *Online public access catalogs: the user interface*. (Columbus, OH: OCLC, Inc., 1982).

5. Conger, Lucinda D. "Multiple System Searching: A Searcher's Guide to Making Use of the Real Differences between Systems." *Online* 4 (April 1980) 10–21; Weiss, Susan. "Online Bibliographic Services: A Comparison." *Special Libraries* (October 1981) 379–389; Krichmar, Albert. "Command Language Ease of Use: A Comparison of DIALOG and ORBIT." *Online Review* 5 (No. 3) (1981) 227–240.

6. Meadow, Charles T. "Matching Users and User Languages in Information Retrieval." *Online Review* 5 (No. 4) (1981) 313–322.

7. Meadow, Charles T. *The Analysis of Information Systems*. (Los Angeles: Melville Publishing Co., 1973), p. 23.

8. Yngve, Victor H. "Implications of Mechanical Translation Research." *Proceedings of the American Philosophical Society* 108 (No. 4) (August 1964) 275–281.

9. Hutchins, W.J. "Machine Translation and Machine-Aided Translation." *Journal of Documentation* 34 (No. 2) (June 1978) 119-159.

10. Sparck Jones, Karen and Martin Kay. *Linguistics and Information Science* (New York: Academic Press, 1973).

11. Fishman, Marilyn. "The Transformational Model of Language and Information Retrieval." *Drexel Library Quarterly* 8 (No. 2) 193-200.

12. Montgomery, Christine, "Linguistics and Information Science." *Journal of the American Society for Information Science* 23 (May-June 1972) 195-219.

13. McGrath, William, "Relationships Between Hard/Soft, Pure/Applied, and Life/Nonlife Disciplines and Subject Book Use in a University Library." *Information Processing and Management* 14 (1978) 17-28.

14. Kuhn, Thomas, *Structure of Scientific Revolutions*. (Chicago: University of Chicago Press, 1970).

15. McGrath, p. 22.

16. Wiberley, Stephen E., "Subject Access in the Humanities and the Precision of the Humanist's Vocabulary." *Library Quarterly* 53 (No. 4) (1983) 420-433.

17. Buckland, Michael K. *Library Services in Theory and Context*. (New York: Pergamon Press, 1983) pp. 72-73.

18. For example, see American National Standards Institute, Inc. *American National Standard for Writing Abstracts*. ANSI Z39.14-1979. (New York: ANSI, 1979).

19. *Thesaurus of ERIC Descriptors*. (Phoenix, Arizona: Oryx Press, 1980) p. xv.

20. Westby, Barbara M. *Sears List of Subject Headings*. 12th Ed. (New York: H.W. Wilson, 1982); Subject Cataloging Division, Processing Services, Library of Congress. *Library of Congress Subject Headings*. 9th Ed. (Washington, D.C.: Library of Congress, 1980).

21. Meadow, Charles T. *The Analysis of Information Systems*, pp. 25-27.

22. The following articles and texts discuss principles and concepts of indexing and classification in depth: Goodman, Frederick, "The Role and Function of the Thesaurus in Education." *Journal of Library Automation* 2 (No. 4) (December, 1969) 1-31; Neufeld, Margaret, "Linguistic Approaches to the Construction and Use of Thesauri: A Review." *Drexel Library Quarterly* 8 (April 1972) (No. 2) 135-146; Rogers, Virginia G. "Thesaurus Construction: An Introduction." *Drexel Library Quarterly* 8 (April 1972) (No. 2) 117-124; American National Standards Institute, Inc. *Guidelines for Thesaurus Structure, Construction, and Use*. (New York: American National Standards Institute, 1973); Metcalfe, John W. *Information Indexing and Subject Cataloging*. (New York: Scarecrow Press, 1957); Lancaster, F. Wilfrid, *Information Retrieval Systems: Characteristics, Testing, and Evaluation*. First edition. (New York: John Wiley & Sons, Inc., 1968); Davis, Charles H. and James E. Rush, *Guide to Information Science*. (Westport, Connecticut: Greenwood Press, 1979) pp. 15-60; Soergel, Dagobert, *Indexing Languages and Thesauri: Construction and Maintenance* (Los Angeles: Melville Publishing Company, 1974); Borko, Harold and Charles L. Bernier, *Indexing Concepts and Methods*. (New York: Academic Press, 1978); Lancaster, Frederick W. *Vocabulary Control for Information Retrieval*. (Washington, D.C.: Information Resources Press, 1972); Meadow, Charles T. *The Analysis of Information Systems*. Second Edition. (Los Angeles, CA: Melville Publishing Company, 1973).

23. Shera, Jesse H. "Pattern, Structure, and Conceptualization in Classification for Information Retrieval." *Advances in Documentation and Library Science*, edited by J.H. Shera, A. Kent, and J.W. Perry. (New York: Interscience Publishers, Inc., 1957) pp. 15-38.

24. Jones, Kevin P. "The Environment of Classification: The Concept of Mutual Exclusivity." *Journal of the American Society for Information Science* 24 (March 1973) 157-163.

25. Shera, p. 26.

26. Jones, p. 162.

27. Cooper, William S. "Is Interindexer Consistency a Hobgoblin?" *American Documentation* 20 (No. 3) (July 1969) 268-278.

28. Swanson, Don R. "Searching Natural Language Text by Computer." *Science* 132 (October 21, 1960) 1099-1104.

29. Cleverdon, Cyril W. and E.M. Keen, *Factors Determining the Performance of Indexing Systems. Vol. 1: Design. Vol. 2: Results.* (Cranfield, England: Aslib Cranfield Research Project, 1966).

30. See, for example, Salton, Gerard, "Automatic Text Analysis." *Science* 168 (April 1970) 335-343.

31. Salton, Gerard and Michael J. McGill. *Introduction to Modern Information Retrieval.* (New York: McGraw-Hill Book Company, 1983).

32. Piternick, Anne B. "Searching Vocabularies: A Developing Category of Online Search Tools." *Online Review* 8 (No. 5) (1984) 441-449.

33. Garfield, Eugene. *Citation Indexing: Its Theory and Application in Science, Technology, and Humanities.* (New York: John Wiley & Sons, 1979).

Chapter 3

Database Structure, Organization, and Search

3.1 INTRODUCTION

This chapter deals with the record structure and file organization proce-dures currently used by major database producers and search services. Spe-cifically, it examines the inverted and linear file structures used by major search services and the implications of these structures for online informa-tion retrieval.

The orientation of this chapter, as with the book as a whole, is that of the *user* of online search services—the search specialist or end-user. Design problems faced by systems analysts and programmers creating new databases and designing new search systems are interesting and important but are beyond the scope of this book. Thus, for example, there are many approaches to logical and physical database structure and organization on magnetic tape or disk or other device: indexed-sequential, hierarchical, relational, and the like. For readers wishing to study these subjects, Martin's *Computer Data-Base Organization* [1] is highly recommended. These topics have also been treated from the perspective of library and information science [2]. The con-struction, design, use, and evaluation of personal information systems using general purpose or bibliographic database management software such as dBase III and Finder, respectively, are treated in many articles and texts that are devoted exclusively to these topics [3].

The chapter begins with an examination of the record structures typically found in bibliographic databases accessed through online information retrieval systems. File loading practices and structures imposed on databases by search services will then be treated. Concepts and issues discussed in this chapter include the inverted file structure, linear files, system defaults,

Boolean searching, truncation, parsing rules and phrase searching, stop words, and alphabetizing conventions. Emphasis will be placed not only on these topics themselves, but also on the implications of each concept for online searching.

3.2 BASIC TERMINOLOGY

The concept of *record* has thus far been used rather loosely. As it applies to a book, journal article, or other document, the term index record was used to refer to a document surrogate: a representation of the document for storage and subsequent retrieval. However, the term 'record' may be used to refer to other kinds of objects in addition to documents.

Following Martin [4], objects about which information will be stored are called *entities*. An entity may be a document of some kind: a book, journal article, or doctoral dissertation. But more generally, human beings, corporations, and inventory parts may also be considered entities. Entities are considered in terms of their characteristics, called *attributes*. A particular entity is represented by the *values* of its attributes.

To take a simple example, suppose that the entities under consideration are books. We might then consider the attributes of interest to be a book's author, title, publisher, city of publication, date of publication, and number of pages. For a particular entity, *Methods of Information Handling*, by Charles P. Bourne, values of these attributes are given in Table 3.1.

Attributes and entities are concepts. These concepts are represented by data. In the example, a book is represented by the values of its attributes. Each of these attribute values is called a *field* of data. For a particular entity, the set of fields representing it is called a *record*. Although the example given in Table 3.1 illustrates a bibliographic entity (a document), a record can also refer to other kinds of entities: persons, companies, software packages, and many others. The concept of data is examined more closely in Table 3.2, which illustrates a hierarchy of data elements. From smallest to largest, they are: bit, byte, subfield, field, record, database, and library.

The smallest element recognizable by data processing equipment is the *bit*, represented symbolically by a 1 or a 0. A *byte* is, for the architecture of a particular computer system, the smallest addressable group of bits. Usually a byte refers to a group of 8 bits, and represents a printable character.

A *field* or *subfield* of a record is a set of characters that represent the value of an attribute for the entity under consideration. A field may comprise two or more subfields although some fields may have none. For example, in the MARC format for bibliographic data, the publication statement, or imprint, of a book is regarded as a data field. There are five possible subfields of

TABLE 3.1
Attributes and Attribute Values for the Entity *Methods of Information Handling* by Charles P. Bourne.

Attributes	Attribute values
author	Charles P. Bourne
title	Methods of Information Handling
publisher	John Wiley & Sons, Inc.
city of publication	New York
date of publication	1963
number of pages	241

this field: place of publication, publisher, dates of publication, place of printing, and printer.

The totality of fields and subfields describing the attributes of an entity is the *index record*, or simply *record*, representing that entity. For items that are bibliographic, index records are often called *bibliographic records*. Table 3.3 shows a portion of a bibliographic record from the ERIC database, as it might appear in print, including abstract, descriptors, and identifiers.

This book is primarily concerned with full texts and surrogates of *documents*, and hence, bibliographic records, although attention will be given to other source and referral databases as well (see Chapter 8). The terms entity, attribute, attribute value, field, and record will allow us to discuss these concepts generally, whether they refer to properties of chemical compounds, journal articles, organizations, or books.

TABLE 3.2
Hierarchy of Data Elements

Data element	Example	Text represented
Bit	1 or 0	—
Byte	0100110	&
Subfield	(Place of publication)	Chicago, Illinois
Field	(Publication statement)	Chicago, Illinois: Academic Press, 1985
Record	(An ERIC index record)	(see Table 3.3)
Database	(The ERIC database)	(more than 500,000 records)
Library	(All DIALOG databases)	(more than 200 databases)

TABLE 3.3
A Portion of an ERIC Record

Meadow, Charles T. "Adventures in the Silicon Trade." *Bulletin of the American Society for Information Science* 8 (4) (1981) 15–17.

Abstract: Recounts some of the problems encountered in the use of an Osborne 1 microcomputer for personal purposes by a computing veteran, describes some of the shortcomings of the sales system for microcomputers as it presently exists, and makes some conjectures concerning the impact of those shortcomings on the personal computer industry.

Descriptors: Computer Programs; *Electronics Industry; *Guides; Merchandise Information; *Microcomputers; Problems; Programing; Purchasing

Identifiers: Customer Services; *Osborne 1

3.3 BIBLIOGRAPHIC RECORD STRUCTURES: ERIC

A distinction was made in Chapter 1 between database producers and search services. Database producers build source and reference databases and publish them in machine-readable form. Historically, these databases were often byproducts of a computer typesetting process, in which the primary product was a printed tool. Search services such as BRS, Vu/Text, Compuserve, DIALOG, and SDC contract with database producers to provide access to their databases in an online mode.

The phrase "to provide access to" stands for the completion of several necessary tasks. Levine describes in detail what must be done by a search service that has obtained the rights to offer a new database [5]. These processes include analysis of file format, design of database structure, conversion of machine-readable data from formats used by database producers to those required by the search service, testing of conversion programs and adjusting the original design to accommodate aberrant data, loading (creating and storing) the disk files to be accessed by the search system, and preparation of *documentation*—descriptions of file content and system features. To discuss some of these ideas more concretely, a particular database— ERIC—will be examined in detail.

The ERIC database is a collection of document surrogates produced by the Educational Resources Information Center of the National Institute of Education. It consists of two subfiles: the machine-readable versions of *Resources in Education (RIE)*, an indexing and abstracting journal to "fugitive" publications in education, and *Current Index to Journals in Education (CIJE)*, an index to more than 700 serial publications important to education. The sixteen broad subject areas that are considered to be relevant to education from the point of view of ERIC are listed in Table 3.4. These cor-

TABLE 3.4
Broad Subject Coverage of the ERIC Database

* adult, career, and vocational education
* counseling and personnel services
* early childhood education
* educational management
* handicapped and gifted children
* higher education
* information resources
* junior colleges
* languages and linguistics
* reading and communication skills
* rural education and small schools
* science, mathematics, and environmental education
* social studies/social science education
* teacher education
* tests, measurement, and evaluation
* urban education

respond to sixteen decentralized clearinghouses that share the responsibility for finding, collecting, indexing, and abstracting documents falling within these subject areas, and producing bibliographic records representing these documents.

The remainder of this section is devoted to a examination of the field structure of the RIE portion of the ERIC database, as it can be obtained from the National Institute of Education in machine-readable form. The restructuring of ERIC by search services so that online access can be provided is discussed in the next section of the chapter.

Table 3.5 lists selected data fields for the *RIE* database, as described in extensive documentation produced by ERIC [6]. Readers interested in the structure of the database as it is currently produced should consult the most recent available version of this documentation, because the field structure of databases changes, sometimes significantly, over the passage of time.

Several of the data fields listed in Table 3.5 require further explanation for complete understanding and efficient use on an online search system. For example, what are the codes used to represent "Publication Type"? These and other necessary explanations are found in the documentation produced by search services offering access to ERIC as well as by the database producers themselves. For ERIC, the print versions of *RIE* and *CIJE* provide much useful information. The 1984 edition of the *Thesaurus of ERIC Descriptors* has 20 pages of front matter that discuss several of the data fields, and the documentation offered by search services providing access to ERIC is even

TABLE 3.5
Selected Data Fields and Descriptions from the ERIC Resources in Education Database*

Add date:
Julian date recording when record was added to the file, e.g., 73032 for 2/1/73.

Change date:
Binary Julian date that record was last changed.

Accession number:
A unique number with the two character prefix ED followed by 6 decimal digits, sequentially assigned to records as they are entered into the system.

Clearinghouse accession number:
Accession number assigned by the originating clearinghouses.

Publication type:
Three character codes identifying the class of publication of which the record is a member, e.g., book, legislative hearing, map, research report, dictionary, etc. There are thirty-one classes in all.

Publication date:
The date the publication was published or issued

Title:
The title and subtitle, if any, of the document.

Personal author:
The name of the person(s) who wrote the report.

Institution code:
An alphanumeric code assigned by ERIC to institutions originating the publication.

Sponsoring agency code:
An alphanumeric code assigned by ERIC to the agency that sponsored the publication.

Descriptors:
One or more subfields, where each subfield consists of a term that is a member of the *Thesaurus of ERIC Descriptors*.

Identifiers:
One or more subfields, where each subfield consists of a natural language term that describes an entity or subject dealt with by the document.

EDRS price:
The price of the document for paper or microfiche copies obtained from the Eric Document Reproduction Service (EDRS).

Descriptive note:
Cataloging information augmenting the document description.

Page:
Number of pages in the document.

Level:
Code indicating availability from EDRS.

Issue:
The issue of RIE in which the index record was published.

Abstract:
A brief narrative summary of the document.

Report number:
A unique identifying number assigned to the document by the organization that produced or disseminated the publication.

(continues)

TABLE 3.5 (*continued*)

Contract number:
An alphanumeric code identifying the government contract supporting this publication.
Grant number:
An alphanumeric code identifying the grant supporting this publication.
Project number:
An alphanumeric code assigned by the sponsoring agency to the project under which the publication was issued.
Availability:
Indicates where and in what form this publication is available, other than from EDRS.
Journal citation:
Journal name, volume number, issue number, inclusive pagination, and date.
Geographic source:
An alphanumeric code indicating the country of origin. For the U.S., Canada, Great Britain, and Australia, a second subfield identifies the state, province, or territory.
Governmental status:
Designates official publications of a governmental agency: federal, state, local, foreign, international.
Institution name:
Name of the corporate source.
Sponsoring agency name:
Name of the sponsoring agency.

---

*Source: ERIC Processing and Reference Facility, *ERIC Data Base Master Files: Tape Documentation.* (ERIC Processing and Reference Facility, Computer Systems Department, 1980). A few obsolete data fields or fields of interest principally to programmers have been omitted from the list provided in this source.

more extensive. The searcher who wants to make full use of the potential offered by the ERIC database must consult such documentation.

A complete explanation of the field "Publication type" would describe each of the 31 publication classes and the three-character code standing for that class. These are summarized in Table 3.6.

The importance of consulting search system and database documentation cannot be stressed too greatly. Table 3.5 describes the fields present in the *RIE* database *as the database was prepared by ERIC*. But each search system deciding to provide online access to ERIC will make different decisions regarding the installation of the database on its system. Some data fields established by ERIC may be eliminated from the online version by one service, but not by another. Other fields may be embellished. Still others might be made printable but not searchable. Those fields that are searchable may be indexed in different ways by different search systems and thus may require different searching techniques. In addition to differences in searching, *sorting* of records may be made possible on some fields, but not others. There

TABLE 3.6

Publication/Document Types and Codes, As Used From August 1979 Forward in the ERIC RIE Database*

Code	Publication/document types	Code	Publication/document types
010	BOOKS	110	NUMERICAL/QUANTITATIVE DATA
	COLLECTED WORKS	120	OPINIONS/PERSONAL VIEWPOINTS/POSITION PAPERS/ESSAYS
020	General		
021	Proceedings		
022	Serials		REFERENCE MATERIALS
030	CREATIVE WORKS (LITERARY AND DRAMATIC)	130	General
040	DISSERTATIONS/THESES	131	Bibliographies
050	General	132	Directories/Catalogs
	Classroom Use	133	Geographic Materials
051	Instructional Materials (For *Learner*)	134	Vocabularies/Classifications
			REPORTS
052	Teaching Guides (For *Teacher*)	140	General
055	Non-Classroom Use (For *Administrative and Support Staff, etc.*)	141	Descriptive (Program/Project Descriptions)
		142	Evaluative/Feasibility
060	HISTORICAL MATERIALS	143	Research/Technical
070	INFORMATION ANALYSES/STATE-OF-THE-ART MATERIALS	150	SPEECHES, CONFERENCE PAPERS
071	ERIC Information Analysis Products	160	TESTS, QUESTIONNAIRES, EVALUATION INSTRUMENTS
080	JOURNAL ARTICLES	170	TRANSLATIONS
090	LEGAL/LEGISLATIVE/REGULA-TORY MATERIALS	999	OTHER/MISCELLANEOUS (NOT CLASSIFIABLE ELSEWHERE)
100	NON-PRINT MEDIA		

*Source: ERIC Processing and Reference Facility, *ERIC Data Base Master Files: Tape Documentation.* (ERIC Processing and Reference Facility, Computer Systems Department, 1980), p.56.

are other possible differences between systems as well. These decisions are made by the search service offering access to the database. Since the various search services have approached these questions differently, the searcher must be familiar with decisions made *by the search service being utilized.*

DIALOG, for example, distinguishes between fields such as title, descriptor, etc. that contain soft, subject information, and fields such as journal name and document type that contain relatively hard, factual information. Subject fields are termed *suffix fields* by DIALOG, and are searched by appending suffixes to search terms. The term

indians/de,ab

means that 'indians' is to be searched in the subject fields of descriptor and abstract. Non-subject fields such as journal name are called *prefix fields*, and are searched by attaching the appropriate prefix to the search term, as:

jn = library quarterly

However, other search services treat fields in ERIC and other databases in a different way, and may not make a distinction for searching purposes between subject and non-subject fields.

Some of the information related to a given database, such as syntax rules and the names of searchable fields, may be available online as well as in print form, at the usual online rates. But whether one uses print tools or online sources, there is no substitute for consulting documentation, for each database and search service one wishes to use. Failure to consult documentation not only will drastically limit what can be accomplished, but also will reduce the efficiency with which the work is conducted.

3.4 BASIC FILE STRUCTURES

Search services must go through several processes before offering a new database for online access: analysis, design, conversion, testing, loading, and preparation of documentation. This book is not as concerned with these processes as with their products: machine-readable files ready for online searching.

The basic conceptual structures used by virtually all online search services are the linear file and the inverted index to that file. One may think of the *linear* file (sometimes called the print file) as a set of index records, in which each record describes one item or entity, and are arranged in an order based on the values of one or more attributes. If the entities are employees, for example, a linear file might consist of a card file of employees, one card for each, arranged alphabetically by the last name of the employee. A library's card catalog is another example of a printed linear file, in which the entities are books.

An *inverted index* (sometimes called an index file) consists of records, typically alphabetically arranged, that are created from a linear file. A record from an inverted index consists of an attribute along with a listing of every entity that is associated with that attribute. A back of the book index is an example of a simple inverted file in which the entities are the individual pages in the book and the attributes are the topics or subjects discussed on those pages. Thus a given entry in an inverted index to a book would be the name

TABLE 3.7
The Document/Term Matrix

Documents	Terms					
	t_1	t_2	t_3	t_4	$t_5 \ldots t_n$	
d_1	1	0	0	1	0	1
d_2	0	0	1	0	0	0
d_3	1	0	1	0	$0 \ldots 0$	
d_4	1	0	1	1	$0 \ldots 0$	
d_5	0	0	1	0	$1 \ldots 0$	
d_6	1	0	0	1	$1 \ldots 1$	
.	.	.	.	.	.	.
.	.	.	.	.	.	.
.	.	.	.	.	.	.
d_m	0	0	1	0	0	0

of a topic, followed by a list of all page numbers in the book that discuss that topic.

Table 3.7 illustrates an example of a *document/term matrix*, showing the concept of a simple linear file as well as an inverted index, both as sets of binary vectors. A '1' at the intersection of a document row and a term column means that the term is part of the index record of that document; a '0' means that it is not. The rows of the matrix, d_1, d_2, . . . d_m, represent document records and the columns of the matrix t_1, t_2, . . . t_n, are term records. A row of the matrix is an entire index record from the linear file. For example, row three is the index record for document d_3, and contains the terms t_1, t_3, etc.

Each of the row numbers can be regarded as an *accession number* associated with a record. An accession number is a unique number assigned to an entity by a database producer or search service. Each accession number is assigned to one and only one entity. Thus the accession number stands for, or represents, the entire record. The Social Security Number serves much the same function in files for which the entities are U.S. citizens. See Table 3.5 for a description of the accession number field in ERIC.

When the inverted index is prepared from the linear file, accession numbers associated with a given term are assigned to, or *posted* to that term. Accession numbers are perhaps more usually called simply *postings*.

The columns of the matrix in Table 3.7 are records from the inverted index. For a given term, say t_4, one can see at a glance the index records that contain those terms: d_1, d_4, d_6 (or more simply, documents with accession numbers 1, 4, 6, etc.). Indeed, this is exactly how an online search is conducted using an inverted index; the column vector associated with the attribute of interest is retrieved—simply extracted from the matrix. This vector contains the accession numbers or postings associated with all index records that meet the required condition. For term t_4, postings 1, 4, and 6 would be extracted from the linear file and placed in a retrieval set.

Each search system provides a means for forming the set of postings associated with a given term. On DIALOG, for example, this is done with the command SELECT, abbreviated as S. The formulation

  select positivism

would create a set of accession numbers associated with records in the database being searched that contain the term 'positivism,' by extracting the appropriate column vector from the term/document matrix. Other search systems are designed so that "create a postings set" is *assumed* by the system in the normal search mode, making a command for this action unnecessary. In a system with such a default search mode, simply typing the term 'positivism' would have the desired effect.

There is a curious and interesting dualism between the linear file and the inverted file. To create or add to the term/document matrix, one produces new rows. To search the matrix, one extracts given columns. The database producer creates the linear file while the search service creates the inverted file. Searching is done on the inverted file, but the printing of retrieved records is done using the linear file.

The *postings file* is a brief summary of the characteristics of the inverted index. It is an alphabetically arranged listing showing at a minimum the number of records posted to each term appearing in the database [7]. Some search systems allow the postings file to be consulted online. Figure 3.1 shows the result of the command

  expand statistics

put to the ERIC database on DIALOG. The column labelled "Items" shows the number of records posted to each term in title, descriptor, identifier, and abstract fields in ERIC. The output shows that term E1, the word 'statisticizing,' is found in 1 index record. The number 27 in the column labelled RT indicates that the word associated with that number—the word 'statistics'—is an ERIC descriptor, and that there are 27 words listed under 'statistics' in the *Thesaurus*. The first part of the scope note for 'statistics' is also displayed. Terms E4, E5, and E6 are identifiers, while terms E7 and E8 are examples of misspelled words.

For some databases, search systems may also permit the display of terms in a controlled vocabulary. The EXPAND command is also used for this

```
?expand statistics

Ref   Items  RT  Index-term
E1      1        STATISTICIZING
E2      1        STATISTICOPHOBIA
E3    8686   27  *STATISTICS (BRANCH OF MATHEMATICS DEALING WITH
                 COLLECTIO...)
E4      1        STATISTICS ATTITUDE SURVEY
E5      1        STATISTICS ATTITUDE SURVEY (ROBERTS)
E6      1        STATISTICS INDEXING AND RETRIEVAL PROJECT
E7      2        STATISTICSL
E8      1        STATISTICSLLY
E9      1        STATISTIICAL
E10     4        STATISTIQUE
E11     5        STATISTIQUES
E12     1        STATISTISCHEN


           Enter P or E for more
?expand (phonetics)

Ref   Items  type RT  Index-term
R1    1309        16  *PHONETICS (STUDY AND CLASSIFICATION OF SPEECH SOUNDS,
                      I...)
R2     246   N     8  ACOUSTIC PHONETICS
R3    1012   N    16  PHONICS
R4    2463   B    28  PHONOLOGY
R5     915   R    10  ARTICULATION (SPEECH)
R6     857   R     7  CONSONANTS
R7      43   R     7  DIACRITICAL MARKING
R8     450   R    10  DISTINCTIVE FEATURES (LANGUAGE)
R9      92   R     5  GENERATIVE PHONOLOGY
R10    201   R    10  GRAPHEMES
R11    213   R    12  MORPHOPHONEMICS
R12    367   R    13  PHONEMICS

         Enter P or E for more
```

Figure 3.1 The EXPAND command on DIALOG. Search performed via the DIALOG* Information Retrieval Services, Inc. (*Servicemark Reg. U.S. Patent and Trademark Office).

function in DIALOG, where the descriptor is enclosed in parentheses. Figure 3.1 illustrates the first portion of a display of the terms from the *Thesaurus* as related in any way to the descriptor 'phonetics.'

There are two excellent reasons for occasionally examining these postings files online. First, alternative ways of expressing concepts of interest can be displayed, both in natural language and in controlled vocabularies. Second, in some search systems sets of accession numbers can be created directly from the postings file, by referring to one or more reference numbers (in Figure 3.1, these are E-numbers and R-numbers). Creating sets of postings by selecting reference numbers directly from a display of the postings file can result in substantial savings in the keying time required in a complex search.

TABLE 3.8
A Sample Document/Term Matrix

	Dogs	Cats	Rats	Breeding	Raising	Pets
d_1	1	0	0	1	0	1
d_2	0	0	1	0	0	0
d_3	1	0	1	0	0	0
d_4	1	0	1	1	0	0
d_5	0	0	1	0	1	0
d_6	1	0	0	1	1	1
.	.	.	.	.	.	.
.	.	.	.	.	.	.
.	.	.	.	.	.	.
d_m	0	0	1	0	0	0

3.5 BOOLEAN LOGIC

Many commercial online search systems permit the formation of complex expressions by using Boolean logic to combine retrieval sets. Boolean logic is an algebra of sets. In online information retrieval, Boolean logic is applied to sets of postings.

The major Boolean operators are AND, OR, and NOT. If A and B are sets of postings, these Boolean operators have the following meanings:

AND   A AND B is the set of postings in common to A and B, and is called the *intersection* of A and B. A AND B is represented by the expression A * B on some search systems.

OR   A OR B is the set of postings either in set A or in set B or in both sets A and B, and is called the *union* of A and B. A OR B is represented by the expression A + B on some search systems.

NOT   A NOT B is the set of postings in set A but not in set B, and is called the *difference* between A and B. A NOT B is represented by the expression A − B on some search systems. NOT should be used with caution, since relevant records can inadvertantly be eliminated with NOT.

Example 3.1. Consider the sample term/document matrix given in Table 3.8. The result of searching on the term 'rats' is {2,3,4,5}—the set of accession numbers 2, 3, 4, and 5. Similarly, the set of accession numbers associated with the term 'breeding' is {1, 4, 6}. The index records containing both terms—the result of the Boolean operation rats AND breeding—is therefore

{4}—the set containing the single number 4. Document #4 is the only citation posted to both terms. Similarly, the reader should be able to see each
of the following results:

    a. (dogs OR cats OR rats) = {1,2,3,4,5,6,m}
    b. (breeding OR raising) = {1,4,5,6}
    c. (dogs OR cats OR rats) AND (breeding OR raising) = {1,4,5,6}
    d. cats AND pets = {}
    e. rats AND pets = {}
    f. dogs OR cats = {1,3,4,6} = dogs
    g. (dogs OR cats) NOT pets = {3,4}

    Examples 3.1a and 3.1b illustrate how terms can be treated as equivalent
for a given search problem by combining them with Boolean OR. Example
3.1c illustrates a solution to a more complex information need: information
is wanted concerning methods of breeding certain animals, including dogs,
cats, and rats. Example 3.1d illustrates the general principle that if a set A
has no elements (that is, is *the empty set*) then A AND B = {}, for all sets
B. Example 3.1e shows that the intersection of A and B can be empty even
though neither A nor B is empty. Example 3.1f illustrates the general principle that if a set A is empty, then A OR B is equal to B, for all sets B.

    Example 3.1g illustrates the use of NOT. Records containing the terms
'dogs' or 'cats' are excluded if they also contain the term 'pets.' Evidently
the searcher wants information concerning dogs or cats, but not in their roles
as pets.

    The previous example also illustrates the reason that one should be cau-
tious when using NOT. The records eliminated by using NOT apparently
discuss pets. But they also may discuss other matters of interest to a user:
breeding, feeding, etc. Therefore, to eliminate records because they contain
the word 'pets' will probably eliminate much of interest to the user. This
is not an isolated example. The online searcher should be extremely cautious
when using the Boolean operator NOT.

    It should be observed in passing that Example 3.1 is plagued with poten-
tial semantic problems of the sort discussed in the last chapter: synonymity,
homographs, false drops, and the generic/specific problem, especially if the
terms are to be searched in natural language fields. The formulations in Example 3.1 are not intended to exhibit particularly well constructed search statements; their purpose is to demonstrate the basic workings of Boolean logic
and the inverted index.

    Some readers may find Venn diagrams helpful in understanding Boolean
operators. Figure 3.2 shows Venn diagrams illustrating the basic Boolean
operators, and Figure 3.3 illustrates Example 3.1.g.

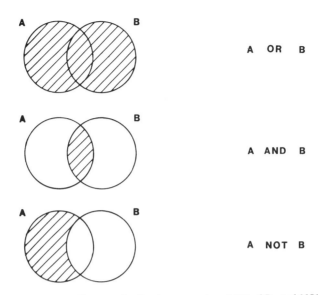

Figure 3.2   Venn diagrams for Boolean operators AND, OR, and NOT.

Example 3.2. Complex combinations of terms can also be expressed using Boolean operators. To evaluate an expression like the following, work from the innermost parentheses out, a step at a time.

((breeding OR raising) AND pets) NOT (cats OR dogs)
= ({1,4,5,6} AND {1,6}) NOT {1,3,4,6}
= {1,6} NOT {1,3,4,6}
= {}

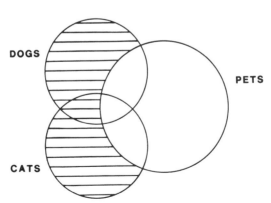

Figure 3.3   Venn diagrams for the formulation: (Dogs OR Cats) NOT Pets.

There are apparently no records in the database that discuss raising pets other than the cat or dog. Again, however, had this been a real search, problems with natural language as well as the use of NOT should make one extremely cautious in coming to this conclusion.

Example 3.2 illustrates the *nesting* of sets of parentheses within one another. Some systems permit nesting to several levels, as in the expression:

(((D OR E) AND F) OR (G OR (H NOT I))) AND A

While perfectly legal syntactically in some search systems, it does not seem useful to formulate such complex expressions online. Not only are these expressions difficult for some searchers to comprehend from a conceptual standpoint, they are also much more difficult to modify online, in cases in which efforts are being made to improve system output. An approach much preferred to the formation of complex Boolean expressions in a single step is to work on one concept at a time, taking several steps to accomplish the building of the final sets. This is essentially the *building blocks* approach, to be discussed in more detail in Chapter 7.

The *order of operations* for carrying out potentially ambiguous Boolean operations (that is, expressions omitting parentheses) is a characteristic of search systems with which one should be intimately familiar. Most search systems do not *require* the use of parentheses, and are able to evaluate complex Boolean expressions that omit parentheses by making assumptions regarding what is intended. These assumptions define the order of operations understood by the search system software.

Example 3.3. Assume that a user wants information regarding formal standards for any of the analytical operations of subject analysis: indexing, abstracting, or classification. The searcher builds the Boolean expression:

indexing OR abstracting OR classifying AND standards

A Venn diagram representing the *desired* result is displayed in Figure 3.4. But as the formulation stands, what is the order in which the Boolean operations will be performed? If the search system performs Boolean operations in order from left to right, or if Boolean OR's are executed before AND's, the result will be what is wanted. But suppose that the search system carries out all AND operations *before* OR operations, in the absence of disambiguating parentheses? Then the result will not be as expected, as Figure 3.5 illustrates. In this case, the majority of the retrieved records will not be relevant to the search formulation; they will treat some aspect of indexing or abstracting but will not include the concept of standards.

As it happens, some (but not all) search systems, will evaluate expressions

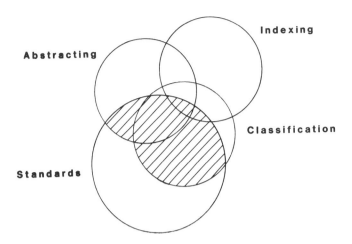

Figure 3.4   Venn diagram for the formulation: (Indexing OR Abstracting OR Classification) AND Standards.

such as Example 3.3 like the Venn diagram in Figure 3.5, contrary to what is wanted and expected by the searcher. If this formulation were put to such a system (for example, the ERIC database on the DIALOG system), nearly all retrieved records would be useless.

Each search system has its own implicit order of operations for the evaluation of Boolean expressions if there are no explanatory parentheses. It is imperative that a searcher be aware of this order, if such expressions are to be formed. However, for clarity of thought and also for simple readability,

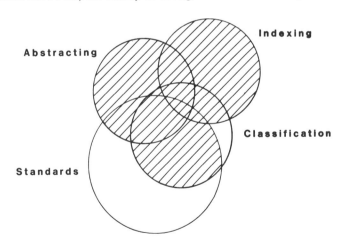

Figure 3.5   Venn diagram for the formulation: Indexing OR Abstracting OR (Classification AND Standards.)

we recommend that parentheses always be used in Boolean expressions to group equivalent sets together. Perhaps even better, the situation can be avoided altogether by never using more than one type of Boolean operator in a single command statement.

3.6 FIELD SEARCHING, WORD PROXIMITY SEARCHING, AND TRUNCATION

A somewhat simplistic approach was taken in the previous section of this chapter. In particular, the discussion of the document/term matrix was simplified to introduce the concepts of inverted and linear files and Boolean logic. As presented in Tables 3.7 and 3.8, the document/term matrix is able to show only the presence or absence of each attribute for a given entity. A term either is, or is not, in the index record associated with a particular document.

While this view is descriptive of early and relatively simple and crude information retrieval systems, several modern online systems store much more information about a term than simply its presence or absence in the record. In addition to the posting number, systems such as DIALOG and BRS include data regarding the *location* of the term in the record. Examples of such locational information are

a	the posting number of the record in which the term occurs
f	the field number in the record in which the term occurs
s	the sentence number in the field in which the word occurs
w	the word number in the sentence in which the term occurs

Example 3.4. Consider a hypothetical search system in which, for each occurrence of each term in each record, a 4-tuple $<a,f,s,w>$ is stored in the inverted index. For example, a piece of the inverted index for the term 'deep' might look like this:

deep: , ... , $<227,3,2,1>$, $<416,2,3,5>$, $<518,2,4,4>$, ...

The 4-tuple $<416,2,3,5>$ says that index record #416 contains the term 'deep.' It is the fifth word of the third sentence of the second field of this record. Now suppose that a second entry in the inverted index is:

structure:,..., $<227,1,3,2>$, $<416,2,3,6>$, $<518,2,4,17>$, ...

By comparing the first two 4-tuples in each listing, observe that 'deep' and 'structure' are both present in record #227, but in different fields. The phrase 'deep structure' actually occurs as a phrase in document #416 (that is, the

TABLE 3.9
Examples of Some Basic Word Proximity Features of DIALOG2

Deep(3w)structure	Requires that 'deep' be within 3 words of 'structure,' and in that order
Minority(w)role	Requires that 'minority' and 'role' be adjacent words in some field, and in that order
Self(f)government	Requires that 'self' and 'government' be present in the same field
Search(c)strategies	Requires that 'search' and 'strategies' be present in the same record
Aged(L)crimes against	Links the subheading 'crimes against' with the main heading, 'aged'
Online(s)systems	Requires in some full text databases that 'online' and 'systems' be present in the same paragraph. Has different meanings in other databases.
Relevance(4n)judgment	Requires that 'relevance' and 'judgment' be within 4 words of one another, in any order

word 'deep' is adjacent to the word 'structure'), occurring in field #2. Finally, 'deep' and 'structure' are present in the same field and sentence of document #518, but are separated by 13 words.

A host of new search formulations to supplement the simple Boolean AND, OR, and NOT are made possible by the additional information stored in the 4-tuple. In particular, in such a system a searcher can require that two search terms be adjacent, or present in a particular field or fields such as abstract or title, or present together in any field, or sentence, or separated by n or fewer words, or any combination of these. These are called word proximity, or free text operators. For illustration, examples of the major word proximity specifications possible with the DIALOG system are displayed in Table 3.9. Thus the following search statement is possible on DIALOG:

    select deep(3w)structure/ti,de

This command requires that 'deep' and 'structure' be within three words of one another in either the title or descriptor fields. The SELECT command causes the system to form a set of postings associated with index records that meet the specifications.

Word proximity commands are different for every search system; the searcher should be aware of all the possibilities and what they mean in terms of the inverted index.

If particular fields are not specified in a search formulation, most systems will make an assumption regarding the fields to be searched. That is, by not specifying fields to be searched, the searcher is in fact specifying the *default* search fields. On DIALOG, for example, if no field is specified, as in the formulation

    select deep(w)structure,

DIALOG'S *basic index* will be searched. This basic index is different for each database available through the search system. In ERIC, for example, it consists of the following four fields: title, abstract, descriptor, and identifier. Note that these fields include controlled vocabulary terms as well as natural language terms. Mixing controlled vocabularies and natural language in this way may not always be a desirable approach to a search, for the reasons discussed in Chapter 2. Nevertheless, for some search systems and databases, the default search fields contain such a mixture. Thus the searcher who carelessly specifies search terms without specifying fields will be searching both natural language and controlled-vocabulary in most DIALOG databases.

DIALOG has been used as an occasional example in this discussion, but it should be observed that other search services also use default search fields. These are, in general, different from each other and from DIALOG, *even for the same databases*. Although now dated, Rouse and Lannom provide an excellent discussion of these issues as applied to three search services: BRS, SDC, and DIALOG [8].

In summary, for effective searching, it is important to know which fields will be searched in a given database and search system if none are explicitly specified by the searcher. For readability and error avoidance it is probably wise to specify fields to be searched even if these coincide with the default fields.

Truncation is another search device based directly on the inverted index structure. To truncate a search term is to search on a piece of a longer word or phrase, usually its leftmost portion. By so doing, the searcher indicates a willingness to accept any terms in the inverted index meeting the "wild card" specification. If the @ sign is used to indicate truncation, then the search term 'libr@' will retrieve the set of postings associated with records that contain any term beginning with the character string 'libr,' including 'library,' 'librarian,' 'libraries,' 'librarianship,' etc.

Used wisely, truncation can save much keying time. Truncating too soon, however, can generate disastrously many false drops. The term 'lib@,' for example, would retrieve records containing the words 'liberty,' 'libra,' 'libation,' 'liberal,' 'libido,' 'libya,' 'libel,' etc., in addition to the 'library' terms. Clearly this particular stem has been truncated too far for effective retrieval. Too much semantic noise has been generated.

Left truncation and imbedded truncation, as in '@computer' and 'wom@n' are also possible with some systems.

Truncation and term proximity search features require a relatively large amount of computer processing time, when compared to simply retrieving vectors from the inverted index and employing Boolean operators. Searching on a term like 'recidivism' requires a simple lookup in the inverted index, and asking that a single term appear in particular fields requires little more.

But requiring that the phrase 'recidivism rehabilitation' appear as a phrase in a particular field requires two lookups in the inverted file followed by a comparison of every pair of accession numbers, field numbers, and word numbers posted to the two terms. If the terms are common in the database, this will take a relatively long time, as with the phrase 'library education,' searched in the abstract field on the ERIC database. Formulations involving truncation can take even much longer, as hundreds of term vectors may need to be compared.

There are three other considerations related to database and file organization that affect one's ability to carry out an online search effectively. These are the parsing rules for creating inverted files from database fields, the use of stop words, and the alphabetizing conventions followed by the system. Each will be discussed in the last section of this chapter.

3.7 SORT SEQUENCES AND PARSING RULES

It is useful to explore in somewhat more depth the concept of binary coding and its implications for online information retrieval. Several different binary coding systems have been developed and used in the history of computing; however, one, the ASCII code, is used in almost all microcomputers and by several online search services. A second code, EBCDIC, was developed by IBM and is used with IBM-compatible equipment. See [9] for a discussion relating the EBCDIC code to online searching.

A *binary code* is a representation of a set of print and special-purpose, non-print characters with strings of binary digits, called code words, so that each character is represented by a unique string of binary digits. Digital computers do not actually manipulate "characters;" they manipulate *bytes*—binary code words *representing* characters. Ordinarily one need not worry about this distinction, but there are times when some knowledge regarding binary coding is useful.

The ASCII 7-bit binary code is represented in Table 3.10. The letters 'r' and 's' are represented by the code words '1110010' and '1110011', respectively, and the character '&' is represented by the string '0100110'. The first several characters in the table are not printable or displayable, but cause other actions. For example, line feed (LF) is represented by '0001010', and carriage return (CR) by '0001101.' The blank, or space (SP), is considered to be a valid character like the others, and is represented by the string '0100000.'

Note that upper case and lower case characters are represented by different binary codes. This means that, in general, computers can and do distinguish between upper and lower case. Most online search systems convert all data in inverted files to the same case before the search process, so that differences between cases disappear for searching purposes. However, some search systems (for example, the Source) do not always do this. In this instance, there will be a differences between upper and lower case. For example, if a system distinguishes between upper and lower case, a searcher will probably need to capitalize the first letter of proper nouns. System responses and search results may depend heavily on this difference, and the user must be prepared for this possibility.

Also, note that the binary code for the letter l ("el") is different from the binary code for the number 1 (one). Similarly, the letter O ("oh") has a different code than the number 0 (zero). While the difference between the two characters means little or nothing to a human reader of printed materials, it means everything to a computer. Using one when the other is intended can cause errors.

The codes used to represent characters have implications for sorting character strings (that is, arranging them in numerical order). Unless complex algorithms are designed to change this order, text strings coded by the ASCII character set will be sorted character by character, in the order given in Table 3.10. The space character precedes all other printable characters. Most punctuation marks precede the numerals, which precede the alphabetic characters. Alphabetic characters and numerals are arranged and will sort in their correct orders: a, b, c, etc. The character codes for EBCDIC are different from those of the ASCII character set, but the sort order is roughly the same. The main difference is that numerals sort *after* alphabetic characters in the EBCDIC code.

Table 3.11 illustrates the results of sorting several character strings representing authors' names, coded in the ASCII character set. There are several interesting things to observe about this order. First, because the space character sorts before the comma, *all* strings beginning 'smith ' will precede *all* strings beginning 'smith, '. Second, because the numeral '1' was typed instead of the letter 'l', 'smith, 1arry' does not appear in its proper place. Third, 'smith-moncriefe' follows all 'smith ' and 'smith, ' strings, because the hyphen sorts after the space and comma. And finally, because ' ' precedes every letter of the alphabet in the sort order, all strings beginning 'smith,' will precede all strings beginning 'smith,x' where x stands for any alphabetic character.

We observed earlier that, in some search systems, a portion of the postings file can be examined online to gain information regarding spellings, alternative word forms, and for other purposes. When this is possible, one gives a command to open a *window* to the postings file at a specified point. Potential problems can result from the sort order in which the postings file is

TABLE 3.10
The ASCII 7-Bit Character Code

Binary	ASCII	Binary	ASCII	Binary	ASCII	Binary	ASCII
0000000	NUL	0100000	SP	1000000		1100000	
0000001	SOH	0100001	!	1000001	A	1100001	a
0000010	STX	0100010	"	1000010	B	1100010	b
0000011	ETX	0100011	#	1000011	C	1100011	c
0000100	EOT	0100100	$	1000100	D	1100100	d
0000101	ENQ	0100101	°	1000101	E	1100101	e
0000110	ACK	0100110	&	1000110	F	1100110	f
0000111	BEL	0100111	'	1000111	G	1100111	g
0001000	BS	0101000	(	1001000	H	1101000	h
0001001	HT	0101001	)	1001001	I	1101001	i
0001010	LF	0101010	*	1001010	J	1101010	j
0001011	VT	0101011	+	1001011	K	1101011	k
0001100	FF	0101100	,	1001100	L	1101100	l
0001101	CR	0101101	–	1001101	M	1101101	m
0001110	SO	0101110	.	1001110	N	1101110	n
0001111	SI	0101111	/	1001111	O	1101111	o
0010000	DLE	0110000	0	1010000	P	1110000	p
0010001	DC1	0110001	1	1010001	Q	1110001	q
0010010	DC2	0110010	2	1010010	R	1110010	r
0010011	DC3	0110011	3	1010011	S	1110011	s
0010100	DC4	0110100	4	1010100	T	1110100	t
0010101	NAK	0110101	5	1010101	U	1110101	u
0010110	SYN	0110110	6	1010110	V	1110110	v
0010111	ETB	0110111	7	1010111	W	1110111	w
0011000	CAN	0111000	8	1011000	X	1111000	x
0011001	EM	0111001	9	1011001	Y	1111001	y
0011010	SUB	0111010	:	1011010	Z	1111010	z
0011011	ESC	0111011	;	1011011	[	1111011	{
0011100	FS	0111100	<	1011100		1111100		
0011101	GS	0111101	=	1011101	]	1111101	}
0011110	RS	0111110	>	1011110	∧	1111110	~
0011111	US	0111111	?	1011111	–	1111111	DEL

arranged. The window that will be displayed is based on the alphabetical position in the postings file of the term entered, and if the term is not typed exactly as it appears in the index, including space characters and punctuation marks, and following proper syntax rules, an unwanted portion of the postings index may be displayed. This can cause confusion and errors.

An example of this is given in Figure 3.6, which shows an attempt using DIALOG to view the terms in the *ERIC Thesaurus of Descriptors* that are listed as being related to the descriptor 'phonetics.' The searcher neglected

TABLE 3.11
**Several Character Strings Representing Authors' Names,
Sorted into Correct ASCII Order.**

smith willy	smith, woodruff
smith woodruff	smith,charley
smith, larry	smith,michael
smith, bill	smith-moncriefe, helene
smith, charley	smithers, bob
smith, michael	smithers, robert
smith, willy	smithers,alice

to close the parentheses properly, and the syntax rule for displaying *Thesaurus* entries was violated. DIALOG then simply expanded *alphabetically* on the string '(phonetics.' Since the first character of the string was the left parenthesis, which occurs before any alphabetic character in the sort order, the terms displayed are the first terms in the inverted index for this database. The strange, potentially confusing display reproduced in Figure 3.6 is the result.

The online searcher must be familiar with the general outline of the binary code used with each search system utilized, as this determines the alphabetic arrangement of all sorted character strings. It is especially important to be aware of sort order when displaying the postings file online.

Another characteristic of machine-readable files that affects online searching is the set of parsing rules used by the search service to construct the inverted file from the linear file. Padin has written a clear introduction to this important subject [10].

When a database is loaded onto a search system for the first time or is being updated, an algorithm called a *parsing rule* is used to prepare the inverted index. A parsing rule is specific to a particular field of a given database. It refers to a set of separating and sorting operations performed by the search service on that data field. The parsing rule is applied when the inverted index is created from the linear file for that database.

The simplest parsing rule is just to make an entry in the inverted index for every word in the field. There are at least two reasons why some modification of this rule for some fields may be useful. First, there are many common, function words in natural language that occur frequently and that would not be useful as search terms (for example, 'and'). Such terms are often eliminated from the inverted index.

Second, there may be reasons for wanting to preserve phrases in certain fields, so that false drops in these fields can be minimized at the time of search. The descriptor field is an obvious example of this. Clearly, little is accom-

```
?e(phonetics

Ref    Items  Index-term
E1         0  *(PHONETICS
E2    388139  A
E3         1  A AND M CONSOLIDATED HIGH SCHOOL TX
E4         1  A B DICK COMPANY
E5         1  A B DICK MODEL 555
E6         5  A B THERAPIST SCALES
E7        11  A BETTER CHANCE INC
E8         1  A BETTER CHANCE, INC
E9         1  A C TEST
E10        1  A CAPPELLA CHOIRS
E11        1  A CHAIR FOR MY MOTHER (BOOK)
E12        1  A CHILDRENS BOOKS

        Enter P or E for more
```

Figure 3.6   Confusing DIALOG display caused by a syntax error and computer sort order. Search performed via the DIALOG* Information Retrieval Services, Inc. (*Servicemark Reg. U.S. Patent and Trademark Office).

plished by indexing documents with phrases such as 'chemical bonding' and then destroying this precoordinated phrase by parsing the descriptor field on a word by word basis. There may be other fields where it would seem useful to preserve a phrase structure, including journal name, author, and others.

Every major search system has defined several *stop words* or words on a *kill list*. Such words are considered to have no value for indexing or retrieval, and receive no entries made in the inverted index. As with other decisions made related to file loading practices, each search service has defined its own list of stop words.

Again using DIALOG as an example, there were originally twelve stop words used with the DIALOG system:

a	for	on
an	from	the
and	in	to
by	of	with

Later, the words 'a', 'in', and 'on' were eliminated from the list of stop words, because of important scientific and technical terms such as 'Vitamin A,' 'in vitro,' and 'on line.' There are today nine stop words on DIALOG. Other search systems have different lists of stop words.

An important question related to the existence of stop words is how one searches for a natural language phrase containing such a word. This depends on the parsing rules used in the search system being employed.

Example 3.5. A searcher wants to look for the material discussing the book *Gone with the Wind*. How should this be done? To answer this question, one must know how stop words are handled by the search service during the parsing operations. On some systems (e.g., DIALOG), although stop words have been omitted from the inverted index, *they are counted* when each word is assigned a sequential number during the preparation of the inverted index. Therefore, to search for the phrase "gone with the wind" using such a system, a formulation specifying that 'gone' be separated from 'wind' by two or fewer words would be necessary to achieve the desired result.

Plainly, the online searcher must be aware of the stop words used with each search system as well as how searches for phrases including one or more stop words must be conducted, based on the parsing rules used to create the inverted indexes.

In addition to eliminating stop words from the inverted index, parsing rules include directions for separating a field into parts. A field is divided into words by searching for blanks, each blank signifying the beginning or the end of a word. Actually, the algorithm must be a bit more complex than this because of the possible occurrence of two or more adjacent space characters, and also because punctuation marks must be stripped from the record. Assuming all punctuation has been removed, a word can be defined as a group of contiguous characters, or *character string*, that does not itself contain a blank character and that is enclosed on both ends by a blank.

There are three main classes of parsing rules, ignoring details involving punctuation and other special characters, case, extra space characters, and stop words. These are

1. Enter the field into the inverted index only once, as a single character string or phrase representing the entire field. Such a field is called a *phrase-indexed* field.

2. Make a separate entry in the inverted index for each word present in the field (except for stop words), where a word is defined as above. Such a field is called a *word-indexed* field.

3. Enter the field both as separate words and as a single character string representing the full field.

For fields parsed by rule 1, records are retrievable only if a search term consists of the exact character string, or a truncated version thereof. In particular, to search for a multiword phrase in a phrase-indexed field one would need to enter the term *exactly* as it appears in the inverted index, including any blank characters, punctuation, and stop words, up to a possible truncation symbol. This parsing rule is used for almost all prefix fields in DIALOG databases, including journal, document type, and several others.

Example 3.6. To conduct a search for articles published in the *Journal of the American Society for Information Science* in ERIC, one enters:

SELECT jn = journal of the american society for information science

Truncating the character string would also serve to retrieve the wanted records.

For word-indexed fields, records are retrievable if searched on any combination of (non stop) words that occurs in the field. The words must be linked by Boolean operators or word proximity symbols, or both. In the DIALOG system, this parsing rule is used, in most databases, for natural language fields: title, abstract, full text, as well as a few prefix fields.

Example 3.7. To conduct a DIALOG search for the *critical path method* in ERIC abstract or title fields, any of the following formulations could be used:

SELECT critical(w)path(w)method/ab
SELECT critical(f)path(f)method/ti
SELECT critical(w)path/ti,ab

However, the formulation

SELECT critical path method/ti

would result in the empty set, since title fields in ERIC are not parsed as full phrases by DIALOG.

DIALOG also parses certain prefix fields on a word by word basis. For ERIC, these are corporate source (cs =) and sponsoring agency (sp =). For searching purposes, DIALOG requires in these cases that the prefix be attached *to each search word.*

Example 3.8. Construct a search on DIALOG for all ERIC records issued by divisions of the Pennsylvania State Department of Education. Either of the following two formulations would do, with the second resulting in some false drops:

SELECT cs=pennsylvania(w)cs=state(w)cs=department(1w)cs=education
SELECT cs=pennsylvania(f)cs=state(f)cs=state(f)cs=education

Since terms appearing in corporate source and sponsoring agency fields are often abbreviated, truncation can also be extremely useful:

SELECT cs = penn?(f)cs = st?(f)cs = ed?

For fields that are both word-indexed and phrase-indexed (rule 3), any of the approaches already discussed can be used. The desirability of preserving the structure of the descriptor and identifier phrases (sometimes called *bound descriptors*) has been discussed. However, an argument can also be made for the usefulness of making entries in the inverted index for each separate word that appears in descriptors and identifiers, in addition to the full phrase. Thus in some search systems, among them DIALOG, descriptor and identifier fields are both word-indexed and phrase-indexed. In such a system the following four entries would be made in the inverted index for the ERIC descriptor 'australian aboriginal languages':

> australian aboriginal languages
> australian
> aboriginal
> languages

A search for any of these four terms would retrieve, among others, records for all items assigned this descriptor. The first of these is especially interesting in its implications for searching. The phrase 'australian aboriginal languages' appears in the inverted index as a long character string containing two blanks. As with any other term intended to search a phrase-indexed field, this character string can be truncated at any point. For example, a search on the term 'australian a@' will retrieve all records assigned 'australian aboriginal languages.' However, because of the presence of the embedded space character, and because titles, abstracts, and full texts are word-indexed, 'australian a@' will retrieve *only* from descriptor and identifier fields.

The example discussed in the previous paragraph suggests an efficient approach of searching for long multi-word descriptors, or any string parsed by rules 1 or 3: truncate after the first blank.

Of course, there may be other phrases (e.g., identifiers that meet the specified criteria, depending on where the string is truncated. In the example given there are several ERIC records indexed by two identifiers meeting the criteria: 'australian academy of sciences' and 'australian aborigines.' Thus the formulation results in false drops. Truncating a bit later in the string would eliminate these entirely.

Example 3.9. Assume that one wants to retrieve records assigned the descriptor 'child development disorders' and the descriptor field is parsed using rule 3. What will searching for the following character string accomplish?

> child@ devel@ disord@

If individual words are to be truncated, word proximity operators must be used. Since there are no proximity operators in the expression, the system will assume that the 21-character string

'child@ devel@ disord@'

is the search term. It will find no entry for that string in the inverted index, and will return a finding of zero postings.

This is not the first time an example of zero postings resulting from a logical, syntax, or spelling error has been discussed. The online searcher should beware a result of zero postings. It may mean that the database has nothing of interest on the topic to be searched, but more usually, it reflects an error by the searcher.

Example 3.10. We have discussed the idea of the order of execution of Boolean operations. The same kind of ambiguity can result from more than one proximity operator in the same expression. Suppose, for example, that a searcher were interested in the concept of education for information science. Following are two DIALOG formulations for this subject, which ought to yield the same search result, intuitively, but which do not.

    (a) information(w)science(f)education
    (b) education(f)information(w)science.

Formulations (a) and (b) result in *different* retrieval sets using the original DIALOG search system. Using Version 2, formulation (b) results in yet a third different set.

The explanation has to do with the order of operations of word proximity operators in DIALOG, which is *from left to right*.

To avoid inaccurate retrieval results, the DIALOG manual recommends that formulations including more than one proximity operator should proceed from the most specific to the most general, in order from left to right (in the example, formulation (a)). The online searcher is advised to know the order of execution of adjacency operators on the search system being utilized and to plan search formulations accordingly.

Example 3.11. There is another type of controlled vocabulary that requires further discussion: the subject heading with subheading, as:

    television, computer applications

On the COMPENDEX database, DIALOG parses each *piece* of the subject heading as if it were a separate descriptor. These pieces can be linked at the time of search using the (L) proximity operator. However, the entire entry

```
File8:COMPENDEX - 70-84/May
Copr. Engineering Information Inc.)

        Set Items Description
        --- ----- -----------

? s television, computer applications
          1      0 TELEVISION, COMPUTER APPLICATIONS

? s television(1)computer applications
          2     51 TELEVISION(L)COMPUTER APPLICATIONS

? s television/de and computer applications/de
               6274 TELEVISION/DE
              16374 COMPUTER APPLICATIONS/DE

          3    139 TELEVISION/DE AND COMPUTER APPLICATIONS/DE
```

Figure 3.7 Example showing use of subheading operator (L) on DIALOG. Search performed via the DIALOG* Information Retrieval Services, Inc. (*Servicemark Reg. U.S. Patent and Trademark Office).

is *not* searchable as a single string. Figure 3.7 illustrates this, in an example due to Padin [11]. Note that if one searches for the entire heading (including the subheading), the empty set is the result (set #1). Linking the subheading 'computer applications' to 'television' produces 51 postings, while the intersection of the two descriptor phrases increases this to 139 postings. In this last formulation, there need be no particular semantic relationship between "television" and "computer applications."

This chapter has examined principles and concepts related to file loading practices. For illustration, the DIALOG language has been discussed extensively. However, there has been no attempt to provide full information regarding the syntax, parsing rules, or other file loading practices for any search system, including DIALOG. Rather, the emphasis has been on discussing principles and concepts related to file loading practices. These will remain unchanged even if a search system changes its command language, as DIALOG has done with its DIALOG2. The online searcher concerned with these matters will need to review carefully the documentation for all search systems used, and to keep up with system changes.

In the long run, everything one does online should depend on the parsing rules, stop words, sort order, order of Boolean and word proximity operators, and system defaults followed by the search system for given fields and databases. Effective retrieval requires an understanding of these and how they affect retrieval.

The problems that follow should be attempted by every reader.

PROBLEMS

1. Examine the most recent documentation for ERIC that you can find, from as many sources as you can, e.g., the front matter of recent issues of *Resources In Education*, the *Thesaurus of ERIC Descriptors, Current Index to Journals in Education,* search service documentation, reference [6], etc. List and discuss any differences among these that you detect.

2. Carefully examine the documentation for the search system of your choice to answer the following questions:

a. Can several levels of parentheses be nested in a Boolean expression? How many?

b. What is the name of the command used to create a set of postings from the inverted index? Is there any limit to the number of sets that can be created? To the number of postings?

c. What is the default order of operations for Boolean expressions with no parentheses?

d. What is the default order of operations if different word proximity operators are used in the same search formulation?

e. What is the default order of operations if word proximity operators and Boolean operators are used in the same search formulation?

f. What command is used to print an index record?

g. What are the default search fields for the search system (specify a particular database)?

h. What command is used to display a portion of the postings file? Can sets of accession numbers be created by directly selecting from this display? What are the syntax rules for these commands?

i. How is the descriptor field parsed (specify database)?

j. What command is used to combine two or more sets using Boolean operators?

3. Carefully examine the documentation for the search system of your choice, and answer the following questions:

a. How are descriptors with parenthetical qualifiers such as the ERIC descriptor 'RELE-VANCE(INFORMATION RETRIEVAL)' parsed?

b. How are heading/subheading searches conducted, as in 'AGED, CRIMES AGAINST'?

c. How are punctuation marks handled in the parsing process? In particular, how are hyphenated words such as 'on-line' parsed? Words including apostrophes? Initialisms such as U.S.A.? Your answer should distinguish between phrase-indexed and word-indexed fields.

d. Is it possible to conduct a search for all records containing a single word descriptor (specify database)?

e. If the answer to (d) is 'yes', is there any way to restrict retrieval to *only* those records assigned the *single word* (and not retrieve records assigned multi-word descriptors that contain the single word)? An example in ERIC is to retrieve records assigned the descriptor 'television' but not records assigned the descriptor 'television violence.'

f. The following formulations are valid in DIALOG:

   (i)   s family(w)structure/de
   (ii)   s family(w)structure
   (iii)   s family(w)structure/de,ti

   1. Is it possible to accomplish this exact result on the search system you have selected?

   2. Arrange sets (i) - (iii) in order of size, from smallest to largest.

   3. Can you say anything about the probable relevance of each of the three formulations to an information need concerning (the effects of high technology on) the structure of the American family?

   4. Which of the above questions is a function of the database searched? Which is not?

g. Sketch Venn diagrams for each of the following. For each pair, decide which diagram would describe the operation as it would be performed on the system you have selected, if *no* parentheses were present in the expression.

   (i)   (A AND B) NOT C; A AND (B NOT C)

    (ii) (A NOT B) AND C; A NOT (B AND C)
    (iii) (A AND B) OR C; A AND (B OR C)
    (iv) (A OR B) AND C; A OR (B AND C)

4. Formulate an expression to create a set of accession numbers accomplishing each of the following (if possible), for the search system and database of your choice:

    a. all records containing any of the words 'irascibility', 'crossness', 'acerbity', 'petulance', or 'pugnacity' in the default search fields

    b. all records containing any of the words 'excess', 'excessive', or 'excessively' in titles or descriptors.

    c. all speeches delivered by Thomas C. Wilson

    d. all bibliographies on library automation

    e. all records containing the phrase 'probabilistic indexing' in titles

    f. all journal articles in *Library Quarterly* applying principles of operations research to an analysis of browsing in libraries

    g. 'aims and objectives' as a subheading of the descriptor 'adult education'

    h. all records containing the descriptor 'information retrieval'

    i. all records of documents appearing in the *Journal of the British Society for Psychoanalytic Thought and Expression*

    j. the research paper entitled "Community Politics and the Death of Democracy in American Education"

    k. all records containing (book or books) and (catalog or catalogs) in the same field

5. If A = {1,2,3,4,5,6,7,8,9}

       B = {2,4,6,8,10,12,14}

       C = {3,6,9,12,15,18,21}, and

       D = {}, find

    a. A OR B AND C

    b. A AND B NOT C

    c. (A OR B) AND C

    d. A AND (B NOT C)

    e. A OR D

    f. A AND D

6. Arrange the following DIALOG commands in order of the size of the sets that will be created by each, from smallest to largest. Assume that 'feeding behaviors' is a descriptor parsed both by individual words and by full phrase, and that it is also sometimes used as a subheading.

    a. s feeding(w)behavior?

    b. s feeding behavior?

    c. s feeding behaviors

    d. s feeding behavior/ti,de,id

    e. s feeding(w)behaviors

    f. s feeding(3w)behaviors

    g. s feeding(w)behaviors/ti

    h. s feeding(c)behaviors

    i. s feeding AND behaviors

    j. s feeding(f)behaviors

    k. s feeding(f)behaviors/ti

    l. s feed?(w)behav?

    m. s horses(l)feeding behaviors

    n. s feeding(n)behaviors

    o. s feeding(s)behaviors

7. Re-examine the "intelligent interface" problem of Table 2.5. This time, try to structure a Boolean formulation for a search that captures the subtle meaning of several of the terms, going beyond their simple Boolean union. You will need to create at least a second concept, and to employ Boolean AND and perhaps NOT as well as OR. It may also be necessary to add additional vocabulary elements.

8. Explain truncation in terms of the inverted index. That is, when the command is given to search on a truncated stem, what does the system do with the inverted index entries? Discuss any implications of your answer for searching.

9. Discuss a philosophy or set of decision rules for deciding how a given field of a database should be parsed to maximize its usefulness for retrieval, from the point of view of a search service. Give examples from a specific database, e.g., ERIC.

10. Select a search system and a database offered by that system. Apply the philosophy developed in Problem #9 to an evaluation of the choice of parsing rules used by the search system to index each field of the database.

NOTES AND REFERENCES

1. Martin, James, *Computer Data-Base Organization*. Second edition. (Englewood Cliffs, New Jersey: Prentice-Hall, Inc.: 1977.)

2. Heaps, H.S. *Information Retrieval: Computational and Theoretical Aspects*. (New York: Academic Press, 1978); Davis, Charles H. Guide to Information Science. (Westport, Connecticut: Greenwood Press, 1979); Meadow, Charles T. *The Analysis of Information Systems*. Second edition. (Los Angeles, California: Melville Publishing Company, 1973); Salton, Gerard and Michael J. McGill. *Introduction to Modern Information Retrieval*. (New York: McGraw-Hill Book Company, 1983).

3. For example, Kenealy, Patrick, "Database Software Packages for Micros." *Mini-Micro Systems* (September 1982) 193–202; Blair, John C., "Creating Your Own Database." *Database* (August 1982) 11–17; Cowart, Bob, "An Introduction to dBase II." *User's Guide to Systems and Software* 1 (No. 5) (September 1983) 8–15; Bove, Tony and Cheryl Rhodes, "Subscription Fulfillment with dBase II: Part 1." *User's Guide to Systems and Software* 1 (No. 5) (September 1983) 32–41.

4. Martin, pp. 48–51.

5. Levine, Gwen Reveley, "Developing Databases for Online Information Retrieval." *Online Review* 5 (1981) (No. 2) 109–120.

6. ERIC Processing and Reference Facility, *ERIC Data Base Master Files: Tape Documentation*. (ERIC Processing and Reference Facility, Computer Systems Department, 1980).

7. This is not quite accurate; *stopwords* do not appear in the inverted index. Stopwords are discussed later in the chapter.

8. Rouse, Sandra H., and Laurence W. Lannom. "Some Differences between Three On-Line Systems: Impact on Search Results." *Online Review* 1 (No. 3)(1977) 117–132.

9. Padin, Mary Ellen, "The 63-character Alphabet." Online 1 (No. 2) (April 1977) 28–30.

10. Padin, Mary Ellen. "How to Study an Online Bibliographic Database." *Online* 2 (No. 3) (July 1978) 82–85.

11. Padin, Mary Ellen. "Unfriendly Commas." *Online* 5 (No. 1)(January 1981) 80–81.

Chapter 4
Reference Databases

4.1 INTRODUCTION

A general classification for machine-readable databases, adopted from that developed by Cuadra Associates [1], was introduced in Chapter 1. *Reference Databases* contain representations of original sources of data, information, or knowledge. Hence their name; they *refer* the searcher to more complete, printed information sources. Records in reference databases are distillations, created through the analytical processes of cataloging, indexing, abstracting, and classification. Reference databases are intended to serve information retrieval functions; through their indexing they filter the information sources so that, theoretically at least, the searcher is referred to relevant material but not to the great mass of remaining records.

Reference databases comprise two classes: bibliographic databases and referral, or directory, databases. *Bibliographic databases* contain clues concerning the intellectual content and physical characteristics of pieces of the graphic (printed) record of humanity. *Referral databases* lead to information sources other than print materials, such as persons, organizations, research projects, and forms of non-print media. For evaluation purposes the two classes will be treated together in Section 4.4. But first, some of the most important characteristics of the two classes will be identified and briefly discussed.

4.2 BIBLIOGRAPHIC DATABASES

Most bibliographic databases provide references to journal articles in areas of science and technology, and to a lesser extent in disciplines of the social sciences and humanities. But there are also bibliographic databases containing references to news, sports, and other current affairs, law and govern-

TABLE 4.1
Large Bibliographic Databases in Several Subject Areas

Discipline	Approximate number of records in January, 1986
Agriculture	
AGRICOLA	2,000,000
BIOSIS PREVIEWS	4,700,000
Books and monographs	
BOOK REVIEW INDEX	1,500,000
BOOKS IN PRINT	1,800,000
LC MARC	2,000,000
REMARC	5,000,000
Business and economics	
ABI/INFORM	360,000
MANAGEMENT CONTENTS	300,000
Chemistry	
CA SEARCH	7,000,000
Current affairs	
MAGAZINE INDEX	1,700,000
PAIS	300,000
UPI NEWS	varies
Education	
ERIC	600,000
Medicine and biological sciences	
BIOSIS PREVIEWS	4,700,000
EMBASE	3,000,000
MEDLINE	4,800,000
SCISEARCH	6,500,000
Multidisciplinary	
DISSERTATION ABSTRACTS	900,000
CONFERENCE PAPERS INDEX	1,200,000
Science and technology	
COMPENDEX	1,400,000
INSPEC	2,400,000
NTIS	1,100,000
SCISEARCH	6,500,000
Social science and humanities	
HISTORICAL ABSTRACTS	230,000
PSYCINFO	460,000
SOCIAL SCISEARCH	1,500,000
SOCIOLOGICAL ABSTRACTS	120,000

ment, business and economics, and interdisciplinary fields. Table 4.1 lists some of the largest bibliographic databases in several subject categories.

The basic data structure introduced in Chapter 3 describes most bibliographic databases quite well. The "entities" described in a bibliographic database include journal articles, books, newspapers stories, laws, theses and dissertations, curriculum guides, editorials, technical reports, and other published materials. Bibliographic records comprise data fields and subfields.

Each field and subfield represents an attribute, or characteristic of interest. The characteristics selected by a database producer for representation are those attributes thought to be of greatest potential usefulness for the solution of information problems.

Bibliographic databases differ widely in the data fields they include. Fields conveying subject information can include titles, subject headings, descriptors, classification codes, abstracts, full texts, identifiers, and others. Besides communicating the subjects or topics treated in the source document, data fields describe other aspects of the publication as well. Table 4.2 summarizes the search fields present in four bibliographic databases as they have been loaded on DIALOG. Each database covers topics important to the areas of medicine: BIOSIS PREVIEWS, MEDLINE, EMBASE (formerly EXCERPTA MEDICA), and SCISEARCH.

There are several observations that should be made regarding Table 4.2. First, there are only a few search fields in SCISEARCH, with the cited reference field being unique to this database. Clearly, the cited reference field and the interdisciplinary nature of the database constitute the greatest strengths of SCISEARCH.

The lack of standardization among databases is also suggested by Table 4.2. Even though the databases deal with similar subjects, they have few fields in common. Of the forty-one fields listed, only five are found in all four databases: author, journal name, language, article title, and update. Only three additional fields are common to at least three of the four databases: corporate source, descriptor, and publication year. The remaining 34 fields are found in only one or two of the four databases.

For effective use of bibliographic databases, it may be necessary to consult special printed and online tools, generically called database documentation. Lists of descriptors and subject headings, hierarchical classification schemes, and other controlled vocabularies, as well as special codes for geographic areas, languages, journal names, document types, and many other non-subject fields are described in such tools. For example, the National Library of Medicine cites ten of its own publications as useful search aids for Medline searchers. Among these are *List of Serials and Monographs Indexed for Online Users, Medical Subject Headings—Tree Structures, Medlars Indexing Manual (Part 1): Bibliographic Principles and Descriptive Indexing,* and *Medlars Indexing Manual (Part II): Indexing Principles.*

It may also be necessary to consult search service documentation. Of particular importance are lists of special codes and other terminology constituting controlled vocabularies, parsing rules for each data field, and how to properly use the system command language to invoke each action that can be performed.

By and large, there are two main purposes for conducting an online search of a bibliographic database. First, there is the need to create a customized bibliography of items treating a research, scholarly, or topical *literature* of

TABLE 4.2
Data fields in SCISEARCH, BIOSIS, MEDLINE, and EMBASE, as Loaded on DIALOG in 1985

	SCISEARCH	BIOSIS	MEDLINE	EMBASE
abstract		X	X	X
abstract indicator		X	X	
accession number			X	
author	X	X	X	X
author affiliation		X		
biosystematic code		X		
biosystematic name		X		
call number (NLM)			X	
CAS registry number			X	
check tag			X	X
cited references	X			
CODEN		X		X
concept code		X		
concept name		X		
contract/grant number			X	
corporate source	X		X	X
country of publication			X	X
descriptor		X	X	X
descriptor code			X	X
document type	X		X	
identifier			X	X
ISBN				X
ISSN			X	
journal announcement			X	
journal code			X	
journal name	X	X	X	X
language	X	X	X	X
manufacturer's name				X
named person			X	
publication year	X		X	X
publisher				X
rotated headings (MESH)			X	
section heading				X
section heading code				X
series				X
subfile			X	X
summary language			X	X
tag code				X
title	X	X	X	X
trade name				X
update	X	X	X	X

interest. Scientists, scholars, and students all have occasional need for this kind of investigation—for a *literature search* and review. The result of a literature search is not information per se but citations to a literature. Eventually, the original sources will be read, analyzed, and synthesized into a more complete understanding of the literature treating the problem area that motivated the search.

The second main purpose of searching bibliographic databases is for *fact*, or *data retrieval*. In such cases, what is wanted is not a literature, but particular pieces of data or information. Such quick, factual information searches are sometimes called *ready reference* inquiries. While there is reason to believe that reference librarians are not using online bibliographic databases as frequently as they might for ready reference purposes, they are being increasingly used for quick fact/subject searches and for citation verification [2]. This topic will be further addressed in Chapters 7, 8, and 9.

4.3 REFERRAL DATABASES

Referral or directory databases are reference databases that lead to non-print information sources such as persons, companies, businesses and other organizations, research projects, and forms of non-print media. If bibliographic databases are diverse in the data fields they provide, referral databases are more so. Because of their great diversity, it is difficult to state generalizations concerning them. However, a few tentative statements can be made regarding differences between referral and bibliographic databases:

1. Referral databases refer not to documents but to other classes of homogeneous entities.

2. There are usually some *numeric* fields in referral databases. Numeric fields include numbers on which some arithmetic computations can be performed, including at a minimum the inequality and equality comparison operators ' $<$ ', ' $>$ ', and ' $=$ '.

3. Subject searching is, in general, less important in referral databases than for bibliographic databases. Although subject searching is probably possible in most referral databases, *name searching* is much more common: company names, personal names and other proper names, as well as other non-subject data fields. If anything, database documentation is even more important when planning a search on referral databases, to ensure that correct syntax, codes, and symbols are used for these non-subject fields.

4. Sorting—arranging records in numerical or alphabetical order by a specified field or fields—is generally possible on many more data fields in referral databases than in bibliographic databases. This is because sorting often

is more useful to do in the latter. Sorting output is typically done as the final step before printing in most referral searches.

5. There is probably a higher proportion of *fact searching* in referral databases than in bibliographic databases.

Bibliographic databases contain records referring to printed information sources. Referral databases are much more diverse. Table 4.3 lists some examples of referral databases currently available on commercial search services. The "entities" described can be from any population of people or things: software packages, persons, associations, companies, private foundations, government and industry standards, grants, and many others. The potential for introducing additional referral databases for online searching is virtually unlimited, and their number is expected to increase significantly in the future.

Table 4.4 illustrates the data fields of TRINET ESTABLISHMENT DATABASE, produced by TRINET, Inc. TRINET ESTABLISHMENTS provides basic directory information regarding U.S. industrial and non-industrial establishments. DISCLOSURE II, another database dealing with (publicly owned) companies, has no fewer than 96 data fields, providing extremely detailed financial and ownership information about each company indexed.

The fact that some fields in referral databases are numeric is an especially important characteristic. Some data in bibliographic records may appear to the reader to be numeric since they are represented by numerals (for example, year of publication). However, in bibliographic databases such numerals are treated as character strings instead of numbers. This can have odd consequences. For example, for the numbers 2 and 13254,

$$2 < 13254$$

However, when treated as character strings, '2' > '13254' (that is, would appear after '13254' in an alphabetical sequence), since the binary code for '2' follows the binary code for '1', and character strings sort character by character. Numeric data fields in referral databases are treated as numbers, not character strings, and can be added, ordered, and otherwise manipulated as a number. Although the statistical routines actually possible to conduct are limited in general purpose commercial search systems like DIALOG, BRS and SDC, this is likely to change with time. Currently, sophisticated numerical analyses are possible using numeric database systems (see Chapter 8).

Although subject searching is less important in referral database searching, it does sometimes take place. Several databases use modified versions of the Standard Industrial Classification Code (SIC) to assign descriptors

TABLE 4.3
Examples of Referral Databases Available through Commercial Search Services

ELECTRONIC YELLOW PAGES
Offered in several subfiles (for construction, financial services, manufacturing, professionals, retailers, services, and wholesalers), these files are generated from yellow page listings appearing in 4,800 telephone books from all over the United States. They include full directory listings as well as modified Standard Industrial Classification (SIC) codes for subject access, county, city size, and details of the yellow page ad. A special file contains an index to the other seven.
TRINET ESTABLISHMENT DATA BASE
Provides directory information on more than 400,000 public and private U.S. establishments in all sectors of industry, with 20 or more employees. Subject access is provided with modified SIC codes. Also includes corporate links.
FOUNDATION DIRECTORY
Directory information and detailed descriptions of more than 3500 foundations with assets exceeding $1,000,000 and grants totaling more than $100,000 annually. Foundations included account for nearly 90 percent of the assets of all foundations in the U.S. and 85% of all grants by foundations. Includes information regarding grants, scholarships, statement of purposes and activities, number and amounts of grants. Subject access is provided through descriptors, purpose, and activities.
.MENU (formerly INTERNATIONAL SOFTWARE DATABASE)
Lists and describes more than 15,000 software packages for microcomputers, minicomputers, and mainframes. Classified and searchable by type of computer, operating system, application, vendor, minimum memory required, manufacturer, terms of sale, warranty availability, price, and other characteristics. Subject access is provided through short abstracts, title, descriptors, identifiers, and notes.
MARQUIS WHO'S WHO
Self-reported biographical information from 75,000 individuals in business, sports, government, the arts, entertainment, and science. Includes detailed personal information relating to vital statistics, career, education, achievements, political, religious, and other affiliations, family, address, and creative works. More then 50 searchable data fields, many in free text.
STANDARDS AND SPECIFICATIONS
Records of U.S. military and federal and private sector industry standards and specifications relating to performance testing, safety, materials, products, and other requirements. Subject access through descriptors, identifiers, notes, and title.
DISCLOSURE II
Extracts from reports filed with the U.S. Securities and Exchange Commission (SEC) by 9,000 publicly-owned companies with at least 500 shareholders and one million dollars in assets. Information is extracted from 10-K, 20-F, 10-Q, Proxy statements, 8-K, and Registration statements provided by companies to the SEC. Records include extremely detailed public financial and management information concerning the company, with more than 95 searchable data fields.
D & B MILLION DOLLAR DIRECTORY
Current information on more than 120,000 U.S. commercial and industrial establishments having a net worth of $500,000 or more. The online version of Dun and Bradstreet's *Million Dollar Directory*. Subject access provided through company name, descriptors, SIC codes, and secondary trade names.

TABLE 4.4
Data Fields of TRINET ESTABLISHMENT DATABASE

descriptor
country name
company name
city
number of employees
headquarters city
headquarters name
headquarters state
headquarters telephone area code
headquarters zip code
Metropolitan Statistical Area (MSA) code
primary Standard Industrial Classification (SIC) code
two-digit primary SIC code
three-digit primary SIC code
sales
special feature
share of market (%)
state
telephone area code
TRINET number
ticker symbol
zip code

and subject codes to companies and other entities. Figures 4.1 and 4.2 provide excerpts from the classification and its index [3]. Note that the *Classification* is hierarchical. Major Group 39 stands for "Miscellaneous Manufacturing Industries," of which group 391 is "Jewelry, Silverware, and Plated Ware," and subgroup 3911 is "Jewelry, Precious Metal." On some databases and search systems "cascaded" searches on a group and simultaneously on all its subgroups can be conducted.

The SIC Classification Manual includes agriculture, forestry and fishing, mineral industries, construction, manufacturers, wholesale trade, retail trade, financial and insurance institutions, and selected service industries (see Figure 4.2). Unfortunately, SIC codes are assigned inconsistently by database producers to companies, especially diversified companies [4]. SIC codes are no different from other controlled vocabularies in their potential disadvantages. However, they are widely used in referral databases for subject access to companies and corporations. SIC codes are used by several of the databases listed in Table 4.3: ELECTRONIC YELLOW PAGES, TRINET ESTABLISHMENTS DATABASE, DISCLOSURE II, AND D & B MILLION DOLLAR DIRECTORY. However, modifications to the basic SIC classification schedules are made by most database producers, and database

Major Group 39.—MISCELLANEOUS MANUFACTURING INDUSTRIES

THE MAJOR GROUP AS A WHOLE

This major group includes establishments primarily engaged in manufacturing products not classified in any other manufacturing major group. Industries in this group fall into the following categories: jewelry, silverware and plated ware; musical instruments; toys, sporting and athletic goods; pens, pencils, and other office and artists' materials; buttons, costume novelties, miscellaneous notions; brooms and brushes; morticians' goods; and other miscellaneous manufacturing industries.

Group No.	Industry No.	
391		JEWELRY, SILVERWARE, AND PLATED WARE
	3911	Jewelry, precious metal

Establishments primarily engaged in manufacturing jewelry and other articles, worn on or carried about the person, made of precious metals with or without stones (including the setting of stones where stones are used), including cigarette cases and lighters; vanity cases and compacts; trimmings for umbrellas and canes; and jewel settings and mountings. Establishments primarily engaged in manufacturing costume jewelry from nonprecious metals and other materials are classified in Industry 3961.

3912 Jewelers' findings and materials

Establishments primarily engaged in manufacturing unassembled jewelry parts, and stock shop products such as sheet, wire, and tubing. Establishments primarily engaged in lapidary work are classified in Industry 3913.

3913 Lapidary work and cutting and polishing diamonds

Establishments primarily engaged in all types of lapidary work, and cutting and polishing diamonds. This industry also includes establishments primarily engaged in cutting and polishing other precious stones; recutting and setting stones; preparing jewels for instruments, tools, and for watches and chronometers; and preparing real and imitation stones for settings.

3914 Silverware and plated ware

Establishments primarily engaged in manufacturing flatware (including knives, forks, and spoons), hollow ware, toilet ware, ecclesiastical ware, and related products made of sterling silver; of metal plated with silver, gold, or other metal; of nickel silver; of pewter; or of stainless steel.

393   MUSICAL INSTRUMENTS AND PARTS

3931 Musical instruments and parts

Establishments primarily engaged in manufacturing pianos, with or without player attachments; organs; other musical instruments; and parts and materials for musical instruments.

Figure 4.1   Page from *Standard Industrial Classification (SIC) Manual.*

documentation must be consulted for accurate information regarding SIC codes as they are used in a given database.

We have already commented on the importance of sorting search output, either in ascending order (most useful for alphabetic fields) or descending order (often most useful for numeric fields). One can imagine occasions in which it would be useful to sort records in TRINET ESTABLISHMENTS DATABASE on any of the following fields: company name, city, headquarters name, state, zip code, MSA code, number of employees, sales in millions of dollars, and share of market, among others. The following search

J

3569	Jack screws	3913	Jewel preparing, for instruments, tools, watches, and jewelry
1961	Jackets, bullet: 30 mm. (or 1.18 inch) and below	3911	Jewel settings and mountings, precious metal
2337	Jackets, except fur: women's, misses', and juniors'	2645	Jewelers' cards, made from purchased materials
2371	Jackets, fur: women's, misses', and juniors'	3912	Jewelers' findings and materials
3443	Jackets, industrial: steel plate	3423	Jewelers' hand tools
2328	Jackets, overall and work	3559	Jewelers' machines
2311	Jackets, sport: oiled fabric, suede, leatherette, melton, blanket lined—men's, youths', and boys'	3079	Jewelry boxes, plastic
		3172	Jewelry cases, regardless of material
3569	Jacks, hydraulic: for general industrial use	3961	Jewelry, costume: except precious metal and precious or semiprecious stones
2499	Jacks, ladder: wood	3479	Jewelry enameling, for the trade
3423	Jacks: lifting, screw, and ratchet (hand tools)	3911	Jewelry, made of precious metal or precious or semiprecious stones
3552	Jacquard card cutting machines	3912	Jewelry parts, unassembled
2645	Jacquard cards made from purchased materials	3911	Jewelry soldering, for the trade
		3541	Jig boring machines
3552	Jacquard loom parts and attachments	3541	Jig grinding machines
2211	Jacquard woven fabrics, cotton	3544	Jigs and fixtures
2221	Jacquard woven fabrics, man-made fiber and silk	2751	Job printing, except lithographic and offset
3442	Jalousies, all metal or metal frame	2711	Job printing and newspaper publishing combined
2431	Jalousies, glass: wood frame	3553	Jointers (woodworking machines)
2033	Jams	3566	Joints, universal
2833	Japanese gelatin	3272	Joists, concrete
3111	Japanning of leather	3441	Joists, open web steel: longspan series—not made in rolling mills
3567	Japanning ovens		
2851	Japans, baking and drying	3221	Jugs (packers' ware), glass
3461	Jar crowns and tops, stamped metal	3429	Jugs, vacuum
3069	Jar rings, rubber	3634	Juice extractors, electric
3221	Jars (packers' ware), glass	3551	Juice extractors, fruit and vegetable: commercial type
2033	Jellies, edible	2033	Juices, fruit and vegetable: canned, bottled, and bulk
2256	Jersey cloth, made in knitting mills		
2253	Jerseys and sweaters, made in knitting mills	2631	Jute liner board, made in paperboard mills
3722	Jet assisted take-off devices (JATO)	2514	Juvenile furniture, metal
3722	Jet propulsion engines, aircraft	2519	Juvenile furniture, rattan and reed: padded or plain
3519	Jet propulsion engines, except aircraft	2512	Juvenile furniture, upholstered on wood frames
1929	Jet propulsion projectiles, complete		
3912	Jewel bearings, synthetic	2511	Juvenile furniture, wood except upholstered
3913	Jewel cutting, drilling, polishing, recutting, or setting		

Figure 4.2   Page from index to *Standard Industrial Classification (SIC) Manual.*

problem is an example of what can be done quickly and efficiently on TRI-NET ESTABLISHMENTS:

Example 4.1. I want a list of all manufacturers of jewelry and similar articles. Manufacturers should employ 20 or more people, and be limited to certain states in the Midwest. The output should be provided in the following order: first, companies should be listed in ascending order by state; then in ascending order within state by city, and finally, in descending order, within city by sales in millions of dollars.

Obviously there are many other potentially useful sort orders for this information problem. Sorting is a fundamental final step in many referral database searches.

We now turn to a discussion of criteria for the evaluation of bibliographic and referral databases.

4.4 EVALUATION AND SELECTION

The remainder of the chapter discusses principles and issues related to the evaluation and selection of bibliographic and referral databases. The literature contains several introductions to this topic [5]. The criteria to be discussed are summarized in Table 4.5.

Evaluation criteria must concern not only characteristics of databases themselves, but also the search systems through which the databases are made available for online searching. As they are provided by database producers, machine-readable databases possess certain intrinsic characteristics. But databases are made accessible for online access by search services in a variety of ways that differ in their potential usefulness.

In a given database, for example, a particular field may exist in machine-readable form but may be eliminated by a search service providing access to that database. Another search service offering access to the same database may permit free text searching of the field using word proximity operators. A third may permit searching of the field on a character by character basis (as a phrase) but not through free text searching. A fourth may allow the field to be displayed online or printed but not searched.

Thus the potential offered by a given reference database can differ significantly from one search system to another. Evaluation criteria must consider not only database content but also access to the database on particular search systems. Table 4.5 lists a set of criteria for the evaluation of reference databases. There are thirteen main classes of evaluative criteria. These are

* Coverage
* Size
* Local Availability of Primary Sources
* Currency
* Indexing and Cataloging Practices
* Error Rates
* Treatment of Research

TABLE 4.5
Criteria for the Evaluation of Reference Databases

1. Coverage
    a. subject emphases
    b. type of material indexed
    c. focus of material indexed
    d. inclusive dates of material indexed
    e. selection policy
    f. quality of material indexed
    g. proportion of "world's literature" covered
    h. interdisciplinary nature of subject coverage
2. Size
    a. number of records
    b. number of subfiles
    c. growth rate
3. Local Availability of Primary Sources
4. Currency
    a. time lapse between primary source and paper copy
    b. time lapse between primary source and online version
    c. frequency of update
5. Indexing and Cataloging Practices
    a. use of controlled vocabulary
    b. presence of abstracts
    c. presence of full texts
    d. searchability of abstracts, titles, and full texts
    e. integrity of information
    f. quality of indexing
    g. depth (exhaustivity) of indexing
    h. specificity of indexing language
    i. weighting of index terms
    j. authority control in non-subject data fields
    k. consistency of indexing and cataloging practices
6. Error Rates
    a. number of errors
    b. factual errors
    c. clerical errors
    d. indexing errors
7. Treatment of Concepts of Research
8. Record and File Structure
    a. subject fields (i) displayable and (ii) searchable
    b. non-subject fields (i) displayable and (ii) searchable
    c. cited reference capability
    d. what constitutes default index
    e. parsing rules for subject fields
    f. parsing rules for non-subject fields
    g. free-text searching possible in which fields
9. Printing and Sorting Capabilities
    a. default sort order
    b. sortable fields

(continues)

TABLE 4.5 *(continued)*

---

    c. possibility for multiple sorts
    d. availability of printing formats
10. Cost
    a. connect hour charges
    b. online print charges
    c. offline print charges
    d. database royalty charges
    e. subscription charges
    f. per search charges
    g. CPU time charges
    h. cost in searcher time when compared to alternatives (ease of use)
11. Database Aids
    a. availability of
    b. clarity
    c. accuracy
    d. completeness
12. Differences between Online and Print Version
    a. access points to records
    b. coverage
    c. currency
    d. output
    e. time required
    f. cost
13. Review Literature
    a. analytical reviews
    b. comparative reviews

---

* Record and File Structure
* Sorting and Printing Capabilities
* Cost
* Database Aids
* Differences between Online and Print Versions
* Review Literature

These will be discussed in the pages that follow.

Coverage

The *subject emphasis* of a database refers to the topical areas it covers. Some search systems offer print and online tools (indexes to indexes) that can help determine the databases providing the best subject coverage of given topics and problems, e.g., DIALOG's DIALINDEX, SDC's Data Base Index and BRS/CROS. However, these tools should be regarded as preliminary guides at best, because while they indicate the presence or absence of terminology, and even can handle Boolean combinations of terms, they ignore other evaluative criteria.

One's initial "common sense" assumption regarding the lack of applicability of a given database to a search problem may be premature and incorrect. Many search problems are highly interdisciplinary and have subliteratures in what may at first appear to be unlikely databases. For example, a significant amount of material of interest to the scholar of English and American literature has been reported in Medline [6].

In one sense, subject emphasis is the most important of all the criteria for evaluation. If the database does not cover the fields of interest, none of the other criteria need be applied. By definition, there in no likelihood that the database will be useful. However, the converse of this proposition is not true. There are literally hundreds of reference databases available for searching, and one must go well beyond an analysis of subject emphases to evaluate them intelligently.

The *type of material* indexed is another aspect of coverage. Is a database limited to journal articles? Does it, like ERIC, include access to unpublished "fugitive materials"? Does it include access to speeches, congressional hearings, conference proceedings, doctoral dissertations, non-print materials, ongoing research projects, or books? Few databases offer access to all possible forms of information that might be of interest.

The *focus of the material* indexed is also important to consider. Is the information "popular" or research-oriented? What is the overall orientation of the database? For example, a database including information relating to an animal species might have a focus of environmental concerns; in another the focus might be on biological characteristics; in a third the focus might be on food production; and a fourth might concentrate on trade and market information.

The *inclusive dates* associated with the material indexed is another important aspect of coverage. Most reference databases in machine-readable form cover only recent publications, and do not go back nearly as far as their print counterparts. This may not be of great consequence for most search problems in the harder sciences and social sciences, but for the softer disciplines and the humanities, it can be a crucial consideration. DISSERTATION ABSTRACTS ONLINE goes back to 1861, but such complete coverage is rare. The beginning dates associated with PHILOSOPHER'S INDEX, MLA BIBLIOGRAPHY, and AMERICA: HISTORY AND LIFE are 1979, 1976, and 1964, respectively. These ranges are closer to the norm for databases in machine-readable form.

Database coverage may change as older materials are converted retrospectively. However, such conversion projects are taking place currently in only a few databases. Probably print materials of interest to scholars in the humanities will never be well covered by databases in machine-readable form.

The *selection policy* and the *quality of material indexed* by the database producer are also important issues affecting coverage. Some database producers such as EXCERPTA MEDICA, MEDLINE, AND AGRICOLA are selective in coverage. Others, such as the *Current Index to Journals in Education* (CIJE), index everything appearing in the journals covered. Still others, such as ERIC's *Resources in Education* (RIE), have reputations of accepting contributions that are sometimes less than the high quality that might be hoped for.

For comprehensive searches demanding the retrieval of a high percentage of materials published on a subject, another issue of importance is the *proportion of the "world's literature"* in the discipline of interest that is covered by the database. The Institute for Scientific Information's *Science Citation Index* (SCISEARCH) claims to include 90 percent of the world's significant scientific and technical literature [7]. Other databases may include only a small proportion of the total literature of a field.

Another important consideration is the interdisciplinary and multidisciplinary nature of the materials covered by the database. Because of the heterogeneous nature of the materials indexed, multidisciplinary databases such as SCISEARCH and DISSERTATION ABSTRACTS contain more homographs in natural language fields. Thus when used for subject searching, these databases will lead to a higher incidence of false drops than will more homogeneous databases. On the other hand, these databases will provide access to information treating a search problem from a variety of disciplines.

Size

Related to issues of coverage and currency are questions of size and growth. The number of records in a database affects one's strategy for searching that file. Files containing millions of records present difficulties not present in small files. Some search systems have upper limits to the number of postings that can be stored in retrieval sets, and these limits are easy to exceed in large databases like BIOSIS. In some search systems, sets no longer needed can be erased, helping to relieve this problem.

Because of their size, some databases may be split up into *several subfiles* by the search service. Currently, most commercial search services require that separate searches be conducted on each database. (The Wilsonline search system is an exception to this.) Rerunning the same search on several databases can be inconvenient, time-consuming, and expensive for a complex, comprehensive search, since the execution time required for a search is directly proportional to the number of files searched.

Some search systems have the capability of saving searches and re-executing them in as many databases as wanted. This can save the connect time and effort related to rekeying search formulations for each database searched.

Local Availability of Primary Sources

Reference databases are surrogates to original materials. The *local availability* of these primary sources is, strictly speaking, not an evaluative criterion to be applied to databases or search systems. Rather, availability is a measure of how efficiently the local information system or library can furnish the needed sources on demand. Since the next step after receiving a list of references is the obtaining of the primary sources themselves, the ability to furnish these materials must be an issue of some concern to a search specialist who is attempting to evaluate the suitability of a database for use for a given information problem. Interlibrary loans increase dramatically in institutions that institute online search services, presumably because it is much easier online to learn about information sources that are not available locally.

Currency

The *currency* of reference databases refers to the up-to-datedness of the information contained in a database, when compared to the information being indexed. Currency is a function of *frequency of update*. Databases that are updated on a daily or weekly basis are obviously much more current than those updated only semiannually.

For bibliographic databases, a lack of currency refers to a long time lapse between the date of publication of the published materials indexed and the availability of the database containing the surrogates of those materials. This can be years for some databases, and only a few weeks for others.

Especially for referral databases, currency also refers to the accuracy of information contained in data fields. For example, in the ENCYCLOPE-DIA OF ASSOCIATIONS, the entities being indexed are nonprofit American organizations of national scope. Obviously, while new organizations are added each year, and others become defunct, the majority of organizations remain the same from year to year. However, changes of potential importance regularly take place in the record referring to such organizations: the name of the executive director, address, telephone number, and other facts. Similar examples can be given for the ELECTRONIC YELLOW PAGES, DISCLOSURE II, FOUNDATION DIRECTORY, and other referral databases. Perhaps more than any other factor, the currency and accuracy of the data provided determine the value of a referral database.

Indexing and Cataloging Practices

There are many aspects of indexing and cataloging practice worthy of discussion, and an entire book could be devoted to an in-depth treatment of these issues. Some of the more important concepts will be introduced in this section of the chapter, and the interested reader is encouraged to explore other texts as well [8].

The first question one should ask regarding the indexing and cataloging provided in a reference database is whether controlled vocabularies are employed, and if so, to what extent and for which data fields? Are descriptors used? A hierarchical classification system? Broad, general subject headings?

The appropriateness of the controlled vocabulary available, if any, to the information problem is important to consider. Are there elements of the controlled vocabulary that appear to describe key concepts of the information problem?

The nature of any natural language fields present in the record may also be important. Are *abstracts* included? If so, are they descriptive or evaluative? That is, do they merely summarize the paper or do they also make some attempt to evaluate the paper and its findings? Are they long or short? Do they seem well written and informative? A key question is whether abstracts are *searchable*, using free text proximity operators, as opposed to being only displayable. Similar questions can be asked for *titles*. Are they searchable? Are they descriptive, as in most research reports in the hard sciences? Or are many titles merely cute, useless for information retrieval? [9]

For bibliographic databases, another natural language field is the full text of the document itself. There has been little research studying large full text databases as they can be searched on commercial search systems [10]. But one suspects that for comprehensive searches, full texts will require different search methods than those that work well for other subject fields. However, full text databases may be ideally suited for *fact* searching.

The *integrity* of the information provided is another question of interest. This is perhaps especially important for referral databases. Are data provided generally reliable and precise? Or does the database have a reputation for factual errors and inaccuracies? Such information can be gleaned from reviews of databases appearing in such journals as *Database, Special Libraries, Online,* and *Online Review.* For example, Nichol reported finding seven errors in fewer than 20 lines of printout on a search of DISCLOSURE II [11]. Word of mouth is another valuable source of information. Obviously such judgments will take time to render, will be difficult to obtain, and will be somewhat subjective.

If controlled vocabularies are used in the database, what is the *quality of the indexing*? Even more than the previous criterion, this is a difficult, subjective issue. Indexing errors include the omission of concepts that should have been indexed as well as the representation of concepts by inappropriate index terms. For certain classes of problems, some databases are recognized by search specialists as being superior to others in indexing quality. An awareness of this will come with experience.

Another issue related to subject indexing is the *depth*, or *exhaustivity* of the indexing provided. Exhaustivity of indexing refers to the number of concepts treated in a document (or other entity) that are indexed by the database producer. If "all" the concepts of a document are indexed, the indexing is said to be exhaustive. If only major concepts are indexed, the indexing is less exhaustive. If only a single subject heading or classification code is assigned each document, then the indexing is not exhaustive at all.

Exhaustive indexing is most useful for highly comprehensive searches, in which the searcher wants to find a high proportion of items relevant to the search question, even those only peripherally related to the question. In contrast, in a database in which the indexing is not exhaustive, only those entities treating the concepts in a central way will be indexed and retrieved in a search, and more peripheral items will be missed.

The *specificity* of the indexing language is another important characteristic affecting retrieval. Can highly precise concepts be represented in the controlled vocabulary? Or are index terms broad and encompassing? For a particular search problem, can the specific concepts of interest be represented adequately in the controlled vocabulary? The descriptors or subject headings used in some databases are so broad that they are almost useless for most searches.

Although presently found in only a few databases and search systems, *weighted index terms* can be extremely useful for retrieval. Assigning weights to descriptors or other controlled elements of a controlled vocabulary can reflect the relative degree to which concepts are treated in a document as compared to other concepts in that document (major concept, minor concept, peripheral treatment, etc.). The ERIC database weights descriptors in this way. Or, term weighting might reflect the relative degree of treatment of that concept as compared to other documents in the database. Term weighting might reflect the frequency of occurrence of terms in documents, or frequency of occurrence normalized by some measure of the relative importance of the term. Finally, term weights might be used to reflect "the probability that a document will be found useful" by a user.

There are other possible interpretations of term weights. The question of term weighting has been heavily studied in a theoretical sense in the information retrieval literature, but has not been much utilized in operational systems. As new full text databases continue to make their appearance, an increased interest in this question is likely, both theoretically and for operational systems [12].

Considerable time was devoted in Chapter 2 discussing controlled vocabularies for the representation of subjects. The question of *authority control* of non-subject data is also important to consider. Standardizing the representation of such data as journal name, author name, company name, and similar data fields is crucial for effective retrieval for some search problems. However, this tends to be not well done in bibliographic databases. For example, in a study of the form of entry of the journal title element in seven databases indexing physics journals, Williams found that two were found to be "completely free form," three were 'almost" standardized, and another three were judged "standardized" [13]. Another revealing study of errors in journal names was published by Keck [14].

Since they are author-supplied, it is likely that even worse problems exist with such fields as corporate source and authors' names. For example, many authors publish under several different forms of their names but most database producers and search services typically make no attempt to standardize the form of entry. That it would be extremely difficult for them to do so does not alter this situation. Exceptions to this generalization are the Library of Congress MARC records for books and other forms of publication (but not journal articles). Search problems with proper names are thoroughly explored in [15].

Finally, the *consistency of indexing and cataloging practices* is an important criterion for evaluation. Indexing terminology should grow and change with the literatures being indexed. Has this in fact happened in the database of interest? This is an important initial question. But, given that a controlled vocabulary has developed and changed over the years, how do the database producer and search system treat documents assigned the older, now discarded or changed, headings? The problem is ignored by some databases, producing a confusing mish-mash of entries that threatens to confound the most able searcher. For other databases, the search system has undertaken a massive reloading, producing consistent usage over the entire database.

We have noted that some search services divide some large databases into several subfiles, each of which must be separately searched for the comprehensive treatment of an information problem. Consistency of usage is important as well. If a searcher must change vocabulary for each subfile of a multi-part database, clear communication, ease of use and efficiency are threatened.

Error Rates

Related to indexing and cataloging practices are the error rates associated with records in the database. There are three kinds of errors: factual errors, typographical errors, and indexing errors. Factual errors consist of non-typographical mistakes in numerical or other non-subject data such as publication date, number of employees, amount of annual sales, address, or telephone number. Factual errors may be the result of carelessness or lack of currency in data.

Typographical errors are simple clerical keystroking errors that do not play major roles in searching printed bibliographic databases because the reader has the benefit of seeing the context of all errors. However, clerical errors are more important in online information retrieval because, as has been stressed, computers search for character strings, not concepts. If a character string contains a typographical error, it will not be retrieved in response to a search for the correctly spelled character string. Clearly, typographical errors in numerical data fields and other fields of referral databases can have an important effect on retrieval.

Indexing errors are errors of judgment—conceptual errors made during the analysis and term assignment stages of the indexing process. These are highly subjective and elusive and will not be discussed further.

Treatment of Research

There are many kinds of publications that are cited in most bibliographic databases. Especially in the softer sciences and social sciences, there are many opinion papers, polemics, argumentative or thought pieces, "glad tidings," and descriptions of "how we did it good in our institution." And then there is the research literature, which in many databases is lumped in with the rest of the literature of the field. We are not suggesting that research publications are good and all else is bad. Rather, we are observing that it would be extremely useful if more databases made it easier to identify publications that report research findings. In many environments, the identification of research is an extremely important requirement. Currently this is not easy to do in most databases.

Some bibliographic databases, such as DISSERTATION ABSTRACTS and the SMITHSONIAN SCIENCE INFORMATION EXCHANGE, include research exclusively. Others, such as ERIC, MEDLINE, and BIOSIS, include a mixture of literature forms. Still others, such as MAGAZINE INDEX and UPI NEWS, contain no research. The second and largest of these categories presents the major problem. How can a searcher sift out the research treating a topic like "online public access catalogs," from the remaining literature? The latter category may well constitute as much as 90% of the literature on this subject.

Atkinson and Dolan have explored in depth issues and problems related to the identification of research in online searches [16]. Among other suggestions, the authors recommend using the structure of a research paper as a guide to the searcher. The authors focus on techniques useful for searching five databases: BIOSIS, ERIC, MEDLINE, PSYCINFO, and the National Clearinghouse for Mental Health (NCMH).

To be most useful, a database will offer elements of a controlled vocabulary that permit indexers to recognize and to specify as concepts the general idea of "research;" aspects of research as a social process, such as schools of thought and ethical questions; aspects of the research problem, such as independent and dependent variables, hypotheses, assumptions and definitions; aspects of methodology, such as sampling, measurement techniques and populations studied; and results [17].

Record and File Structure

Knowing which subject fields are present in a given reference database is important. But as stated, this criterion is somewhat ambiguous. Is a given subject field searchable (that is, are entries made in the inverted index for the field) or is it merely displayable? If searchable, in what ways can it be searched?

Before 1984, the abstracts provided in DISSERTATION ABSTRACTS, as mounted on the DIALOG system, were displayable in retrieved records but were not searchable. The subject elements that were searchable on this database included dissertation titles and extremely broad subject headings. Even though the titles of doctoral dissertations are notoriously dense, lengthy, and descriptive, this database was seriously limited in subject access, with its exceptionally broad controlled vocabulary and lack of searchable abstracts. Access to records in DISSERTATION ABSTRACTS through DIALOG is vastly improved now that abstracts are searchable as well as displayable.

To take another example, while the full text of the *Academic American Encyclopedia* is offered by several search services, it is *searchable* using free text methods in only some of these systems. In the remaining systems, access to records is limited to article titles. The full text can be printed but cannot be searched. This seriously limits the usefulness of this tool.

Non-subject fields may also be displayable but not searchable, although examples of wide generality are difficult to cite. Generally speaking, search services provide access to all non-subject fields for which search access is important. For specific search problems, however, this may be an important issue in some databases.

Depending on one's approaches to an information problem, the availability of *cited references* for searching can be a major advantage. However, if subject access through subject fields (rather than cited references) is wanted, the Institute for Scientific Information's SCISEARCH and SOCIAL

SCISEARCH provide no controlled vocabulary or keyword indexing for records, nor are there abstracts available for searching. Subject access is provided only in title fields. This can be extremely limiting, particularly in soft social sciences. Subject searches in ISI's databases should be done very cautiously because of these limitations.

Besides knowing whether a given data field is searchable, one must know how it can be searched. As described in Chapter 3, knowledge of the parsing rules used to separate and sort fields into entries for the inverted index are crucial here. Are fields parsed word-for-word, full phrase only, in each of these ways, or in yet another way? What are the stop words? How is punctuation handled? Is free text searching using word proximity operators possible? In which data fields? The answers to these questions may help a searcher decide whether to search a particular database on one system as opposed to another. This observation applies as well to non-subject fields. It is also important to be aware of the fields that are included in the default, or basic search index used for a given database on a particular search system. Default search fields vary widely among search services, and affects the planning and even the evaluation process.

Printing and Sorting Capabilities

The searcher should be aware of the *default sort order* in which retrieved records will be displayed and printed, for each search system used. On some systems, if records are not sorted before the output step, they will be printed in reverse accession number order, that is, in the opposite order in which they were input into the system. Although accession number order is not the same as the arrangement produced by sorting by publication date, there may be a close relationship between the two orders produced in some databases.

Some search systems offer a variety of fields on which sorting, or alphabetical and numerical arrangement of records is possible. That is, the default order in which records print and display can be changed by sorting. This may be particularly important for searches on referral databases. For some information problems using bibliographic databases, it may be useful to sort output by authors' last names, or journals, or corporate source. Multiple sorts may be desirable for some search problems. For example, it might be useful to sort a set of records first by corporate source and within corporate source by author.

Questions to ask then, for a particular database/search system, are What is the default sort order? On which fields can sorting be done? Are multiple sorts possible? These are especially important questions for searches on referral databases.

Printing can also often be done in a variety of formats, ranging from the full record to accession numbers only to a customized format of the searcher's own design. What formats are desirable for a given problem? Which are possible?

Cost

A consideration that cannot be ignored is cost, both the monetary cost of conducting the search and the cost in the searcher's or client's time and money that is saved by the search. A significant proportion of searchers report that monetary considerations constitute the *primary* criterion for terminating a search [18]. While cost is certainly an important consideration, it should not be the primary criterion, otherwise surely the most intelligent posture would be not to conduct a search at all! Cost *and* effectiveness must be considered together; if a search cannot be conducted effectively for the money available, then it should not be done at all. The searcher should have an approximate idea in advance about what the probable costs of a search are likely to be, and clients should be so counseled, during the reference interview (see Chapter 6).

Costs are assessed by online search services in several ways. Among methods used are connect time charges (based on the proportion of a clock hour that the computer terminal is online with the host computer), database royalty charges, online print charges, offline print charges, subscription charges, per search charges, and computer resource charges (CPU time). One or more of these may be absent, hidden, or absorbed into another category.

One cannot simply compare one or more of these charges for two search systems and conclude that system A is superior to system B, since the time required to use a system to carry out a specified task also helps to determine the cost effectiveness of the system. A given system may appear to be less expensive on paper but may be more difficult to use, or more consuming of computer connect time or CPU time, or both. With either condition, overall charges may in fact be higher, rather than lower. There have been only a few studies that compared the cost effectiveness of several search systems in solving the same information problem. However, because of changes in the capabilities of search systems and in their usage load, the findings of such studies soon become dated and lose their usefulness.

Database Aids

A vital set of considerations in evaluating one's potential use of a given database involves database aids: the tools provided by database producers and search services to enhance a searcher's effective use of the database. Database aids include the following kinds of printed tools:

* user search manual, including detailed examples and discussion
* thesaurus
* classification schedule
* list of subject headings
* list of journals indexed
* list of classification codes for geographical area, type of product, document type, and other attributes

Less common but potentially useful are (among others):

* term frequency lists
* guidelines for subject indexing
* guidelines for the use of names and acronyms
* guidelines for bibliographic description
* guidelines for the preparation of abstracts

Sometimes tools such as these will be provided free to searchers by database producers. More often, database aids must be purchased, often at considerable expense. If databases will be used only infrequently, this can present a serious problem. Since effective searching often demands study of printed aids, not having the appropriate tool can be a major stumbling block. This is probably the primary obstacle standing in the way of effective end-user searching. It is not a problem that has a simple solution in the foreseeable future.

Online database aids are often also available, at the cost of connect time charges, through such commands as HELP and EXPLAIN. We recommend that the use of such commands be minimized because of the associated costs and because "print your own" documentation is sloppy, difficult to organize and read, and easy to lose. This remark is directed more towards end-user systems such as The Source, Compuserve, and Dow Jones News Retrieval than library oriented systems such as DIALOG, ORBIT, and BRS. The latter all offer relatively complete and well-written documentation for their systems and the majority of their databases. However, end-user searchers using offshoots of these systems (BRS/After Dark and DIALOG's Knowledge Index) will not ordinarily have access to these database aids. It is difficult to see how effective searches for complex problems can be conducted under these circumstances. This issue is discussed more completely in Chapter 9.

Database aids and other documentation for effective searching should be evaluated critically, first for their existence, and second, for their clarity, accuracy, and completeness. There is no point in struggling with poor documentation if there are alternatives at hand.

Differences between Online and Print Version

Although the same database is used to produce both the online version and the print version of reference databases, there are differences between the two that can be important in determining whether an online search should be conducted, or whether a manual search of the printed version will suffice. The principal differences between print and online versions lie in the number and type of access points provided by the search system to records in the database. For most information problems, this weighs heavily in favor of online searching. There are other important points of comparison as well, including the coverage dates of the material covered, the ability of the search system to produce sorted and otherwise customized output, the currency of the information, and the time and estimated cost required to conduct the search.

Review Literature

Many of the issues discussed in this chapter are difficult to address, with definitive answers possible only after many hours of experience by an expert working with a database and search system and studying the relevant documentation. Fortunately, several writers have published critical and comparative reviews of related databases, answering at least temporarily many of the questions raised here, for some databases and search systems. It should be stressed, however, that change is always taking place, both in databases and in search systems. The chances are good that if a particular aspect of a database was criticized heavily five years ago, it may no longer be a "feature" of that database today.

With the above caveat in mind, we suggest that the following journals are good places to find critical discussions and comparisons of databases: *Database, RQ, Journal of the American Society for Information Science, Online, Special Libraries,* and *Online Review.* There have been many such analyses published in these journals [19]. Published proceedings of national and international online conferences are also excellent sources of analytical and comparative information concerning databases.

PROBLEMS

1. Find examples and compare the selection policies for three abstracting or indexing databases.

2. Find two or more databases covering approximately the same discipline, and examine the documentation provided for each:

    a. Study the "list of journals indexed" by the two databases. Compare the coverage of the databases by analyzing the overlap among these journals.

b. Compare their focus.

c. Compare the type of material indexed.

d. Compare their controlled vocabularies, if any.

3. Obtain the output from three different online searches conducted on different databases. Check the journals, books, research reports, etc. listed in the output of the search (or a random sample drawn from this output) for local availability, and compute the proportion of items that are available locally (without going through interlibrary loan). Are there any major differences between the three databases?

4. Select a database for study and examine its controlled vocabulary for terms representing concepts or aspects of research. How adequate are the terms provided?

5. Conduct a detailed comparative analysis of three databases available on one or more search systems that treat a *specific* subject area of your choice, such as forestry, philosophy, history of science, paleontology, etc. Try to apply as many of the criteria presented in this chapter as possible.

6. Compare and contrast two search systems that provide access to the same database. Apply criteria relating to file structure, printing and sorting capabilities, cost, and database aids to an analysis of the two search systems. Use the database you have identified as the basis of comparison.

7. Using all available database aids, identify three databases likely to provide the desired information for each of the following brief statements of topical information needs. Discuss advantages and disadvantages of each. Since there can be no reference interview, you may need to make certain assumptions regarding the information need. If you do need to make assumptions, *state them explicitly.*

a. brain parasites in sea mammals

b. styles of nineteenth century watercolor artists

c. windmill power as an energy source

d. all available information concerning the physicist Marc Kastner

e. the effect of herbicides on the health of smokers of Mexican-grown marijuana

f. the relationship between alcoholism and thumbsucking

g. funded research in the application of simulation and game theory to administrative practices

h. curriculum materials for the training of paraprofessionals in academic libraries

i. sex role stereotyping in children's literature

NOTES AND REFERENCES

1. Cuadra Associates, Inc. *Directory of Online Databases* 6(1) (Fall 1984).

2. Hitchingham, Eileen. "A Survey of Database Use at the Reference Desk." *Online* 8 (March 1984) 44–50.

3. U.S. Technical Committee on Industrial Classification. *Standard Industrial Classification Manual.* (Washington, D.C.: U.S. Government Printing Office, 1972).

4. Pagell, Ruth A. "SIC Codes: The SIC Confusion in Comparing Codes." *Online* 7 (November 1983) 49–55.

5. Nichol, Kathleen. "Database Proliferation: Implications for Librarians." *Special Libraries* 74 (1983) 110–118; Wanger, Judith. 'Multiple Database Use: The Challenge of the Database Selection Process." *Online* 1 (No. 4) (October 1977) 35–41; Williams, Martha E. "Criteria for

Evaluation and Selection of Data Bases and Data Base Services.'' *Special Libraries* 66 (December 1975) 561-569.

6. Robbins, Simone B. "Literature in MEDLINE . . . A Bibliographic Anomaly?'' *Database* 8 (February 1985) 38-42.

7. DIALOG Information Retrieval Service, *SCISEARCH* (Bluesheet). (Palo Alto, CA: DIALOG Information Retrieval Service, 1983).

8. Metcalfe, John W. *Information Indexing and Subject Cataloging.* (New York: Scarecrow Press, 1957); Lancaster, F. Wilfrid, *Information Retrieval Systems: Characteristics, Testing, and Evaluation.* First edition. (New York: John Wiley & Sons, Inc., 1968); Davis, Charles H. and James E. Rush, *Guide to Information Science.* (Westport, Connecticut: Greenwood Press, 1979). pp. 15-60; Soergel, Dagobert, *Indexing Languages and Thesauri: Construction and Maintenance*; Lancaster, Frederick W. *Vocabulary Control for Information Retrieval.* (Washington, DC: Information Resources Press, 1972); Meadow, Charles T. *The Analysis of Information Systems.* Second Edition. (Los Angeles, CA: Melville Publishing Company, 1973).

9. An otherwise thoughtful and thought-provoking recent article by Fred T. Friedman in *Library Journal* provides a good example of this, although many other examples could equally well be given. Its title is: "Something There Is That Doesn't Love a Computer (Nor Hate It Either),'' *Library Journal* (June 15, 1984) 1190-1193.

10. Research bearing on full text searching in large databases is reported in Tenopir, Carol. "Full-Text Databases.'' *Annual Review of Information Science and Technology* 19 (1984) 215-246.

11. Nichol, p. 113.

12. See Harter, Stephen P. "Statistical Approaches to Automatic Indexing,'' *Drexel Library Quarterly* 14 (April 1978) 57-74, for a review of the literature on automatic indexing through statistical approaches and term weighting in particular.

13. Williams, Martha. "Lack of Standardization of the Journal Title Data Element in Databases.'' *Journal of the American Society for Information Science* 32 (No. 3) (May 1981) 229-233.

14. Keck, Bruce L. "An Investigation of Recall in the ABI/INFORM Database when Selecting by Journal.'' *Online Review* 5 (No. 5) 395-398.

15. Lobeck, von Martin A. "Namensrecherchen.'' *Nachr. f. Dokum* 32 (May 1980) 20-26.

16. Atkinson, Steven D. and Donna R. Dolan. "In Search of Research Studies in Online Databases.'' *Online* 7 (March 1983) 51-63.

17. Atkinson and Dolan, p. 62.

18. Harter, Stephen P. "Online Searching Styles: An Exploratory Study.'' *College and Research Libraries* 45 (July 1984) 249-250.

19. Excellent, if somewhat outdated examples of analytical and comparative studies of databases are: Girard, Anne and Stuart M. Kaback. "APILIT and APIPAT: Petroleum Information Online.'' *Database* 1 (December 1978) 46-67; Wagers, Robert. "ABI/INFORM and MANAGEMENT CONTENTS on DIALOG.'' *Database* 3 (March 1980) 12-36; and Dolan, Donna and Carol E. Heron. "Criminal Justice Coverage in Online Databases.'' *Database* 3 (March 1980) 10-32.

Chapter 5

The Process of Online Searching

5.1 THE ONLINE SEARCHER

The last three chapters have examined principles and concepts that are important to the conduct of online information retrieval. Little has been said, however, regarding online information retrieval as a *process*, as it might be carried out by a specialist or an end-user. A few articles have been published that provide an analysis of the online process. Benson and Maloney discuss the search process in a way equally descriptive of traditional reference librarianship and online information retrieval [1], and Dolan has constructed a flowchart of the process in a preliminary way [2].

As the process was introduced in Chapter 1, for a particular information retrieval system and searcher, online searching can be represented as a set of discrete but interrelated steps, to be carried out approximately in the order given. These are reproduced in Table 5.1.

Several of the actions listed in Table 5.1 have already been discussed, and others will be treated later in the book. In this chapter, we are particularly interested in not one or another of the individual steps, but in the overall philosophy, personal style, or approach underlying and affecting the entire online searching process.

In a conceptual framework for research, Fidel and Soergel have identified several broad classes of factors that potentially affect the quality of this search process. These include

* institutional setting
* user characteristics
* characteristics of the search problem

TABLE 5.1
Steps in the Online Searching Process

1. Understand the information need of the user. Here, attention must be given to distinguishing between what the user needs as opposed to what he or she wants, or says he or she wants.
2. Formulate search objectives. What will the search attempt to accomplish? The listing of a comprehensive bibliography? The discovery of a fact? Citations to a few pertinent documents?
3. Select one or more databases and search systems.
4. Identify major concepts or facets and indicate their logical relationships with one another.
5. Select an overall approach (strategy) for attacking the information problem.
6. Identify a variety of ways to express the concepts in words, phrases, symbols, etc., expressed in natural language, descriptors, subject headings, etc.
7. Identify the fields of the records that will be searched in the databases selected.
8. Translate decisions made in (2)-(7) into formal statements expressed in the command language of the search system.
9. For each of the steps (2)-(7) above, consider and plan alternatives in case initial attempts do not meet search objectives
10. Logon to the search system of choice and enter the initial search statements formulated in (8)
11. Evaluate the intermediate results against the search objectives.
12. Iterate. That is, on the basis of the results of the evaluation obtained in step (11), and considering the alternatives planned in step (9), as well as new ideas obtained through system feedback, decide whether to print the results and stop or continue with the search. If it is decided to continue, one might return to any of the steps above, perhaps even step (1). The process continues until satisfactory results are obtained.

* characteristics of the database
* characteristics of the search system
* personal characteristics of the searcher [3]

This chapter concentrates on the last of these categories. In particular, it examines opposing philosophical approaches to the activity of online searching as an intellectual process. An excellent review of research in this general area has been published by Fenichel [4].

What personal qualities does the effective online searcher possess? There have been several attempts to answer this question by writers who describe characteristics that they believe are important to the process [5]. Many characteristics associated with effective online searching, in the opinions of these and other authors, have been identified. These are summarized in Table 5.2.

The first five of these characteristics clearly depend on an understanding of concepts and principles of information retrieval that can be learned in educational settings, whether these be formal or informal. Most of these concepts and principles have already been introduced in this book.

The next characteristic listed in Table 5.2 refers to how well the searcher understands the nature of the information problem. A clear understanding

TABLE 5.2
Personal Characteristics Important to Online Searching

Concepts and Principles of Information Retrieval
  1. understanding of command language vocabulary and syntax, search systems defaults, etc.
  2. understanding of basic principles of searching, including Boolean logic, truncation, inverted index, etc.
  3. understanding of concepts and principles of controlled vocabularies and natural language and advantages and disadvantages of each
  4. understanding of concepts and principles of file and record structures: sort order, parsing rules, field structure, etc.
  5. understanding of characteristics of the databases to be searched, and the ability to use database documentation effectively

The Information Problem
  6. understanding of the problem for which information is wanted as well as the problem's conceptual and social context

Personal Abilities and Qualities
  7. typing ability
  8. subject knowledge in the problem area to be searched
  9. ability to communicate effectively with end-users, people-oriented
  10. logical, analytical, conceptual abilities
  11. self confidence
  12. enthusiasm
  13. courage and the ability to make quick decisions
  14. creativity
  15. intelligence
  16. masculinity/femininity
  17. self-esteem

Personal Attitudes
  18. willingness to grow
  19. willingness to persevere, patience
  20. willingness to think flexibly, to look at a problem in more than one way
  21. willingness to conduct an interactive and iterative dialog with a search system
  22. willingness to view an information retrieval question as a poblem to be solved; problem-solving attitudes and skills
  23. appreciation for and understanding of science and the scientific method of inquiry
  24. willingness to question: to be critical with documentation, controlled vocabularies, system output, and oneself

is crucial to effective online searching. This is not a consideration if the individual with the information need is also the searcher (that is, an end-user). However, if the searcher is a professional intermediary—a librarian or other information specialist—then communication of the information need from client to searcher is crucial for effective results. Issues related to this communication process are discussed in depth in Chapter 6.

The next several of the characteristics listed in Table 5.2 are personal abilities and qualities such as subject knowledge, logical ability, self confidence, and enthusiasm. Little can be done to develop most of these traits in an individual if they are not initially present.

The last six qualities in the list directly address a philosophy or set of attitudes for the conduct of online information storage and retrieval. Several writers have suggested that an open-minded, flexible, *learning* mode will produce the most effective results for online information retrieval. Viewed in this way, online searching is a problem-solving process. Attributes such as a willingness to learn and grow, persevere, and *question* are crucial for success, at least for the most difficult information problems. On the other hand, other philosophical approaches are possible and are commonly found among online searchers. In the remainder of this chapter, alternative approaches addressing online searching as a human activity will be examined. Research related to the *practice* of online searching will also be reviewed. We begin by suggesting an overall problem solving approach, having much in common with the conduct of scientific inquiry, as a useful model for online information retrieval.

5.2   ONLINE SEARCHING AS SCIENTIFIC INQUIRY

There are many characteristics identified by experts as possibly being important to success as an online searcher. In an article published in the *Journal of the American Society for Information Science*, Harter presented an argument supporting his belief that among these many qualities, the most critically important are problem-solving abilities and attitudes [6]. Whatever a searcher's other qualities might be, consistently effective online information retrieval requires attitudes that will permit the development and use of these qualities. The article proposed scientific inquiry as a philosophical and behavioral model for online information retrieval and for the online search specialist.

The general perspective taken in reference [6] is not entirely new. It is based on the idea of viewing library reference work, and more specifically, information retrieval, as a trial-and-error, problem solving process. This point of view has been cogently stated in papers by Don R. Swanson [8], Linda Smith [9], and Marcia Bates [10]. However, the idea is carried further in reference [6], in which the argument is put forth that science itself, as perhaps humanity's most prominent and successful example of problem-solving, serves as a useful model of the online search process. The discussion that follows is based largely on this paper.

The conduct of scientific inquiry is an iterative, trial-and-error process in which science collectively moves ever closer to 'truth,'' and in which, over the passage of time, knowledge cumulates. The scientist's choice of problems for investigation depends in part on how well existing knowledge and theory describe the empirical universe. It is the anomaly, the unexplained phenomenon, the missing piece of the puzzle, that is the prime candidate for scientific inquiry.

After a research problem has been discovered and selected for study by a scientist, the next stage in scientific inquiry is to identify important *variables*—concepts or factors bearing on the problem to be investigated. Then declarative statements of relationship between the variables, thought by the investigator to be likely to reflect or explain empirical data, are formulated. These statements are called *hypotheses*. Hypotheses are "intelligent guesses" concerning relationships between variables. They depend on experience and knowledge of the general problem area, and may originate through mental processes such as intuition, analogy, and the identification of commonly held assumptions.

After hypotheses have been formulated, methods and procedures are designed to gather data to test the hypotheses. These methods are pragmatic, being guided by what seems to work and by what the community of scientists finds collectively acceptable. The object of these methods and procedures is to test the hypotheses with empirical data.

Although scientists' choices of procedures and methods are guided by pragmatic considerations, they must also be concerned with questions of validity and reliability. *Operational definitions* of variables are formulated by the investigator, intended not only to measure accurately the specific phenomena of interest but also to do so consistently. Loosely, these are the concepts of *validity* and *reliability*, respectively. Since science is a collective, social pursuit, it depends heavily on precise communication. Thus operational definitions must be clear, unambiguous, and replicable.

Assumptions are also important in scientific inquiry. In a given study, assumptions are statements of relationships between variables that are accepted as though they were true, for that study. Of course, assumptions may later be tested as hypotheses by the original investigator or by others. Assumptions may be false.

When operational definitions for the variables of interest, assumptions, and procedures and methods for conducting the research have been defined clearly, the hypotheses can then be tested by gathering and evaluating empirical data. The results of hypothesis testing may have several outcomes. Data collected may tend to support one or more hypothesis, or may tend to disprove some or all. But whatever the results, information of value is derived from the investigation.

If the data collected do not support the hypotheses, the investigator may suspect the correctness of an assumption or definition. Or, the reliability of certain procedures or methods may be questioned and ways be seen of improving them. Perhaps no fault can be found in the research design, and it may be concluded that a hypothesis is without foundation. Or, the results may suggest the need to pay increased attention to certain variables. They may even suggest new hypotheses. Some of these ideas may be pursued in further research conducted by the original investigator, or by others. In this way a body of knowledge is developed, building on itself. As the iterative and cumulative process of science continues over the years and decades, humanity's knowledge of the physical and behavioral universe continues to advance.

When the philosophy and methods of online information retrieval are compared to those of scientific inquiry, these two human activities can be seen to be analogous in many ways. We believe that scientific inquiry can serve as a model providing significant insights into the philosophy and methods of online searching.

If an intermediary is used, the online search process begins with a reference interview, during which the search specialist identifies the concepts or facts bearing on the topic or problem for which information is wanted. These concepts are analogous to the variables in a scientific inquiry; they are the concepts that are related to one another in hypotheses, definitions, and assumptions. In online searching, concepts are linked with the Boolean operators AND, OR, and NOT. Such statements can usefully be regarded as hypotheses—conjectures regarding combinations of concepts that will retrieve records relating to the topic or problem of interest.

Now operational definitions must be provided for these variables. In online information retrieval, concepts are operationalized as search terms. Words and phrases selected from natural language and controlled vocabularies are used to represent the concepts of interest, just as variables must be defined operationally in scientific inquiry. The importance of vocabulary in information retrieval has been noted earlier. The choice of natural language or controlled vocabularies, the specific vocabulary elements selected, the fields to be searched, and whether and how truncation and word proximity searching are used are all important decisions. Each of these decisions involves operationally defining the concepts of interest in such a way that communication with a database and a search system will effectively retrieve index records relevant to an information need.

Just as validity and reliability are important concepts in scientific inquiry, so are they for online searching. Words and phrases represent concepts or ideas. Search terms are valid if they represent accurately the concepts they are supposed to represent, the concepts of the topic or information problem as it is perceived by the person with the information need.

Reliability is also important. Search terms will be reliable if they produce consistent results, that is, if they retrieve index records associated with documents that treat the same or similar topic or problems. Homographs in the database cause ambiguity of meaning. Such terms retrieve records not consistently on the subject requested. As we have seen, this can happen easily, especially in natural language fields. Truncating words too early also produces unreliable results.

A major quantitative difference between scientific inquiry and online information retrieval lies in the time required for the inquiry to be conducted. In online searching, the process of perceiving and formulating the problem, identifying important variables, stating hypotheses, operationalizing variables, gathering data, and testing hypotheses can all be conducted in minutes. In scientific research, these processes may take years. Because of this difference, assumptions should be avoided in online searching. Instead, all tentative ideas should be regarded as hypotheses and tested by gathering data. The initial planning process should include the statement of several alternative hypotheses, each of which can be tested rapidly online. There is never any need to make assumptions in online searching.

In summary, online information retrieval consists of identifying variables, stating hypotheses, and establishing procedures and methods for testing the hypotheses. These take the form of search statements formulated in the command language of the search system. In these formulations, variables are defined operationally as vocabulary elements and search fields. In this way the hypothesis underlying each search statement can be tested by reviewing a sample of the data generated by executing a command—that is, by examining a sample of index records in a retrieval set.

It should be observed that a given search formulation represents only a tentative guess as what combination of vocabulary elements, search fields, etc., will be effective at retrieving records on the subject or information problem at hand. From among the infinite number of statements that might be constructed to test each of these mental hypotheses, only a few are selected. It follows that one's initial approach to an online search may not be a particularly effective formulation. In fact, it is likely to be a relatively poor effort. Perhaps only for the simplest of searches might an assumption of initial excellence be justified, and then only with the greatest of caution. Thus we believe that it is useful to regard online searching, just as scientific inquiry, as an iterative process in which one's first efforts are likely to be unsatisfactory. But

As revisions are formulated, tested, refined, and retested, the final goal is approached ever more closely. Eventually, this trial-and-error process will end, not because the methodology is perfect, but because, for the stated constraints, the data gathered are acceptable to the requester [11].

Suppose that an initial hypothesis has been stated and a search formulation constructed to test it. The formulation can be put to the search system and a retrieval set produced and printed. These index records are the data that will be used to test the hypotheses. The records can be examined quickly by printing a sample in a short display format, for example, document titles, or titles along with assigned descriptors.

Sampling retrieved records will often show that there are major problems with the initial formulation: that there are too many false drops, or that the subject treated in retrieved records is too general, or not precisely on the topic wanted, or even irrelevant to the information need. The reasons that non-relevant records were captured by the formulation can be explored, by analyzing retrieved records. On inspection of the search output it might be discovered that the retrieval set is too large to print in full, or too small to represent the entire literature that is known to exist on the subject. Modification of the search formulation is required in all these cases, and others.

There are an infinite number of changes that might be made in the initial search formulation. First, changes in the original hypothesis might be considered. Perhaps a concept should be added to or deleted from the search formulation. The Boolean combination of concepts may have been done in error, following a careless or incorrect assumption regarding order of operations or a parsing rule. Perhaps Boolean OR was used instead of Boolean AND by error. Or it may be decided to intersect or subtract an additional concept from the previous formulation.

There are also many semantic changes that might be considered. The overall decision to use natural language or controlled vocabularies might be reexamined. On reflection, it might be clear that some of the search terms used in the formulation were too narrow in meaning, or too broad, or off the subject, or examples of homographs, or entirely irrelevant. Additional synonyms or near synonyms might be added to one or more facets using the Boolean OR operator. Or perhaps peripheral terms might be deleted from a facet.

There are also various non-semantic approaches to reducing the volume of a search that might be considered: limiting the output by language, type of document, or year of publication, among others.

In addition, in most databases there are several options regarding the choice of fields to be searched; perhaps some change in the original choices might be made. Word proximity operators may be modified to change the require-ments for retrieval, for example, for retrieval to take place if words are present anywhere in the same field rather than occurring as a phrase. Truncated terms might also be examined and adjusted. Based on case study analyses of five searchers, Fidel has offered some preliminary evidence that online searchers either prefer and use semantic, language approaches to constructing and modifying an online search, or non-semantic devices, using features of the command language and file structures [12]. Fidel calls the former "concep-tualists" and the latter "operationalists."

Among all the logical, semantic, and file structure approaches to modify-ing a search formulation that exist with a given search problem, database, and search system, a gifted searcher will be able to assess the possibilities that offer the best chances of improvement of a search formulation, through heuristics. *Heuristics* may be regarded as mental operations, or tactics, or behaviors, or attitudes, that, when followed, tend to produce useful results in problem solving situations. By their nature, heuristics cannot be proved; they are empirical and inductive, and, indeed, are not always effective.

Heuristics are learned through experience and practice. Proverbs such as "an oak is not felled at one stroke" are examples of heuristics guiding human behaviors and attitudes. Many heuristics for online searching have already been stated in this book. Examples include: "beware of zero postings" and "one should consider searching using natural language if the literature to be searched is poorly defined, belonging to a 'soft' discipline." Many others have been stated as well. These and other heuristics appearing in this book have been found by experts to be useful rules of thumb to follow, as one carries out the activity of online information retrieval. They will continue to appear throughout the book (see especially Chapter 7).

5.3 BEHAVIORAL CHARACTERISTICS
OF ONLINE SEARCHERS

In the last section of this chapter an argument was put forth for what the activity of online searching *ought* to be like. An analogy was made between online information retrieval and scientific inquiry. It was argued that the two human activities have much in common, including their overall iterative nature as well as the applicability of the concepts of problem statement, vari-ables, hypotheses, assumptions, testing of hypotheses, formulation of meth-odology, operational definitions, validity, and reliability.

As viewed by the model of scientific inquiry, online searching is an inter-active, evolutionary process in which the searcher is an inquirer: construct-ing, testing, refining, and retesting hypotheses through the gathering of empirical data in an effort to approach optimal results as closely as possible. This view of the importance of searcher/system interaction and attention to system feedback is shared by virtually every expert contributing to the online searching literature.

The description of online searching summarized in the previous paragraph does not reflect accurately what is known about the actual behavior of online searchers, as this behavior has been reported in published research. In fact, if the results of most of this research are accepted at face value, it can be concluded that many searches involve little or no modification of search formulations, or, indeed, little interaction with the search system of any other kind. If the model of scientific inquiry is used to evaluate such searches and searchers, one's judgment would have to be that most online searching is analogous to bad science carried out by poor scientists. A summary and evaluation of some of this research follows, and an attempt is made to explain what appear to be major differences between theory and practice.

Early research in the use of online systems produced substantial evidence concluding that many searchers conduct extremely simplistic searches. For example, it was reported that 'remarkably little attention' is paid to file differences by searchers, and that poor selection of vocabulary and search formulations often result [13], that most searchers are too uncritical about their work [14], that several system commands are *never* used and most of the remainder are only rarely used [15], that commands for searching and printing account for two thirds of those issued [16], that the full interactive capabilities of systems are little used [17], and that between 46 percent and 78 percent of all searches conducted are not modified at all after the initial formulation [18].

In her doctoral dissertation [19], Carol Fenichel studied 72 searchers using the ERIC ONTAP file on DIALOG. One of the most interesting findings of Fenichel's findings was the striking simplicity of searches conducted by *experienced subjects* [the emphasis is mine]. Fenichel reported that there was no modification of the original search formulation in half of the searches studied. Moreover, in more than two thirds of the searches examined, the subjects did not sample records for relevance to the search problem before printing the final bibliography and terminating the search. Novice searchers performed "surprisingly well" when compared to moderately experienced and to experienced searchers. Fenichel also reported "enormous variability in searching behavior . . . [even] in searches of persons in the same experience groups . . . " [20].

In efforts to explain these results, Fenichel commented on the cognitive complexity of many system commands, suggesting that this might be a heavier load on short term memory requirements than many searchers can handle, thereby causing disuse of many commands. Vigil agreed with Fenichel's assessment and proposed strategies to reduce the cognitive strain felt by online searchers [21].

In a study similar to Fenichel's, Howard studied a group of ERIC searchers and reported that while experienced searchers achieved the most cost-effective results, the novice searchers achieved the highest levels of precision. (See Chapter 6 for a discussion of recall and precision.) Differences in the output values between the experience groups was not great, although they were statistically significant [22]. Lowry also reported observing wide individual variability within the same experience groups [23].

In another extensive controlled experimental study, Wanger, McDonald, and Berger studied a group of MEDLINE searchers for the National Library of Medicine, examining the relationship between several variables and search performance. Examined were source of education and training, organization type, and amount of National Library of Medicine searching experience [24].

Among many other findings, the investigators concluded that about half of the searchers studied did no intermediate printing or browsing. Asked later in a questionnaire how often they planned alternative strategies for use if the original formulation did not meet the objectives online, only about thirty percent of the searchers answered "over 75% of the searches" or "always." However, when asked whether they plan searches in detail and formulate them on paper before going online, more than seventy percent of the searchers responded "over 75% of the searches" or 'always." These results suggest careful planning but little interaction during search execution, for a majority of individuals studied. They also suggest a lack of awareness of the possibility that one's initial formulation might fail to be effective. The authors noted that searchers tended not to browse titles or descriptors of retrieved citations, and generally did not begin to make full use of the interactive features of the search systems. They coined the term *fast batch* to refer to this mode of use:

> a number of searchers are using the online system in a "fast batch" mode. When they enter a set of terms in whatever combination, they expect the retrieved citations to contain those sets of terms, and this is apparently sufficient for their purposes [25].

Like Fenichel, Wanger and her colleagues suggest that fast batch searchers may have been affected by time and cost considerations. Other hypotheses suggested by the authors to explain this behavior included the following: that searchers do not feel that they have a responsibility for evaluating search results, that searchers believe that if terms requested are present in an index record, the record must, *ipso facto*, be relevant to the request, or that searchers have "blind faith" in the system and the vocabulary.

The Wanger study also reported a wide variability among searchers. The reasons for this widespread finding is not so clear. Online *experience* was not found by any study to be an important determinant of online search behavior. Wanger reported that type of training was not a significant factor either. Thus individual differences among online searchers (other than experience and type of training) appear to be extremely important when related to output variables. Bellardo tested several of these, including creativity, level of intelligence, degree of masculinity or femininity, and self-esteem. None were found to relate significantly to effective retrieval performance [26].

There are many additional individual differences noted by past researchers that might be offered as possible explanation of the wide individual variation observed in reported research. In addition to those individual differences already mentioned, institutional setting may significantly affect online behavior. A lack of complete or accurate knowledge regarding system capabilities may explain some differences. Some searchers may have a naive view of the effectiveness of using controlled vocabularies, not recognizing that errors and differences in judgment and perspective are not uncommon among indexers. Or searchers may vary widely in attitudes or in problem-solving skills.

The findings reported above all support the notion that there are many online searchers who use online systems in a "fast batch" mode, using few system capabilities, not interacting with the system, and not conducting iterative searches. Should one then conclude that the problem solving approach to online searching espoused by so many writers and, in particular, the model of scientific inquiry, are just wrong-headed ways of looking at online information retrieval? This is certainly a possible explanation, but there are others. There seem to be three alternative explanations.

First, it may be that the interactive, iterative, heuristic approach to online searching is not necessary for most searches, and that a fast batch approach will produce cost/effective searches a large percentage of the time. In such situations, much or all the necessary formulation and testing of hypotheses would be done offline, applying powers of reason and knowledge of printed documentation to a solution of the information problem. If this explanation were true, it would mean that the conventional wisdom that fast batch searching is bad searching may be unfair and incorrect. Although this possibility has not been explored seriously in the online searching research literature, it raises interesting questions for future research.

A second possibility is that many online searchers are in fact doing a poor job. If online searching as a process ought to be interactive and iterative to be effective, as so many have stated, and it is also true that few searchers conduct their work in this way, then one must conclude that most searchers are bad searchers, most of the time. This raises serious questions regarding educational and training programs for online search specialists as well as for evaluation mechanisms.

A third possibility exists. It might be that much of the research conducted has methodological flaws that explain in part the finding that fast batch searchers are as prevalent as they appear to be. The well-known "Hawthorne effect" encapsulates the idea that the act of measuring human behavior can affect in significant ways the phenomenon that is being measured. Controlled experiments of online searching may affect search behavior in important ways. In particular, it may make searchers reticent (for whatever reasons) to be interactive online, to experiment, to use heuristics, to explore. One's tendency in such situations may be to be "safe and sure" and perhaps especially, cheap. Caution may prevail, overwhelmingly.

All three of these explanations are consistent with the findings of past research. This author's belief is that there is some truth to each of the three conjectures. However, the extent to which this assertion is justified must await further research.

All the explanations discussed in the previous paragraphs suggest that at least some online searchers carry out simplistic, algorithmic searches. An *algorithm* is a procedure for accomplishing a task in a finite number of steps, a set of well-defined rules to be followed to accomplish a goal. In arithmetic, every child learns algorithms for the basic operations of addition, division, and the like. Computer programs or pieces of programs are also sometimes called algorithms.

An algorithmic online searcher is one who devises a strategy and sticks to it, who has an unquestioning attitude toward the search and its results, who makes little use of the interactive features of the system and is inflexible, who fails to adapt plans to the database being searched. In essence, the algorithmic searcher is a fast batch searcher.

Just as algorithms can be contrasted to heuristics, algorithmic searchers can be contrasted to interactive, iterative, problem-solving searchers, who anticipate a range of possible outcomes and responses, who investigate a database for a search problem much as the scientist conducts a scientific inquiry.

We have suggested that because of methodological questions, the prevalence of the true fast batch searcher is unclear. However, in a study of self-reported behaviors of Florida online searchers, relatively small percentages of fast batch searchers were found [27]. Only 4 percent of the respondents to a questionnaire survey reported that they do not interact with the system at all in a typical search, and only 17 percent of those responding reported that, while they typically interact with the system, they do not usually assess the relevance of preliminary retrieval sets.

Thirty-six percent of the survey respondents stated that they typically browse titles but not descriptors of retrieved records, and 43 percent of the respondents—the largest of the four percentages—reported that their usual style of searching included browsing samples of both titles and descriptors. These results suggest that fast batch searchers are far less prevalent than they are reported to be in previous research and than is commonly supposed.

It seems possible that the behaviors exhibited by the fast batch searcher are in part a product of held attitudes. In a study conducted by Harter, an attempt was made to understand the rationale underlying certain behaviors of the online search specialist. In particular, the study established positive relationships between reported behaviors and the following variables: attitudes, level of experience, and institutional setting [28].

Fast batch searchers were found to have different attitudes than interactive searchers in several important respects. Interactive searchers were found to believe strongly in the value of trial and error methods in information retrieval. Fast batch searchers tend to believe that careful preparation before the search will lead to effective searching, and that trial and error methods reflect fuzzy thinking and are unnecessary and unduly expensive. They also believe that a carefully planned search using descriptors will produce effective results, and that searches conducted using a controlled vocabulary will result in the retrieval of "all, or nearly all" of the relevant records in database.

Fast batch searchers believe that browsing among retrieved titles in search of additional search terms is a waste of time and money. They do not like the idea of being flexible at the terminal, and consider cost to be much more important in determining when a search should be stopped than do interactive searchers [29].

Harter confirmed results of earlier research that online search specialists vary widely in their reported online search behaviors as well as attitudes. To some extent, this can be traced to organizational setting and experience. Searchers from academic libraries were found to be more cost-conscious and expressed more more faith in the use of controlled vocabularies than their colleagues in special libraries. While online searching experience was found to have no relation to the reported use of system features investigated, experience was found to be related to a flexible, trial and error attitude toward online searching [30].

There was found to be a wide variation among searchers. What is apparently a common behavior for one searcher is never done by another; and this was found to be true for every behavior examined. Among its most important results, Harter's research found there to be great differences in reported behaviors among online searchers, and provided some evidence for the notion that these behavioral differences are due to differences in attitudes and beliefs.

This raises interesting questions regarding the educational process as well as the evaluation process. We have expressed some concern in this and previous chapters regarding the *validity* of certain attitudes, for example, belief in the panacean qualities of controlled vocabularies. However, while writers like Fenichel have indicated their surprise at the striking simplicity of so many searchers (and we must agree with this surprise), this does not in itself show that fast batch searchers are wrong. Research is needed to test the extent to which careful offline planning using a controlled vocabulary will produce effective search results with little or no online interaction. Conceivably, fast batch searching may not be bad after all, for a majority of search problems. This hypothesis needs to be explored through research.

5.4 SUMMARY

We are not likely to know soon with any certainty those personal qualities that make the "best" online search specialists. Much more research will be needed to address with any degree of assurance the many questions raised in this chapter. Indeed, it is by no means even clear what makes a good online *search*. This question is concerned with the pragmatics of the online interaction, and will be addressed in the next chapter.

Table 5.1 listed twelve steps composing the online searching process. Consider these as being clustered into three main categories: Planning, Execution, and Analysis. Again, it is worth stressing that not even these main classes can be regarded as mutually exclusive. They interact with one another in many ways.

1. *Planning.* If an intermediary is used, the searcher must first understand the information need of the user. This usually requires one or more interviews, in which attention is given to the information problem underlying the formal search request that may have been made (see Chapter 6). On the basis of information gathered in the reference interview, and based on database characteristics and search system capabilities, the searcher selects one or more databases and search systems. Regardless of whether an intermediary is employed, the information need must be translated into achievable results. That is, search objectives must be formulated.

Next, major concepts or facets must be identified, their logical relationships with one another established, and the concepts of interest operationalized in natural language or controlled vocabularies. Decisions also must be made regarding fields to be searched. These steps require careful study of search system and database documentation, with attention given to questions of validity and reliability.

At the same time, the many alternatives at each decision point must be considered. Plans should include a variety of alternatives to be used if one's most promising hypotheses fail to meet the search objectives. As a teacher of online information retrieval, the explanations offered me regarding why a search went badly frequently begin with the three words "I assumed that." An especially valuable heuristic for online searching is that *one should never assume anything.* Instead, the searcher should formulate ideas and conjectures as hypotheses and test them by gathering the appropriate data.

All decisions made at the planning stage eventually need to be translated into formal statements expressed in the command language of the search system. However, the searcher should be careful that these pre-prepared formulations are not followed too slavishly. One must be able to adjust search statements to fit current conditions. Since these are not entirely predictable in advance, all pre-prepared search statements should be treated with great caution at the time of execution.

2. *Execution.* When all planning has been completed, the searcher connects to the search system of choice and enters the initial search statements. Typing skill is helpful here. If planning has been properly done, the execution stage can be uneventful. The most important thing one needs to do during this step is to stay calm and collected and to try to react appropriately to system feedback. Thorough planning is obviously important at the execution stage. It is difficult for one to remain calm and collected if it has become obvious that everything is going wrong, for example, from botched planning.

On the other hand, it is impossible to plan for everything that might happen in a search (see the PROBLEMS for this chapter). The telecommunications system and the search service computer sometimes experience hardware or software difficulties that have implications for searchers. Moreover, no one is perfect. Untoward events as well as human errors will occur. And some events *cannot* be planned for. One must be ready to react online to almost anything.

Sometimes, the best action that one can take is to logoff and consider what has happened and what one should do next. Since online search services charge for connect time, this can save money and improve search results as well. However, under these circumstances, the searcher should take steps to ensure that the search sets created will not be lost.

At the execution stage one must evaluate the intermediate results against the search objectives by displaying retrieved titles and by iterating with alternative formulations if necessary. Hypothesis testing is unavoidable if this step is to be accomplished properly. How can one know if the objectives have been met unless the output is examined? To answer this question with a statement of faith would not be acceptable to a scientist, nor, we believe, should it be to an online searcher. Browsing retrieved records can also be important to generate new ideas, vocabulary, etc. One hopes that recent changes in charging policies in which charges are assessed for titles displayed online will not adversely affect browsing and more formal hypothesis testing online. If they do, results will be likely to suffer.

3. *Analysis.* The act of analysis is actually going on throughout the planning and execution processes. It has been listed separately here to stress its importance and also to suggest it as a *post search* exercise, not only for learners, but also to practice on a regular basis for professional searchers.

To analyze is to break into components, to separate into parts, to examine in detail, on a step by step basis. The object of analysis is to fully and completely *understand.* An online search is not a series of random happenings, nor is it a gestalt experience that defies examination. It can be broken down into a linear sequence of steps, actions, and consequences, each one of which can be understood. When the steps are each understood in sequence, then the whole will likewise be understood.

In long-established, well documented, and fully debugged search system it is rare that a system response cannot be explained. And when this does happen, the response is almost never reproducible. One should never assume that a particular system response is the result of a telecommunications or search system error, although these do occur. Much more frequently, unexpected system responses result from searcher error or failure to understand command syntax, spelling, file or record structure, Boolean logic, database indexing policies, parsing rules, or concept formulation. Or perhaps the controlled vocabulary is too broad, resulting in a problem in indexing specificity, or too few descriptors have been assigned to documents, resulting in problems related to indexing exhaustivity. Perhaps the searcher has overspecified or underspecified the search problem. The searcher may even be in the wrong file. Only very seldom are "gremlins" the cause of the problem [31].

We recommend that post-search analyses of search transactions be undertaken on a regular basis. Especially for students, such analyses should conclude every online session. Preparing detailed annotations of search output can be extremely useful. In such analyses, one should attempt to understand *every* system response, no matter how bizarre it may appear to be. Sometimes the explanation can be obscure, but for nearly every system response there is a rational explanation that will help one's understanding and future performance. Some search systems offer an 800-number hotline if all else fails.

Critical examination of search output, whether during search execution or post search analysis, should concentrate on the interesting, unexpected, and unusual. Initially, as one is beginning study of online information retrieval, such events may occur frequently. They never disappear completely. We strongly recommend that online searchers read and try to understand all search output. And always ask "Why?"

PROBLEMS

1. Examine the documentation for one or more search systems and answer each of the following questions for that system:

a. Compile a list of hardware or software "happenings" that are occasionally likely to disrupt the normal flow of an online search. An example of this is being abruptly disconnected from (dropped by) the host system. Look in sections of documentation discussing error messages, trouble shooting, system messages, telecommunications messages, hardware problems, etc.

b. What specific actions can be taken to respond to each of the conditions identified in (a)?

c. Some search systems have a way of reassuring the searcher that the system is still working on the command issued, as a kind of anxiety-reducer for commands that require a lengthy execution time. Does the system you have selected use such a feedback mechanism? What is it?

d. If you are dropped from the system, are the sets of accession numbers that you created lost (erased)? What if you logoff? Under what conditions, if any, will the sets be retained? For how long?

e. Is there any way of displaying a summary of what you have done online in an online session, to reduce the cognitive strain of trying to remember the details of what you have done?

f. What is the system's response if you misspell a command keyword? Give several examples to illustrate.

g. What is the system's response if Boolean logic is used inappropriately? Give examples to illustrate.

h. What is the system's response if a search term is misspelled? A command? Give examples to illustrate.

i. What is the system's response if a command language syntax error is made? Give examples to illustrate.

j. Does the system have an 800 "help" number that one can call if all else fails? If so, evaluate its effectiveness with a sample 'problem.''

2. Try to list all the general classes of careless, logical, conceptual, file structure, and language "errors" that a searcher might make in an online search.

3. In future online sessions, analyze all system output thoroughly, as suggested in Section 5.4. Try to understand *every* system response.

4. Read and discuss reference [31]. What can be done about the problems identified?

5. Using all available database aids, identify three databases likely to provide the desired information for each of the following brief statements of topical information needs. Discuss advantages and disadvantages of each. Since there can be no reference interview, you may need to make certain assumptions. If you do need to make assumptions, state them explicitly.

a. legal and ethical considerations associated with cloning

b. use of microprocessors for energy conserving applications in the home

c. commercially available filmstrips and slides on the Pilgrims

d. proposed bills and legislation dealing with privacy protection in the private sector

e. federal and state regulations concerning poultry additives

f. international standards for emission controls for automobiles

g. the use of optical fiber transmission in the public telephone system

h. detrimental side effects of drugs used for the treatment of schizophrenia.

NOTES AND REFERENCES

1. Benson, James and Ruth Kay Maloney. "Principles of Searching." *RQ* 14 (No. 4) (Summer 1975).

2. Dolan, Donna. "Flowchart of the Search Formulation Process." *Database* 2 (No. 4) (December 1979) 86-88.

3. Fidel, Raya and Dagobert Soergel. "Factors Affecting Online Bibliographic Retrieval: A Conceptual Framework for Research." *Journal of the American Society for Information Science* 34 (No. 3) (1983) 163-180.

4. Fenichel, Carol Hansen. "The Process of Searching Online Bibliographic Databases: A Review of Research." *Library Research* 2 (1980) 107-127.

5. Dolan, Donna R. "The Quality Control of Search Analysts." *Online* 3 (April 1979) 8-16; Van Camp, Ann. "Effective Search Analysts." *Online* 3 (April 1979) 18-20; Wanger, Judith. "Multiple Database Use." *Online* 1 (October 1977) 35-41; Vigil, Peter J. "The Psychology of Online Searching." *Journal of the American Society for Information Science* 34 (No. 4) (1983) 281-287; Harter, Stephen P. "Scientific Inquiry: A Model for Online Searching." *Journal of the American Society for Information Science* 35 (No. 2) (1984) 110-117; Hock, Randolph E. "Who Should Search? The Attributes of a Good Searcher." In: *Online Searching Technique and Management*, edited by J.J. Maloney. (Chicago: American Library Association, 1983).

6. Harter, "Scientific Inquiry," p. 113.

7. Neill, S.D. "Problem Solving and the Reference Process." *RQ* 14 (Summer 1975) 310-315.

8. Swanson, Don R. "Libraries and the Growth of Knowledge." *Library Quarterly*. 49(1): 3-25; January 1979; Swanson, Don R. "Information Retrieval as a Trial-and-Error Process." *Library Quarterly*. 47(2): 128-148; April, 1977.

9. Smith, Linda C. "Artificial Intelligence in Information Retrieval Systems." *Information Processing and Management*. 12: 189-222; 1976.

10. Bates, Marcia J. "Idea Tactics." *Journal of the American Society for Information Science* 30 (September 1979) 280-289; Bates, Marcia J. "Information Search Tactics." *Journal of the American Society for Information Science* 30 (July 1979) 205-214.

11. Harter, "Scientific Inquiry," p. 113.

12. Fidel, Raya. "Online Searching Styles: A Case-Study-Based Model of Searching Behavior." *Journal of the American Society for Information Science* 35(4) (1984) 211-221.

13. Betty K. Oldroyd and Charles L. Citroen, "Study of Strategies used in On-Line Searching," *Online Review* 1: (Dec. 1977) 295-310.

14. Oldroyd and Citroen, p. 297.

15. Standera, Oldrich. "On-Line Retrieval Systems: Some Observations on the User/System Interface." In *Information Revolution*, Proceedings of the 12th ASIS Annual Meeting, vol. 12 (Washington, D.C., American Society for Information Science, 1975), p. 38-40.

16. Brown, Raymond N. and Agrawala, Ashok K. "On the Behavior of Users of the MEDLINE System," in *Changing Patterns in Information Retrieval*, edited by Carol Fenichel. Tenth

Annual National Information Retrieval Colloquium, May 3-4, 1973. (Washington, D.C.: American Society for Information Science, 1974), p. 36-38.

17. Lancaster, F. Wilfrid. "Evaluation of On-Line Searching in MEDLARS (AIM-TWX) by Biomedical Practitioners," University of Illinois Graduate School of Library Science Occasional Paper No. 101. (Urbana, Ill.: University of Illinois Graduate School of Library Science, 1972).

18. Pollit, A.S. *CANCERLINE Evaluation Project: Final Report*. (Leeds, England: University of Leeds School of Medicine, Medical Library, 1977).

19. Fenichel, Carol H. *Online Information Retrieval: Identification of Measures that Discriminate Among Users with Different Levels and Types of Experience.*" (Ph. D. dissertation, Drexel University, 1979).

20. Fenichel, p. xvi.

21. Vigil, Peter J. "The Psychology of Online Searching." *Journal of the American Society for Information Science* 34 (4) (1983) 281-287.

22. Howard, Helen. "Measures that Discriminate Among Online Searchers with Different Training and Experience." *Online Review* 6 (Aug. 1982), p. 324.

23. Lowry, Glenn R. "Improving the Initial Performance of Novice Online Search Intermediaries." In *Proceedings of the 45th ASIS Annual Meeting*, vol. 19 (Columbus, Ohio: American Society for Information Science, 1982), p. 173-175.

24. Wanger, Judith, Dennis McDonald, and Mary C. Berger. *Evaluation of the On-Line Process* (Bethesda, Md.: National Library of Medicine, 1980).

25. Wanger, p. iv-46.

26. Bellardo, Trudi. "Some Attributes of Online Search Intermediaries that Relate to Search Outcome." (Ph. D. dissertation, Drexel University, 1979).

27. Harter, Stephen P. "The Online Information Specialist: Behaviors, Philosophies, and Attitudes." In *The Online Age: Assessment/Directions*, Proceedings of the 12th ASIS Mid-Year Meeting. (Lexington, Kentucky: May, 1983), p. 201-212 (microfiche).

28. Harter, Stephen P. "Online Searching Styles: An Exploratory Study." *College and Research Libraries* 45 (July 1984) 249-258.

29. Harter, "The Online Information Specialist."

30. Harter, "Online Searching Styles: An Exploratory Study."

31. Pemberton, Jeff. "Faults and Failures: 25 Ways that Online Searching Can Let You Down." *Online* 7 (September 1983) 6-7.

Chapter 6
Effective Communication

6.1 INTRODUCTION

A model of communication proposed by Claude Shannon and Warren Weaver was introduced in Chapter 1. In the Shannon/Weaver model, communication consists of three levels, the technical, the semantic, and the effective, or pragmatic [1]. See Figure 1.3.

Chapter 2 considered concepts affecting semantic communication—the transmission of *meaning*—in the specific context of online information retrieval. In Chapter 3 principles and concepts of technical communication related to the organization and searching of data records and files in an online setting were examined. In this chapter, we will examine pragmatic communication in two parallel activities of online information retrieval, especially as they are conducted through an intermediary: the reference interview and the evaluation of search results.

6.2 THE REFERENCE INTERVIEW

The literature on the reference interview, or the *question negotiation session*, as it has come to be called in the context of online searching, divides itself into the theoretical and the applied. As is too often the case in library and information science, there are few explicit connections between these two literatures. They exist almost as two unrelated subjects.

Viewed from a theoretical perspective, discussion of the reference interview implies an understanding of the information seeking behaviors of human beings. This is a large and interdisciplinary subject, potentially drawing from the disciplines of management science, artificial intelligence, management information systems, decision theory, information science, psychology, and

144

library science. It involves the elusive notions of *information* and *relevance*, as well as how to measure these concepts. It may involve discussion of cognitive styles, models of human information seeking, and analysis of information needs. Finally, it may specifically address interviewing styles and techniques, drawing on the voluminous literature produced by other service-oriented fields such as medicine and social work, as well as the literature of survey research [2].

There is not space in this book even for an introduction to some of these problem areas. Rouse and Rouse have published a review of literature related to human information seeking which should be helpful to the reader wishing to begin the study of interdisciplinary underpinnings [3]. The remainder of this section will discuss theoretical and applied treatments of the reference interview from the restricted perspective of library and information science.

Information retrieval always begins with a *question* posed by an information seeker or client. However, one may hypothesize the existence of several stages or conceptual levels at which one might pose a given question. The classic model proposed by Robert S. Taylor is useful to consider in this context. Taylor's perspective is illuminating:

> Most experimental work with retrieval systems and most attitudes toward reference questions look upon the inquiry and the relevance of answers as single events. This is mistaken. An inquiry is merely a micro-event in a shifting non-linear adaptive mechanism. Consequently, in this paper an inquiry is looked upon not as a command, as in conventional search strategy, but rather as a description of an area of doubt in which the question is open-ended, negotiable, and dynamic [4].

Taylor continues:

> Without doubt, the negotiation of reference questions is one of the most complex acts of human communication. During this process, one person tries to describe for another person not something he knows, but rather something he does not know [5].

Taylor's model distinguishes between four levels of questions:
Q_1 the visceral need
Q_2 the conscious need
Q_3 the formalized need
Q_4 the compromised need [6]

The *visceral need* is the underlying "information need" which eventually generates a question. According to Taylor, it represents a conscious or even unconscious need for information, and probably is not yet expressible linguistically.

The *conscious need* is fuzzy and ill-defined. Its linguistic expression will probably be ambiguous and rambling. Taylor suggests that at this stage the inquirer may talk to colleagues in the hopes of understanding these ambiguities.

The *formalized need* is a precise, concrete, unambiguous linguistic expression of need. At this level the statement of need is qualified, and may not include consideration of the context in which the problem originated.

The *compromised need* is the question as presented to an information system—a library, a librarian, or an online information retrieval system. At this level "the question is recast in anticipation of what the files can deliver" [7]. Note that the information seeker is likely to have an incomplete and incorrect idea regarding the actual file content, structure, and capability of response of the information system. (Certainly this is true of most end-users of online information retrieval systems.) Hence the compromised need may be poorly framed and if carried out as stated, may generate unsatisfactory system responses.

Now, based on the Taylor model and assuming an information seeker has posed a question to an information system or specialist, one must ask: at what level was the question posed? If the information specialist is viewed as a colleague, the question may be at level Q_2 [8]. But more likely, the compromised question Q_4 has been put to the system, where the librarian or information specialist is regarded as part of the system. That is, the question posed to an information specialist often has already been (perhaps badly) transformed from its original expression (Q_2—the conscious need) as well as from its formal expression (Q_3—the formalized need). This is why question negotiation is necessary: so that the results will address the underlying information need instead of the specific question posed.

Knapp gives an interesting example of this, in which a patron has asked for information regarding sign languages used with children who are not deaf. Searched online as stated the request produced no useful citations. After a belated question negotiation session, the information need underlying the question was determined: methods of nonverbal communication used with autistic children [9].

Taylor's theory has been supported and reinforced by numerous studies [10], but has remained essentially untested and unchallenged in the literature of library and information science. Markey's elaboration of the Taylor model for online searching represents the first major challenge to and modification of the model [11]. In Markey's model, levels Q_2–Q_4 are negotiated levels rather than isolated levels as in Taylor's model. "If the client at level I-Q3 [the isolated formalized need of Taylor's model] interacts with the librarian, the remainder of the negotiation takes place as a joint process, and negotiated conscious (N-Q2), formalized (N-Q3) and compromised (N-Q4)

TABLE 6.1
Broad Classes of Concern to be Addressed in the
Question Negotiation Session

Understanding the problem context
Using interpersonal communications skills
Understanding the problem and its literature
Selecting a database and search system
Selecting search vocabulary
Selecting an overall strategy
Establishing search formulations and alternatives
Setting retrieval goals
Setting limitations or qualifications
Deciding on output format
Educating the user
Conducting the post search interview

---

levels are enacted'' [12]. Markey suggests a method for testing the validity of the amended model using state transition analysis.

Following the Taylor/Markey model, the purpose of the question negotiation session or reference interview is for the information specialist, working with the client, to work backwards, through a process of negotiation, from the isolated Q_4 of the client to N-Q3 and perhaps even to N-Q2. If the problem is understood at these levels by the searcher, it will then be possible, using the specialized knowledge of the system (vocabulary considerations, record structure, file organization, command syntax, etc.), to translate the need to negotiated level N-Q4, where a successful interaction with the system can take place.

With the notable exception of Markey's work and the task analysis studies of the online pre-search interview conducted by Cochrane [13], most of the online searching literature has focused on suggested techniques and attitudes instead of theoretical considerations. Tasks to be addressed in the question negotiation session fall into the broad categories listed in Table 6.1. These are discussed briefly in the paragraphs that follow.

Understanding the Problem Context

The importance of carefully probing the context of the information problem cannot be overemphasized. Often the user's personal point of view determines whether a retrieved item will be found useful [14]. Why does the user want this information? What will be its function and purpose? Is the search exploratory? Is it a particular fact or citation that is wanted? Is information regarding details of methodology or the results of hypothesis testing the real object of the search? Particular pieces of data? Does the client want to find evidence that a research problem has never been addressed? To write a comprehensive literature review? To write a short paper for a college undergraduate class? Is a focus on *research* wanted? Or will opinion and descriptive accounts be equally useful? Will a brief short search of a few print tools do just as well? What does the client already know related to the problem? Can pertinent authors, journal articles, or research locations be identified? These and other questions permit the searcher to understand the context of the proposed search, and how it fits into the overall goals and objectives of the client.

Even members of the same client group, such as university faculty or graduate students, can have quite different purposes for a literature search. Thesis students, for example, can be at various stages of proposal-writing [15]. But even at the thesis stage, a computer search may not be the best approach:

> Users who do not have an overview of their topic, who have not done any exploratory reading, and who do not know the literature of their field do not need a computerized search at this stage in the thesis development. Such users are operating in a vacuum and place the searcher in the untenable position of guessing what the user wants or needs [16].

Thus information specialists should also ask themselves whether an online search is really necessary for a given question.

Using Interpersonal Communications Skills

If the information specialist is viewed as a colleague, the search specialist will be much more likely to hear the initial problem in its original conscious formulation: at level Q_2. This goal can be best achieved by attempting to ignoring any differences in status between client and searcher:

> The timid student who almost dares not make the request is as poor a communicator as the doctor or administrator who perceive themselves as "above" negotiating their needs with those who are there to serve them. Search analysts who come across as "This is your Captain speaking" are as inhibiting as they are annoying. At the other extreme, we have "Your Obedient Servant" at the terminal, wasting time and money doing exactly what the user commands, even to sinking the ship [17].

The information seeker must be put at ease in such a way that there is mutual respect and trust between the two participants. This can be accomplished by listening attentively and by asking open-ended questions [18]. 'How,', 'when,' 'where,' 'why,' 'what,' and 'who' are good starting points [19]. Also, "It is important to develop and maintain credibility with the user" [20]. Thus the online search specialist should try to achieve a climate of mutual respect, as between two intelligent, interested colleagues.

The search specialist will not ordinarily be an expert in the subject matter of the request. But *as a layperson* in a field one can still achieve an intelligent and collegial interest in another person's work. This is the level the search specialist should try to achieve.

White stresses the holistic nature of the reference interview. According to White, there are two clusters of concerns for the librarian conducting a reference interview. The first group of concerns deal with obtaining specific information needed to carry out particular tasks, such as developing search strategy. The second group of concerns deal with tactics for encouraging the information seeker to cooperate. In this second group are characteristics of the interview itself: structure, coherence, pace, and length. These are explored in depth by White [21]. There is a voluminous interdisciplinary literature on the development of interviewing skills. White's bibliography provides a convenient place to start the study of this topic.

Understanding the Problem and Its Literature

The information problem or topic is a statement, partially of what is known, and partially of what is not known. It involves concepts and ideas, and relationships between them. It concerns ideas that are understood and about which a literature has been produced.

The information specialist must, from the point of view of a layperson, obtain an understanding of the information problem that goes beyond its linguistic expression. The representation of concepts by symbols, words, and phrases is an important step; however, before this can be done, the underlying ideas must be grasped in sufficient depth to structure a successful search.

It is also useful to have some idea of the size and nature of the specific literature and related literatures, as part of the planning process. Asking the client to produce articles known to address the topic or problem can be extremely useful. Often clues, especially regarding terminology, can be gleaned from these.

Selecting a Database and Search System

The searcher's choice of database and search system should be guided by the considerations outlined in Chapter 4, that is, by such database characteristics as indexing exhaustivity, specificity, subject coverage, database focus, searchable fields, and the many other criteria discussed in Chapter 4. The choice of search system is largely dictated by the databases carried and the access offered to them.

The client can be helpful in the choice of database. Some clients may be familiar with the print equivalent to a database. Lists of journals indexed can also be useful to review with a client to help determine a choice of database. However, the final choice of database must lie with the online searcher.

Selecting Search Vocabulary

The choice of search vocabulary may be the single most important set of decisions a searcher must make. Good semantic communication must take place between the client and the searcher, especially concerning the meaning of words and phrases in the search. The search specialist will rarely be a subject expert in the problem area to be investigated. Therefore the client must generate the majority of search terms that will be used. Thesauri and other controlled vocabularies can be helpful in suggesting possible search terms, but it should be the client who makes the final determination of whether a given term captures the intended meaning of a concept. Thus it is important to review all print tools with the client. The client's own mind is often an invaluable source of search terms as well, especially for natural language searching.

If possible, one or more journal articles or other documents that the client feels are relevant to the search problem should be examined. Such articles can be invaluable as guides to vocabulary. Potentially productive authors and corporate sources can also be identified.

Although the client is a major source of potential search terms, the online searcher must be the final judge of the words, phrases and fields that will be searched. Chapter 2 discussed characteristics of controlled vocabularies and natural languages. These characteristics, as they apply to the databases to be searched, should be the determining factor in this decision.

Selecting an Overall Strategy

We have not yet discussed overall search strategies that might be employed in a search, a topic that will be discussed in the next chapter. However, the decision regarding strategy belongs solely to the search specialist, although information bearing on this decision must be gathered at the reference interview. For example, if a given problem area has arisen from a "classic," or seminal paper, then a cited reference approach might be ideal. Obviously, since the searcher is not ordinarily a subject expert, this information must come from the client, during the reference interview.

Establishing Search Formulations and Alternatives

If the client is not present during the search, the search analyst should prepare for alternative search formulations ahead of time. In this case, the librarian systematically covers all potentially relevant topics, perhaps gathering more information than actually necessary to provide a basis for decisions during the search. Any assumptions may be verified verbally since there is little chance for gathering additional information later if they are incorrect [22].

However, if the user is present at the search, the interview may be integrated much more completely into the conduct of the search itself:

> Because the user can make interim relevance judgments or provide additional information on demand, some information gathering [at the question negotiation stage] may be postponed [23].

However, there are disadvantages in having the user present at the terminal. Search connect times may tend to be longer because some clients may tend to wander, following interesting leads, or chat. Nervousness by the searcher may also be a problem. For these reasons, some authorities believe that having the user present is not a cost-effective approach to online searching [24]. The decision regarding whether the user should be present at an online search must be made on the basic of individual personality characteristics of the searcher and, if known, the client. There are clear advantages and disadvantages associated with each alternative.

Setting Retrieval Goals

The comprehensiveness of the search question must be determined, and realistic goals set for retrieval. Is a complete bibliography on the problem or topic wanted? A few pertinent papers? Or something else? And what are the cost limitations of the search problem? This topic will be more fully addressed later in this chapter.

Setting Limitations or Qualifications

In many databases and search systems, output can be reduced in size by imposing limitations such as date of publication, language, country of publication, document type, and other non-semantic conditions on the retrieved records. Information regarding possible useful limitations to impose on search output must be gathered at the reference interview process, if it is to be effectively incorporated into the search planning process.

Deciding on Output Format

In many databases and search systems there are several options for specifying how the records from the linear file will be printed. Also, there may be options for sorting output records in various ways before printing. Decisions regarding these matters must be addressed in the reference interview, if they are to reflect the wishes of the client.

Educating the User

In most search settings, end-users who have not used online search services previously should be instructed in such matters as search connect time and printing costs, print formats, and the time lapse between initiating a search and its completion [25]. Perhaps more important, clients should understand the basic concepts of Boolean logic, the effects of using controlled vocabularies versus natural language fields for searching, and especially the fact, by no means obvious to everyone, that computers use character strings to represent concepts. Once this fact is understood, the user will be much more willing and able to assist in an active way in representing the concepts of the search accurately.

Another concern that the librarian should have is the possible need to *re-educate* the user. All but experienced users will approach the reference interview with certain misconceptions that will require discussion and clarification.

Corrected statements of possible misconceptions include the observation that computer searching of bibliographic databases is usually not based on searching the full texts of documents, nor is it limited to articles located in the library. Thus the full texts of retrieved articles will still have to be obtained following the search, and this may often be difficult or impossible. Databases do not usually include references to older literatures, and often will not answer questions directly. Online searching will not write papers for clients, nor will it clarify or substitute for fuzzy concepts or thinking. Perhaps especially, the client (and searcher) should recognize that online searching is not a panacea. It is easy to do badly and difficult to do well.

The expectations of clients should reflect these and other 'truths'' of online searching realistically. Arlene Somerville discusses additional considerations for dealing with new users and problem users [26].

Conducting the Post Search Interview

When the search has been completed, the search specialist should meet with the client (especially new users) to explain the results of the search. Many of the items retrieved may not be held by the local library. This should be explained to the client, and the interlibrary loan process introduced. Depending on the database searched, it may be necessary to explain the contents of several data fields. Also, the search results should be evaluated by the client during the post search interview. The question of evaluation is more fully addressed in the next section.

6.3 EVALUATION BY END-USERS

Evaluation can be looked at from several perspectives. From the internal perspective of the search specialist, there are many areas in which lapses in judgment, incomplete knowledge or skill levels, or carelessness may have played a significant role in the process of conducting a given search [27]. Some "errors" may be related to the search system or database, e.g., database indexing policies. It seems reasonable to assume that an awareness of indexing and other problems in a given database, as well as search system characteristics and conceptual problems experienced by a searcher will make the searcher better prepared to carry out future searches in that database and system. We will return to the problem of evaluating online searching from the searcher's point of view later in the chapter.

From the external perspective of the information seeker, criteria that might be used to judge the results of online information retrieval are directly related to the information problem and its context. If one accepts the Taylor model of information question formation, the central (really the only) question from the user's point of view must be: How well has the search succeeded in meeting my *visceral* information need, or at the least, my *conscious* need? We hypothesize that this will be a visceral reaction for the client, a single, overall feeling of satisfaction regarding how well the information need has been met. If this hypothesis is true, a single question put to the client will measure accurately the success of the search. An example of such a question is the following:

Please indicate your overall reaction to the search:

    a. extremely disappointed
    b. disappointed
    c. reasonably satisfied
    d. pleased
    e. extremely pleased

In a short written questionnaire, providing a place following this question for open-ended comments will succeed in soliciting information regarding the major areas of success and failure in the search.

The overall reaction of the end user will measure the search effectiveness from an external, *macro* level. There are, of course, many output factors contributing to the success or failure of a search at the *micro* level. The most

TABLE 6.2
Characteristics of Search Output Determining Client Satisfaction

---

Time required for results to be obtained
Appearance, print format, and organization of output
Effort required by the user
Limitations or qualifications placed on search output
Monetary cost of the search
Capabilities of search system: command language, file structures, etc.
Personal attributes of the search specialist
Quality, coverage, etc. of databases searched
Retrieval effectiveness
Novelty and usefulness of search results

---

important of these are listed in Table 6.2. Lancaster provides a detailed discussion of many of these [28]. Note that each criterion must be evaluated *by the requirements of a specific user.*

For example, consider a client who is interested in the online information retrieval process as an intellectual activity, that is, for its own sake, or one who recognizes the need for full participation in the retrieval process. Such an end user may welcome spending personal time and effort and will regard it as time well spent, while a hurried and impatient client will tend to begrudge any personal expenditure of time. This information must be gathered during the reference interview and utilized in the planning, execution, and evaluation of the search.

Each of the criteria listed in Table 6.2 can be measured and elaborated upon in several ways. The first several of these criteria are straightforward checks on elicited user requirements. Actions of the search specialist, characteristics of the search system command language, file structures, and the evaluation of databases have already been discussed.

Possibly among the most interesting and difficult criterion listed in Table 6.2 deals with *retrieval effectiveness.* How well has the search succeeded in retrieving relevant documents and suppressing the retrieval of nonrelevant documents? The effectiveness of information retrieval systems and searches should be a central question for evaluation. There are many approaches that might be taken. The RASD/MARS Committee on the Measurement and Evaluation of Service of the American Library Association has published a sample questionnaire to identify approaches to evaluating retrieval effectiveness and to solicit user feedback to these issues [29]. Information gathered in this questionnaire addresses:

* the client's purpose in requesting the search
* the number of citations retrieved that are relevant to the search question or topic

* the percentage of citations retrieved that are relevant to the question or topic
* the percentage of citations retrieved that are relevant to the overall information need (as opposed to the specific search topic or question)
* the percentage of relevant citations that are new to the client
* the cost/benefit to the client of obtaining the new and relevant documents
* the time lapse between making the request and receiving the results
* the overall value of the search

These ideas incorporate several approaches to the assessment of retrieval effectiveness. Many will be explored in more depth in the following pages.

6.4 EVALUATION OF RETRIEVAL EFFECTIVENESS

Early in this book an information retrieval system was said to be like a sieve, its purpose being to allow relevant documents to pass through but not other documents. Measures of *retrieval effectiveness* assess the extent to which these dual goals have been met. Ideally, an information retrieval system should retrieve all the documents relevant to a search question and suppress the retrieval of all non-relevant documents.

Throughout this book, the concepts of *relevance* and *relevant document* have been left undefined. It has been assumed that, for a particular information need, search question, and document set, there exists a subset of documents consisting of all those documents "relevant" to that information need and question. That is, for each search question, the universe of documents of interest can be partitioned into two parts: the set of relevant documents and the set of non-relevant documents. For the discussion that follows, we continue to make this assumption. The concepts of relevance and relevant document will be examined more closely in section 6.6.

Let a particular search formulation (any command creating a set of postings) be put to an information retrieval system. The collection is thereby partitioned into two parts: *retrieved* documents and *non-retrieved* documents. The result of applying both assumptions to a document collection is to partition the collection into 4 parts. Figure 6.1 shows the results of both assumptions, for a given universe of documents, information problem, and search formulation. (Strictly speaking, documents are not retrieved but records associated with documents. However, to avoid the clumsiness of having to say this continually, we will simply refer to retrieved *documents*.)

Graphically, line 1-1 shows the results of the first partitioning, which divides the collection into relevant and non-relevant documents. Line 2-2 partitions the collection into documents that are retrieved and those that are not

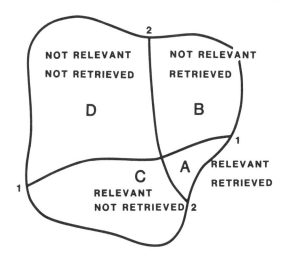

Figure 6.1   A document universe partitioned by a given information need and a given search formulation.

retrieved. Applying the two assumptions to a document collection will divide the collection into four subsets (see Figure 6.2):

Subset A: Documents that are relevant and were retrieved by the formulation. These are called *hits*. There are *a* postings in set A.

Subset B: Documents that are not relevant but were nevertheless retrieved, called *noise, false drops,* or *false coordinations*. There are *b* postings in set B.

Subset C: Documents that are relevant but which were not retrieved by the formulation. These are *missed relevant documents*, or simply *misses*. There are *c* postings in set C.

Subset D: Documents that are not relevant and not retrieved. These are documents correctly suppressed by the system. There are d documents in set D.

Perfect retrieval takes place if sets B and C contain no postings, i.e., are empty sets. In such a case, regardless of the search question, the formulation misses no relevant documents and retrieves no non-relevant documents; all and only relevant documents are retrieved. However, this rarely happens in practice. Usually both B and C are non-empty and the retrieval is less than perfect. The *recall* and *precision* ratios are commonly used to provide a quantitative measure of the extent to which retrieval fails to be perfect.

Let *a* be the number of documents in set A, b be the number of documents in set B, etc. Then *the recall ratio*, or simply *recall*, is defined as the

	Number of relevant documents	Number of non-relevant documents
Number of retrieved documents	a	b
Number of documents not retrieved	c	d

Figure 6.2 Quantitative results of an online search.

proportion of relevant documents in a collection that are retrieved in a given search. Symbolically,

$$R = \text{recall} = \frac{\text{the number of relevant retrieved documents}}{\text{the number of relevant documents}} = \frac{a}{a + c}$$

If all relevant documents are retrieved, then c = 0 and the recall of the formulation is a perfect 1.0 (or 100%). If c is large relative to a, then recall will be low. In the worst case, no relevant documents are retrieved and a = 0 and recall = 0. (Note: the indeterminate form 0/0 is undefined in ordinary arithmetic. We define 0/0 to equal 0 when a = c = 0.) Then $0 \leq R \leq 1$, for all information problems and search formulations. Similarly,

$$P = \text{precision} = \frac{\text{the number of relevant retrieved documents}}{\text{the number of retrieved documents}} = \frac{a}{a + b}$$

If no non-relevant documents are retrieved, then b = 0 and the precision ratio associated with the formulation is a perfect 1.0. If *b* is large relative to *a* then precision will be low. If no relevant documents are retrieved, then a = 0 and precision = 0. Then $0 \leq P \leq 1$, for all information problems and search formulations.

Recall is a measure of the proportion of relevant documents that are captured by a search formulation, while precision assesses the purity of the output: the extent to which retrieved documents are relevant. Other measures have also been proposed, including the *fallout* ratio—the proportion of non-relevant documents that are retrieved—and the *snobbery* ratio—the proportion of relevant documents that are not retrieved [30]. Recall and precision are by far the most commonly used measures of effectiveness, and discussion will be restricted to them.

Observe that it is virtually meaningless to examine only a single measure of effectiveness. Because of the two conflicting goals of information retrieval—to retrieve and at the same time to suppress retrieval—measures must be examined in pairs. For example, perfect recall can be achieved easily, merely by retrieving the entire database. But if this were done in a database of any size, precision would be extremely small, making such a formulation absurd, in spite of the high recall achieved. (This is really the "information retrieval problem," discussed in Chapter 1.) Conversely, suppose that one knows about the existence of a relevant document and creates a set containing a single element—the posting associated with that document. While the precision ratio achieved by this formulation would be a perfect 1.0, the recall ratio would in general be very small.

There are some problems associated with the concepts of relevance, recall, and precision as they are used for the evaluation of retrieval effectiveness. First, it is by no means clear what "relevance" means. Second, there is no obvious way of measuring recall in a search, since its definition requires knowledge of the number of relevant documents *not* retrieved by a formulation, a number not ordinarily known. Finally, it is not clear how an interactive online searcher can make use of these theoretical concepts to conduct an applied online search for a client. Each of these considerations will be addressed in turn, beginning with the latter two problems.

We have seen that the computation of the precision ratio is based on an analysis of retrieved citations, and hence may be computed easily by the information seeker. Calculation of recall ratios, on the other hand, require knowledge of documents *not retrieved* that are relevant to the search request, data that are not usually available to the search analyst. Of what value, then, is recall as a measure of effectiveness for the online searcher?

While recall cannot normally be computed outside the laboratory—that is, cannot be used directly in an online search conducted for a client with a real information need—it can nevertheless remain useful as a theoretical construct. One can discuss ways and means of *increasing* or *decreasing* recall without being able to measure the *extent* of the change, that is, without being able to compute actual recall ratios.

Figure 6.3 illustrates hypothetical results of several search formulations for a given information need. Each point represents the recall and precision ratio associated with a particular formulation. It is assumed that the necessary recall computations could be made, if relevance judgments for the entire database were available.

There are several observations that can be made regarding Figure 6.3. First, point X represents a perfect search, with a recall ratio and a precision ratio

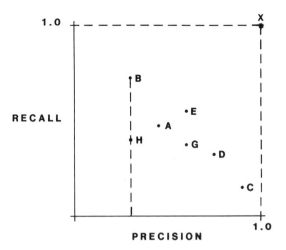

Figure 6.3   Recall/precision points representing the results of several search formulations for a given information problem and for a given database.

of 1.0. Research and experience both suggest that while this result is useful as a point of reference, it is unlikely to be approached in practice. Except for point X, the formulation having the highest recall ratio is point B; however, this point also has the lowest precision ratio. Note that point H has the same precision ratio as B. Since B has a much higher recall ratio than H, B is a superior (or more effective) formulation.

As one moves from formulations B and H to the right and downward in Figure 6.3, the recall ratios decrease and the precision ratios increase. Formulation C is the highest precision search of all, also having, however, the lowest recall ratio.

Online searching has been presented as a heuristic, problem-solving activity, analogous to scientific inquiry. As the searcher constructs formulations, prints and evaluates the relevancy of retrieved citations, and formulates and tests alternative hypotheses, a rational basis on which to proceed is needed. Guidance is offered the searcher by the theoretical concepts of recall and precision. A search is conducted for (or by) an information seeker, who can identify retrieval goals. A client who wants a few documents discussing a topic wants a high precision search. Another client may want a comprehensive, high recall search. When applying heuristics to try to improve retrieval results, then, the searcher should try to move toward the recall and precision goals of the client. The next chapter addresses this idea in more detail. For now, the reader might try to identify actions that would tend to increase the recall or precision of a given formulation. Many such actions have been discussed.

KNOWN FACT: Set 2 is a high precision set that will be printed

QUESTION: Should Set 1 also be printed?

SUGGESTED ACTION: Evaluate Set 3 for relevancy

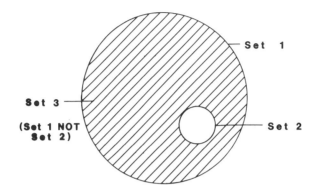

Figure 6.4   A simple example illustrating Vigil's NOT algorithm.

Peter Vigil has suggested a valuable technique for evaluating the retrieval effectiveness of a search in progress [31]. Essentially, the technique uses the Boolean operator NOT to remove redundant postings from multiple sets to facilitate their comparison. The approach allows the comparison of two or more sets consisting of unique documents. References [31] should be read for a detailed discussion of the method. A simple example of Vigil's algorithm is illustrated in Figure 6.4.

In the example, assume that the searcher has created a set of postings (set 2), has examined it for relevancy, and found its precision acceptably high for printing. Indeed, it may have already been printed. Set 1 results from an attempt to increase the recall of the formulation that produced set 2. For example, set 2 might be the result of searching for a given phrase in a controlled vocabulary field, and set 1 is the result of searching for the same phrase in all fields. In this example, set 2 is a subset of set 1, although this is not a necessary condition for the algorithm to be used.

The searcher wants to evaluate set 1 for relevancy. Instead, Vigil suggests evaluating set 3 = set 1 NOT set 2. That is, the redundant records in set 1 are removed before evaluation. In this way the unique contribution of set 1 to the retrieval results can be evaluated. These contributions include not only unique postings to relevant documents, but also unique vocabulary elements associated with these documents. Moreover, the assessment of the precision of set 1 is made only for the new documents not already evaluated (in set 2).

The algorithm is extended by Vigil for multiple sets and iterations. Vigil's algorithm is a highly recommended evaluation technique.

6.5 EVALUATION OF SEARCHER PERFORMANCE

It should come as no surprise to the reader who has come with us thus far in this book that we believe strongly in self-evaluation. An online search can and should be evaluated from the searcher's point of view, in a spirit of healthy constructive criticism and with an aim toward increased understanding and self-improvement.

Several areas of searcher performance can be identified. Indeed, most of this book has been spent discussing concepts and principles of online information retrieval. The extent to which these have been understood, internalized, and used in the online search process constitute clear areas for evaluation. Major evaluation areas include

* Selection of database and search system
* Use of Boolean operators to combine search facets
* Selection of appropriate vocabulary elements to represent concepts of the information need
* Understanding of database documentation and utilization of appropriate characteristics of databases: indexing policies, etc.
* Use of search system command language
* Use of heuristics to improve search output
* Personal qualities relating to the search process: flexibility, willingness to try new ideas, reaction to unexpected search output, etc.
* Extent to which the underlying information need has been met.

There is little in the online searching literature that addresses the process and principles of evaluation [32]. In the information retrieval literature, evaluation is a central subject of discussion. However, evaluation of information retrieval *experiments* rather than operational systems is the main focus of most papers. In spite of its age, Lancaster's evaluation of the Medlars system still stands alone in the comprehensiveness of its analytical evaluation of both system and searcher [33].

Although there is little explicit discussion of evaluation in the online searching literature, much of the content of several professional journals, especially *Online, Online Review,* and *Database* is implicitly related to searcher understanding and hence, at least indirectly, to evaluation. The problem of how to best evaluate online information retrieval searches and searchers as well as systems is a rich area for research and one in which increased rigor and research is badly needed.

6.6 RELEVANCE

The concept of *relevance* underlies theoretical as well as applied work in information retrieval. *Relevance* and *information* are genuine primitive concepts of information science. There have been many attempts to define and explicate relevance, although there cannot be said to have been any definition earning anything like universal acceptance. In this book, relevance has remained undefined up to now. However, the concept cannot be ignored, and a few remarks will be made here.

Relevance has been defined as a random variable [34], as "a member of some minimal premiss set of stored sentences for some component statement of [an information need]" [35], and as "a measure of the effectiveness of a contact between a source and a destination in a communication process" [36], among many others. It has been contrasted with the notions of relatedness, responsiveness, topicality, pertinence, beneficiality, aboutness, and utility [37]. It has been examined by philosophers, logicians, semanticists, psychologists, and information scientists. The historical development of the concept in information science has been clearly outlined by Saracevic [38].

Let us return to Taylor's distinction between the visceral, conscious, formalized, and compromised information needs. The purpose of the question-negotiation session is to work with an individual's compromised and formalized information needs and return to an earlier stage that more truly reflects the underlying motivation for the inquiry. Clearly, if an information specialist or librarian answers a formalized or compromised information need literally, without negotiation, the results may not address the true information need of the client at all well. On the other hand, we believe that documents provided in support of such an effort *may be said to be relevant* to the question asked.

We are not going to break new ground in explicating the concept of relevance. However, there is a perspective regarding the concept of relevance that we believe is particularly useful. This perspective is consistent with some of the literature and with ideas expressed earlier in this book. The term 'relevance' will be used to stand for a relation between documents and questions that is objective and refers to *public knowledge*. The term 'pertinence' will be used for relations that are subjective and refer to private knowledge. This usage is similar to and consistent with that of Foskett [39], Kemp [40], and Weiler [41], but differs from that of Boyce [42], Bookstein [43], Cooper [44], and Buckland [45].

The sense in which the term "relevance" is used here seems to have been first proposed by Foskett [46]. It refers to a *semantic* relation between a document and a question. A document may be said to be *relevant* to a question (that is, a formalized or compromised information need) if it is objectively judged to be so by a consensus of those practicing in a discipline. This view

TABLE 6.3
The Analogy between Relevance and Pertinence to Concepts in other Disciplines*

Discipline	Public	Private
sociology of knowledge, philosophy of science	public knowledge	private knowledge
psychology (especially of learning)	denotation	connotation
linguistics (especially semiotics)	semantics	pragmatics
sociology of knowledge, philosophy of science	formal communication	informal communication
information science (systems evaluation)	relevance	pertinence

*From Kemp, D.A. "Relevance, Pertinence, and Information System Development." *Information Storage and Retrieval* 10 (1974) 37-47.

of an 'objective consensus'' follows Thomas Kuhn's view of a scientific paradigm [47] and especially the idea of "normal science.'' It also agrees with John Ziman's notion of science as public knowledge [48]. Foskett contrasts relevance to pertinence in the following way:

> Relevant means being a part of the paradigm, or public knowledge, or consensus in a field; pertinence means related to the specific pattern of thought in a specific reader's mind [49].

Kemp extended Foskett's notion, relating the concepts of relevance and pertinence to analogous ideas in other disciplines [50]. Table 6.3 summarizes the connections made by Kemp.

In the Foskett/Kemp view, relevance means "fitting into an accepted scientific paradigm.'' It deals with meaning, and, subject to the frailties of human nature, is measurable objectively. It reflects the corporate *Weltanschaung* of a discipline, as that discipline is currently viewed by scientists and scholars working within it. A document relevant to a question is on, or about the topic stated in the formal or compromised information need, as determined by the paradigm currently accepted by the scientific or scholarly establishment. Pertinence, on the other hand, is highly subjective and personal. It is a relation between an individual with an information need and a document.

Ordinarily, relevance is a necessary but not sufficient condition for the relation of pertinence to hold, although conceivably exceptions to this might occur. That is, a client may judge a document as pertinent to an information need, even if the document would not be judged relevant. However, as Boyce points out, such occurrences are probably rare [51]. Thus relevance can be treated as a necessary condition for pertinence without great loss in generality.

In the practice of online information retrieval, the searcher must go beyond mere relevance. An online search must be judged against the personal, visceral information need of an individual. To fail to do so is to fail to move from an expressed, formal statement and a corporate judgment of relevance, or topicality, as a paradigmatic judgment, to the personal satisfaction of an individual. Thus the evaluation of an online search must be based on judgments of pertinence, not relevance. This is the extra dimension brought to the process by the information specialist, or perhaps by the end-user carrying out his or her own search.

However, the evaluation of information systems and databases *per se*, must be based on relevance considerations. To what extent is the system and database able to respond to paradigmatic questions with accuracy, currency, and completeness? These are the kinds of questions that must be asked in the evaluation of databases and search systems. The information specialist must go beyond such questions, in the rendering of a personal, private, subjective service.

What sorts of considerations affect individual judgments of pertinence? Such issues were discussed in Section 6.1. Relevance is nearly always an important factor. In addition, the personal context of the client's information need, the exhaustivity required by the client, as well as non-semantic bibliographic characteristics such as language, document type, and publication date can be important. Besides these, the client may use language in an idiosyncratic way (that is, in a non-paradigmatic way) and pertinent documents should reflect this usage. The comprehensiveness of the search, the novelty of retrieved items, and the cost of the search also can affect pertinence evaluations.

In the context of experimentation and research in information storage and retrieval, the concept of relevance has been a major stumbling block for productive research in information retrieval. To carry out retrieval experiments on a search system and database, some measure of effectiveness is needed, and recall and precision have been commonly used. But then search questions and question/document relevance judgments are required. How can experiments be conducted without significantly biasing one's conclusions? This question introduces thorny methodological issues. The following questions are examples of these concerns:

1. Who is competent to make a relevance judgment? Only the author of the search question? But then isn't the judgment one of pertinence rather than one of relevance? Does this matter?

2. If panels of experts are used to provide relevance judgments, what can be made of the fact that experts sometimes (often?) disagree?

3. On what physical evidence (the document itself, the title of the document, etc.) should relevance judgments be made? If the document itself, how

can the judgment process be made cost effective? If a document surrogate such as title is used, what sorts of bias does this introduce?

4. How should relevance be defined operationally? (Is it a binary variable? continuous?)

5. The use of relevance judges has sometimes led to charges of 'missed'' relevant documents (that is, relevant documents that were not so identified by the judges). For example, The ERIC ONTAP file on the DIALOG search system is an online practice file that has been criticized on this and other grounds [52]. What effect do missed relevant documents have on measures of retrieval effectiveness? What kinds of bias does this produce?

6. Because of the cost of producing a relevance judgment for every document/question pair in a database, a cost which is for all practical purposes impossibly high for a single search question in a moderately sized "real" database like ERIC, other approaches have been used. Lancaster, for example, constructed a *recall base* of documents known to be relevant to search questions. *Estimates* of recall were then made, based on the retrieval results computed for this recall base [53]. But this set of documents is not a random sample of the set of documents relevant to the search question. The obvious question to ask here is What biases does this method of estimating recall introduce into the evaluation process?

These methodological difficulties have been discussed in greater depth in other publications [54]. The reader is directed to these sources for further study of this extraordinarily difficult and important problem.

PROBLEMS

1. Conduct a thorough literature review and write a summary of approximately 10 substantive articles or books from *outside the library and information science fields* relevant to one of the following interdisciplinary topics:
   a. relevance or relevance judgments
   b. reference interview
   c. cognitive styles
   d. human information seeking
   e. nature of information
   f. models of human communication
   g. human/machine online interaction

2. Read Thomas Kuhn's *The Structure of Scientific Revolutions* (Chicago: University of Chicago Press, 1962). Write a short essay discussing the implications for information storage and retrieval of the ideas expressed by Kuhn.

3. Formally define the concepts of recall and precision, and discuss the difficulty in applying these concepts to a "real" information retrieval search.

4. Examine and discuss some of the measures of retrieval effectiveness other than recall and precision that have been suggested in the information retrieval literature. Can you find any examples of *single* measures of effectiveness?

5. Search the online information retrieval literature and earlier chapters of this book for examples of heuristics for increasing the value of recall and precision, or for other purposes, in an online search. Try to identify as many heuristics as you can.

6. Evaluate the assertion that online searching is an *art*. Compare and contrast it to other human endeavors that you consider to be arts.

7. Describe how you would approach a search for the following topic:

"abused children as parents—are they also child abusers?" Provide as much detail as you can regarding possible databases and approaches you might take to this question. What would you try to learn in the reference interview? What potential problems can you identify?

8. Using all available database aids, identify three databases likely to provide the desired information for each of the following brief statements of topical information needs. Discuss advantages and disadvantages of each. Since there can be no reference interview, you may need to make certain assumptions. If you do need to make assumptions, state them explicitly.
  a. market data on mining industries in Brazil
  b. the effects of pollution control devices on power and mechanical performance of automobiles
  c. folklore of early American settlers
  d. a list of drugs approved by the National Drug Administration for the treatment of cancer
  e. methods for raising giant shrimp in fresh water
  f. effects of air and water pollution on the American eagle
  g. sex differences in personal space boundaries
  h. intellectual history of the Italian Renaissance
  i. mating habits of the snail darter

9. Conduct a search on a problem of your choice using controlled vocabulary terms and fields exclusively. Now solve the same search problem in the same database but this time using natural language terms and fields exclusively. Compare the results using Vigil's NOT algorithm.

10. Assume that you are searching in the ERIC database for documents addressing the following information problem: education and training of information scientists. Further assume that the 'education" concept is represented appropriately, and will be intersected to the "information scientists" concept using Boolean AND when the latter has been constructed. Discuss the following representation of the "information scientists" concept in terms of the *relative* recall and precision that will, in your judgment, be likely to result from documents retrieved by the completed formulation. (The symbol @ is the truncation symbol.)
  a. 'information scientists' as a term in titles and abstracts
  b. 'information scientist@' as a term in titles
  c. 'information scientists' as a descriptor
  d. 'information scientists' as an identifier
  e. 'information' and 'scientist@' in the same field
  f. 'information' and 'scientist@' within 3 words of one another
  g. 'information' and 'scientist@' in titles
  h. 'information' and 'scientist@' in titles, abstracts, descriptors, and identifiers
  i. 'information scientist@' as a term in abstracts

11. From now on, when utilizing heuristics to attempt to increase the recall or precision of search formulations, use Vigil's NOT algorithm to evaluate intermediate output.

NOTES AND REFERENCES

1. Shannon, Claude E. and Warren Weaver. *The Mathematical Theory of Communication*. (Urbana, Illinois: The University of Illinois Press, 1964).

2. White, Marilyn Domas. "The Dimensions of the Reference Interview." *RQ* 20 (Summer 1981) 373–381.

3. Rouse, William B. and Sandra H. Rouse. "Human Information Seeking and Design of Information Systems." *Information Processing and Management* 20 (No. 1–2) (1984) 129–138.

4. Taylor, Robert S. "Question Negotiation and Information Seeking in Libraries." *College and Research Libraries* 29 (No. 3) (May 1968) p. 179. © 1968 by the American Library Association.

5. Taylor, p. 180.

6. Taylor, "Question Negotiation and Information Seeking in Libraries." See also Taylor, Robert S., "The Process of Asking Questions." *American Documentation* 13 (No. 4) (October 1962) 391–396.

7. Taylor, "Question Negotiation and Information Seeking in Libraries," p. 184.

8. Taylor, "Question Negotiation and Information Seeking in Libraries," p. 183.

9. Knapp, Sara D. "The Reference Interview in the Computer-Based Setting." *RQ* 17 (Summer 1978) p. 323.

10. Markey, Karen. "Levels of Question Formulation in Negotiation of Information Need During the Online Presearch Interview: A Proposed Model." *Information Processing and Management* 17 (No. 5) (1981) p. 215.

11. Markey, "Levels of Question Formulation in Negotiation of Information Need During the Online Presearch Interview: A Proposed Model."

12. Markey, p. 217.

13. Cochrane, Pauline. "Study of Events and Tasks in Pre-Search Interviews Before Online Searching." *Proceedings* of the Second National Online Meeting, New York, March 24–26, 1981. pp 133–147.

14. Knapp, p. 322.

15. Dommer, Janet M. "Techniques for Conducting Effective Search Interviews with Thesis and Dissertation Candidates." *Online* 6 (March 1982) p. 45.

16. Dommer, p. 45.

17. Knapp, p. 322. © 1978 by the American Library Association.

18. Somerville, Arleen N. "The Pre-Search Reference Interview—A Step by Step Guide." *Database* 5 (February 1982) p. 34.

19. Knapp, p. 324; Jahoda, Gerald. "Reference Question Analysis and Search Strategy Development by Man and Machine." *Journal of the American Society for Information Science* 25 (May–June 1974) 139–144.

20. Somerville, p. 34.

21. White, "The Dimensions of the Reference Interview."

22. White, p. 375.

23. White, p. 374.

24. Somerville, p. 33.

25. Dommer, p. 44.

26. Somerville, p. 37–38.

27. Marshall, Doris B. "To Improve Searching, Check Search Results." *Online* 4 (No. 3) (July 1980) 32–47; Glunz, Diane. 'Maximizing Search Quality through a Program of Peer Review." *Online* 7 (September 1983) 100–110.

28. Lancaster, F.W. "MEDLARS: Report on the Evaluation of Its Operation Efficiency." *American Documentation* 20 (April 1969) 119–142; Lancaster, F. Wilfrid. *Information Retrieval Systems: Characteristics, Testing and Evaluation*. Second edition. (New York: John Wiley & Sons, 1979).

29. Blood, Richard W. "Evaluation of Online Searches." *RQ* 22 (Spring 1983) 266–277.

30. The following references discuss these and other measures of retrieval effectiveness in depth: Robertson, S.E. "The Parametric Description of Retrieval Tests." *Journal of Documentation* 25 (1) (March 1969) 1–27; Robertson, S.E. "The Parametric Description of Retrieval Tests. Part 2." *Journal of Documentation* 25 (2) (June 1969) 93–107; Lancaster, *Information Retrieval Systems*; Hitchingham, Eileen. "Selecting Measures Applicable to Evaluation of Online Literature Searching." *Drexel Library Quarterly* 13 (No. 3) (July 1977) 52–67.

31. Vigil, Peter J. "Analytical methods for online searching." *Online Review* 7 (6) (1983) 497–514; Vigil, Peter J. "The psychology of online searching." *Journal of the American Society for Information Science* 34 (3) (1983) 281–287.

32. An exception to this is Glunz, "Maximizing search quality through a program of peer review."

33. Lancaster, "MEDLARS."

34. Gebhardt, Friedrich. "A Simple Probabilistic Model for the Relevance Assessment of Documents." *Information Processing and Management* 11 (1975) 59–65; Robertson, S.E. "The Probabilistic Character of Relevance." *Information Processing and Management* 13 (1977) 247–251.

35. Cooper, William S. "A Definition of Relevance for Information Retrieval." *Information Storage and Retrieval* 7 (1971) 19–37.

36. Saracevic, Tefko. "Relevance: A Review of and a Framework for the Thinking on the Notion in Information Science." *Journal of the American Society for Information Science* 26 (November–December 1975) p. 325.

37. Buckland, Michael K. *Library Services in Theory and Context*. (New York: Pergamon Press, 1983). pp. 77–94; Cooper, William S. "On Selecting a Measure of Retrieval Effectiveness." *Journal of the American Society for Information Science* 24 (No. 2) (1973) 87–100.

38. Saracevic, "Relevance."

39. Foskett, D.J. "A Note on the Concept of 'Relevance'." *Information Storage and Retrieval* 8 (1972) 77–78.

40. Kemp, D.A. "Relevance, Pertinence, and Information System Development." *Information Storage and Retrieval* 10 (1974) 37–47.

41. Weiler, Gershon. "Relevance Again." *Information Storage and Retrieval* 8 (1972) p. 121.

42. Boyce, Bert. "Beyond Topicality: A Two Stage View of Relevance and the Retrieval Process." *Information Processing and Management* 18 (No. 3) (1982) 105–109.

43. Bookstein, Abraham. "Relevance." *Journal of the American Society for Information Science* 30 (September 1979) 269–273.

44. Cooper, "On Selecting a Measure of Retrieval Effectiveness."

45. Buckland, Michael K. *Library Services in Theory and Context.*

46. Foskett, "A Note on the Concept of Relevance."

47. Kuhn, Thomas S. *The Structure of Scientific Revolutions.* (Chicago: University of Chicago Press, 1962).

48. Ziman, J. *Public Knowledge: The Social Dimension of Science.* (London: Cambridge University Press, 1968).

49. Foskett, "A Note on the Concept of Relevance," p. 78.

50. Kemp, "Relevance, Pertinence, and Information System Development."

51. Boyce, "Beyond Topicality."

52. Jackson, William J. "ONTAP-ERIC: A Critical View." *Online Review* 5 (No. 4) (1981) 335–338.

53. Lancaster, "MEDLARS."

54. Harter, Stephen P. "The Cranfield II Relevance Assessments: A Critical Evaluation." *Library Quarterly* 41 (July 1971) 229–243; Swanson, Don R. "Some Unexplained Aspects of the Cranfield Tests of Indexing Performance Factors." *Library Quarterly* 41 (3) (July 1971) 223–228; Cuadra, Carlos A. and Robert V. Katter. "Opening the Black Box of 'Relevance.' *Journal of Documentation* 23 (4) (1967) 291–303; Taube, Mortimer. "A Note on the Pseudo-Mathematics of Relevance." *American Documentation* 16 (April 1965) 69–72.

Chapter 7

Search Strategies
and Heuristics

The term *strategy* has been used in different ways in the information retrieval literature. For example, some authors comonly refer to a command put to a search system as a strategy. We have reserved the term *search formulation* or simply *formulation* for this concept. 'Strategy' is also sometimes used in the literature to refer to one's action at a particular point in a search, a decision about what might be the best way to proceed, a tactic to serve an immediate objective. But in this book, the term *heuristic* is used to refer to this concept.

The words 'strategy' and 'tactic' are used here in their military sense, a distinction apparently first applied to online searching by Marcia Bates [1]. A *search strategy* is an overall plan or approach for a search problem, while a search tactic or heuristic is a move made to advance a particular strategy. A strategy is broader, more encompassing, and more general than a heuristic. A particular online search may involve a single strategy but many heuristics, employed as necessary as the search develops.

Thus a search strategy may be thought of as an overall plan for achieving a goal, while heuristics are actions taken to meet limited *objectives*, either planned in advance or formulated as the search progresses, to help achieve that goal. The importance of a problem-solving, heuristic approach to online information retrieval has been stressed. One must also plan one's overall strategy as carefully as possible. This chapter addresses global strategies that might be taken toward the solution of a search problem, as well as specific heuristics to achieve more limited objectives [2].

Much of the terminology appearing in this chapter is originally due to Charles Bourne, Barbara Anderson, and Jo Robinson, including the phrases 'building blocks,' 'briefsearch,' 'most specific facet first,' 'lowest postings first,' 'citation pearl growing,' and 'successive fractions' [3]. Many of the ideas expressed in this chapter are probably due originally to the writings of F.W. Lancaster. Lancaster's books and other works are still among the richest sources discussing these topics [4].

The most simple and direct, as well as least expensive approach to an online search is the *briefsearch*. A briefsearch is a single search formulation—a Boolean combination of terms—put to a database, and intended to retrieve a few relevant (or pertinent) records. Only a few search terms are used in a briefsearch and there is little or no interaction between searcher and search system. A briefsearch is a fast, cheap way to get a very rough idea about what a database contains. We know that most concepts can be expressed using words and other symbols in many ways. Because no attempt is made in a briefsearch to find and employ all these, a briefsearch is usually a low recall formulation.

As a "fast batch" approach to online searching, the briefsearch should seldom be used as a model for a completed search, although sometimes it can be a reasonable approach. Example 7.1 describes such a set of circumstances.

Example 7.1[5]. A client wants to prepare a comprehensive bibliography on the psychological concept of "reflection-impulsivity."

> *Discussion.* As this concept is apparently not often referred to by any other terms, a simple briefsearch on the phrase 'reflection-impulsivity' will be not only be a high precision search but will probably also be a relatively high recall search. The search can be broadened by relaxing the requirement that the two terms be adjacent, or through truncation. Whichever of these formulations is used, the briefsearch will be fast and inexpensive, will probably not require the employment of many additional heuristics, and should achieve fairly high recall as well as precision.

A briefsearch might also be employed if a searcher wants to retrieve a few records treating a particular topic to examine the descriptors and other index terms assigned to documents by the database producer. Terms discovered in this way can be added to the original formulation to embellish it. The process can be repeated indefinitely, as needed. (This is essentially the *citation pearl growing* strategy, to be discussed more completely later in the chapter.)

A briefsearch can also be used to retrieve a record for a particular document known to be relevant to a search problem, for bibliographic verification or other purpose. By specifying a few known terms (specific words in

TABLE 7.1
Building Blocks Search Strategy

---

1. Conduct reference interview (question negotiation session)
2. Formulate search objectives: high recall, high precision, or moderate levels of recall and precision
3. Select database(s) and search system
4.* Identify major concepts or facets and their logical relationships with one another
5.* Identify (a) search strings that represent the concepts: words, full-text phrases, pieces of words, descriptors, identifiers, codes, non-semantic bibliographic characteristics and (b) fields to be searched
6.* For each distinct facet of the search, a set of postings will be created for each search string within that facet. The sets are then combined into a single set representing that facet using Boolean OR
7.* Following step #6, the facets sets themselves will be combined with Boolean AND and NOT
8. Plan alternatives
9. Formulate the initial statements of the search in the command language of the system
10. Logon and put the search to the system
11. Evaluate the intermediate results
12. Iterate: that is, use the interactive features of the system to carry out search *heuristics*— tactics, maneuvers, strategies, tricks, devices, approaches, to try to improve search results.

---

*Major components of building blocks approach.

the title, journal, author's last name, etc.) the document can be retrieved quickly and inexpensively.

The briefsearch can be taken as the framework for a full-fledged *building blocks* search. The building blocks strategy has informally and implicitly been used as a model in this book. It is, with its modifications, the most commonly used and useful overall approach to online searching.

The steps in the building blocks approach are listed in Table 7.1. The heart of the strategy is given in steps 4 through 7, and illustrated graphically in Figure 7.1. First, each important concept or facet of the search is identified. A *facet* is a group of concepts that, for a given search, will be considered to be equivalent by the searcher. There may be several facets in a search, but usually there are no more than three or four.

The next step is the selection of terms. In a complex search, dozens of terms may be selected to represent each facet. The terms (words, phrases, classification codes, etc.) within each facet are, for this search, regarded as equivalent by the searcher. For each of these terms a set of postings will be created and their union formed with the Boolean operator OR. This step and the heuristics that normally follow the initial formulations distinguish the building blocks strategy from the briefsearch.

Terms selected to represent a facet group may be synonyms, near synonyms, narrower terms in a hierarchy, or merely related, perhaps only obscurely. The important idea to remember behind the formation of a facet

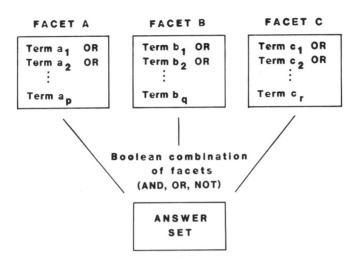

Figure 7.1   Building blocks approach.

is that the sets of postings associated with each term in the group will be combined using Boolean OR into one set. This set is often quite large. The OR operation having taken place, the origin of the postings associated with the individual terms is lost. Visualize all the postings being thrown together into a giant pot, henceforth to be treated equally; this is what is meant by "equivalent."

When the few large facets representing the main concepts of the search problem have been created, they are then combined using Boolean AND, OR, and NOT. The use of OR and NOT at this stage of a building blocks search is rare. Most often, the simple intersection of the main facets, using Boolean AND, is formed. Records associated with the resulting set of postings can then be examined for relevancy and formulations can be modified in various ways using search heuristics. Example 7.2 illustrates a building blocks search.

Example 7.2   A faculty member is preparing a bibliography on the relationship between technology, regulated market structures, and telecommunications. There are actually two related questions of interest: how technology affects markets in telecommunications fields and how regulation affects technological advances in telecommunications. Neither high precision nor high recall was requested by the client.

Discussion.   Three facets can be identified: the concepts of regulation, technology, and telecommunications. An initial building blocks solution to the search request is found by combining the three facets with

TABLE 7.2
Building Blocks Search for Relationships between Technology, Regulated Market Structures, and Telecommunications

Facet 1	Facet 2	Facet 3
REGULATION	TECHNOLOGY	TELECOMMUNICATIONS
FCC	technology	communication
regulation	technical impact	satellite
market structures	innovation	microwave
regulated industries	technological change	broadcasting
monopoly		telecommunication
		telephone
		specialized common carrier
		mobile radio
		land radio
		cellular radio
		telegraph
		television
		cable
		TV

Boolean Combination: REGULATION AND TECHNOLOGY AND COMMUNICATIONS

Boolean AND. Table 7.2 summarizes the facets and some of the terms that might be selected to represent them. Note that the concepts have not been expressed in the language of a controlled vocabulary. Nor have fields for searching been selected, nor such system-specific decisions as truncation and the use of word proximity devices been used. Table 7.2 represents the conceptualization of the major facets as concept groups, and does not attempt to translate these facets into particular search formulations.

Combining the three facets with Boolean AND requires the retrieved records to contain at least one term from each of the three lists. This has led the building blocks approach to be called the "Chinese menu" approach to information retrieval.

Recall and precision can be affected by manipulating the facets and the search strings comprising them. The following actions might be taken with the composition of the search facets of Exercise 7.2:

TO INCREASE RECALL:
—find additional concepts or search terms to add to one or more facets
—delete a facet, e.g., the *technology* facet. The new formulation would retrieve records having anything to do with the concepts of regulation and telecommunications.

TABLE 7.3
Building Blocks Search for Juvenile Sex Offenders

Facet 1	Facet 2
JUVENILES	SEX CRIMES
juveniles	sex crimes
adolescents	sex delinquency
teenagers	sex offenses
youths	
Boolean combination: JUVENILES AND SEX CRIMES	

TO INCREASE PRECISION:

—delete some of the more broader or more ambiguous terms in the facets, e.g., 'technology,' 'innovation' or 'communication.'
—add an additional facet to be intersected with the others

Many other system devices (as opposed to conceptual approaches) for increasing recall and precision were also discussed in earlier chapters, particularly those dealing with languages, search fields, and file structures. Obviously these also should be considered as possible heuristics for achieving search objectives. A fuller discussion of search heuristics for increasing recall or precision is provided later in this chapter.

Recall that the problem of *false drops* can occur when two facets are combined with Boolean AND but when the concepts represented do not appear in the relationship wanted. This is illustrated in Example 7.3.

Example 7.3. A client wants a bibliography on juvenile sex offenders. The client is *not* interested in children as the objects of sex offenses, as in forms of child abuse.

Discussion. The search is composed of two facets: juveniles and sex offenses. Terms representing each of the facets are given in Table 7.3. As in the previous example, there has been no attempt to supply all possible search terms that might be found useful, or to specify particular fields for searching.

Unfortunately, there is in general no way to specify the relationship wanted between the two concepts, that is, juveniles as offenders rather than victims. When this search was carried out, more than 70% of the records retrieved in some databases were false drops. This example illustrates a potential strength of controlled vocabularies. If there existed in a given database a descriptor that *pre-coordinated* the two concepts

TABLE 7.4
Building Blocks Search for Measurement of Risk Tendencies

Facet 1	Facet 2	Facet 3	Facet 4	Facet 5
RISK	MEASUREMENT	RISK AVERSION	BEHAVIORAL DECISION THEORY	INSURANCE
risk	measurement	risk aversion	behavioral	insurance
	assessment	risk avoidance	decision	contract
	choice	risk neutrality	theory	bank
	decision	risk prone		finance
	outcome	risk tendency		stock
				investment
				advertisement

Boolean Combination: ((RISK AND MEASUREMENT) OR RISK AVERSION OR BEHAVIORAL DECISION THEORY) NOT INSURANCE

in the relationship wanted, such as in the phrase 'juvenile sex offenders,' then that descriptor alone could be used, perhaps as the only search term in a briefsearch. In this way a single descriptor might replace two concept groups. Not only would such a search be much cheaper to conduct, it would probably result in higher precision as well.

If high recall is a goal of a search, then it might be decided to create two facets and find their intersection even if appropriate pre-coordinated terms exist. Example 7.4 illustrates this approach.

Example 7.4 Client wants a high recall search for articles dealing with the measurement of risk tendencies.

Discussion. There are some useful terms that are used in the business and psychological literature: 'risk aversion,' 'risk avoidance,' and others (see Table 7.4). However, since a high recall search was wanted, the searcher decided to create additional broad concepts for RISK and MEASUREMENT and to form their intersection. This leads to other problems, however, since the word 'risk' is used in many other senses, especially in the business literature. It might have reference to investments, insurance, banking, etc. (see Table 7.4). Therefore in this example a fifth facet was created to remove the unwanted records using Boolean NOT. It has been noted that one should be cautious when using Boolean NOT because of the danger of eliminating many citations that might be useful. However, in this example the potential rewards of this approach were felt to be worth the risks.

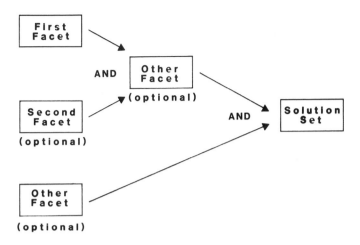

Figure 7.2   Successive facet approaches (adapted from Meadow and Cochrane, p. 137).

7.2 SUCCESSIVE FACET STRATEGIES

A heuristic suggested earlier for increasing the recall of a search was to delete an entire facet. Clearly this is wasteful if the concept group is created, using the building blocks approach, but in the end is not used.

If there is reason to suppose that the intersection of all important facets will retrieve few or no records or if one or more facet of the search problem is relatively ambiguous in meaning, then a modification of the building blocks strategy should be considered. There are two *successive facet* strategies that have been suggested in the literature: the 'most specific concept first,' and the 'fewest postings first.' The 'successive fractions' strategy is closely related to these. All three of the approaches begin with a high recall formulation and move to reduce the retrieval set to a manageable size. They differ only slightly, in the method used to select the initial set of postings.

Figure 7.2 illustrates the successive facet strategies. The basic idea behind these approaches is that facets be constructed one at a time, successively and as needed, rather than all at once. At each step a new facet is constructed and intersected with the previous result. The search stops when the desired recall and precision goals have been met, usually before all facets comprising the search problem have been constructed. Example 7.5 illustrates the approach.

Example 7.5 A search is wanted on the topic of 'members and activities of 4-H clubs' [6]. The topic has three facets: "members," "activities," and "4-H clubs."

Discussion. On the face of it, a reasonable Boolean combination of facets for this search is: 4-H CLUBS AND (MEMBERS OR ACTIVITIES). However, there are several reasons for taking a different approach.

First, the "activities" facet of the search is fuzzy and difficult to represent. Almost anything done by club members can qualify as an "activity," ranging from cockroach racing to picnicking to raising chickens to baking biscuits. Moreover, the first facet, "4-H clubs" is highly specific and is unlikely to have many postings in any database. (At least this seems reasonable as an initial hypothesis.) Third, every facet intersected in a search formulation *requires* that a term from that facet be present in the record. To add a "members" or an "activities" facet to the search will require that a term from that facet be present in the record, a stringent requirement given the fuzziness and breadth of the concept. It is probable that many relevant records will not include the word 'activity' or one of its synonyms, but will instead include the name of one of hundreds of possible activities.

Finally, one can argue that an article about 4-H clubs is likely to be discussing members or activities. Although there are other aspects of 4-H that might be treated in such an article, members or activities are likely to be addressed at least peripherally even in an article focusing on another subject, such as modes of organization. In short, it is hard to imagine an article discussing 4-H clubs that *does not* say something about activities or members.

A recommended first approach for this problem, then, is to search on the single concept of 4-H clubs and assess the output. If the output from this formulation contains a reasonable proportion of pertinent documents and is a manageable size, the searcher should print the results and stop! (Of course, the definition of "manageable" and "reasonable" is largely up to the client.) If the output is too great or the precision achieved is unacceptable, the search will be continued. A topic for which a similar argument can be made is discussed in the next example.

Example 7.6 A client wants a comprehensive bibliography of research on the emotional, physical, and intellectual characteristics of children who have studied violin with the Suzuki method.

Discussion. The literature on this subject is likely to be small, and there are many characteristics of interest, expressible in a variety of ways. Therefore, a reasonable first approach would be to employ successive facets and retrieve and evaluate *everything* that discusses the Suzuki method for studying violin, in a database like ERIC. If too many records are retrieved, additional facets can be added. If not, all retrieved citations can be printed. False drops are likely to occur. Even so, the client may prefer to suffer a few false drops to losing many records by over-specifying. In addition, the cost in connect time of creating additional facets may exceed the cost of printing the entire, more general, bibliography. Finally, in a subject with a small literature, a client often will consider it useful to retrieve peripheral items, which sometimes have buried nuggets of pertinent information that would not be discernible in a search of the bibliographic record.

The rules "lowest postings first" and "most specific concept first" suggest a rule for selecting the facet that will be created first in a successive facet search strategy. Usually, but not always, the most specific concept *is* the facet with the lowest number of postings. If these happen to be different facets, we would recommend forming the most specific concept first, so that the initial set of postings is as semantically well-defined as possible.

The *successive fractions* approach also begins by forming an initial set of postings and reducing its size, step by step, as necessary. As described by Meadow and Cochrane, the essential difference between this approach and the strategies just described seems to be that the initial set is often not a concept group, but is a non-semantic characteristic such as document type, language, and year of publication [7]. Except for this, the successive fractions approach is similar to the other successive facet approaches discussed. All three strategies begin with a set of postings promising high recall and proceed to reduce the size of this set by ANDing additional concepts or by otherwise limiting it. Hawkins and Wagers recommend using the successive fractions approach when the "search topic is fuzzy or broad or when a series of useful but not essential restrictions are possible" [8]. Example 7.7 illustrates this strategy.

Example 7.7. Client wants a high recall search for journal articles published during the past five years treating cost models for public services in libraries.

> *Discussion.* There are three facets to the search: libraries, public services, and cost models. Because of the semantic fuzziness of the latter two concepts, a successive fractions strategy is a useful approach.
>
> First, a "cost" concept can be formed, using such terms as 'cost models,' 'cost analysis,' 'cost measurement,' and others. This facets can then be limited by successively restricting to year of publication (the past five years only) and document type (journal articles only). Finally, the library facet can be added, by searching on the truncated stem 'librar.' The idea of "public services" can be ignored initially, for fear of overspecification.

When this search was conducted on ERIC and ABI/Inform, estimated recall and precision ratios of approximately 80% and 50%, respectively, were achieved, *without* needing to create the public services facet.

There are several less well known strategies using facets or concept groups as a basic model, including the multiple briefsearch, pairwise facets, citation pearl growing, interactive scanning, and implied facets. These are discussed next.

7.3   OTHER FACET STRATEGIES

Successive facet strategies are employed when there is reason to suspect that intersecting all facets of the search problem is likely to produce the null set, because of overspecification. They are especially useful if one or more facet is conceptually fuzzy. In such cases, it may be possible to achieve satisfactory results by ignoring the ambiguous facet. If a danger of overspecification exists but all facets to be intersected are relatively well-defined, another strategy may be even more useful than successive facet approaches. It is called the *pairwise facets* strategy.

Pairwise Facets

Pairwise facets is illustrated in Figures 7.3 and 7.4. The basic premise is simple: if all (usually three) facets of the search problem are roughly equivalent in their precision or specificity of definition, and also in their importance to the information problem, consider taking the intersection of the facets a pair at a time. The resulting three bibliographies can either be printed separately or their union can be created, producing a single list. Example 7.8 illustrates pairwise facets.

Example 7.8. A doctoral student wants a high recall bibliography prepared on the relationship between facial musculature and the physiological (autonomic) responding of emotions, e.g., fear.

Discussion. There are three well-defined facets to the search problem: facial musculature, physiological responding, and emotions. Each of the three facets has a sizable literature associated with it. The client was not aware of any studies that related all three concepts, so expectations were that the result of creating the intersection of the three facets would be the empty set (or at least, a very small number of postings). Initial planning might therefore be for a pairwise facets approach, with each intersection to be further limited if necessary by language, year of publication,

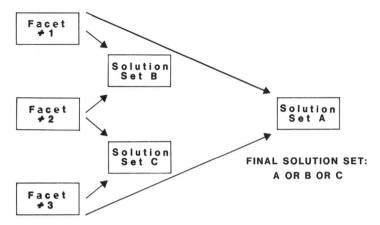

Figure 7.3   Pairwise facets strategy.

human (vs. animal) subjects, and document type. The possibility of needing to further limit the search by moving to a more specific level in one or more facets, reflecting the probable direction of the client's specific research, was also recognized. For example, "facial musculature" might need to become the more narrow "facial expression" and "emotions" become "fear."

When this search was conducted on Medline and PSYCINFO, a total of 130 citations were retrieved from the several intersections created, of which approximately 50 were of direct interest to the client's research problem.

The pairwise facets approach can be generalized to search problems with more than three facets. It may be suitable to use, for example, in a search

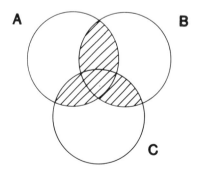

Figure 7.4   Venn diagram for pairwise facets strategy: (A AND B) OR (A AND C) OR (B AND C)

with four facets, where facets are taken in pairs or triplets in most or all combinations.

Multiple Briefsearch

Another approach that can sometimes can be useful is called the *multiple briefsearch*. Like the pairwise facets approach, the multiple briefsearch is occasioned by a high probability of a null set result when the intersection of all the facets of the specific search problem is created. The basic idea of the multiple briefsearch is to conduct a high recall briefsearch on as many databases as can be afforded. Usually, such a search will provide useful background material even if it provides little or no material relating to the specific search problem. The next example illustrates the approach.

Example 7.9. The client wants a comprehensive search of material discussing Carl Sandburg's journalistic style. Client reported being fairly familiar with the literature on Sandburg, and doubted that there is much if anything written on the subject.

> *Discussion.* There are two facets to the search: the poet Carl Sandburg and journalism. A building blocks approach to the search would express the concepts in as many ways as possible, create sets representing the two facets, and find their intersection. However, the client believed that little or no material existed, and a cursory search of selected printed indexes seemed to confirm this.
>
> The overall strategy selected was to search as many databases as possible for the concept of Carl Sandburg. If the resulting set in any database was too large, a journalism facet would be created and the intersection formed. Otherwise, all citations retrieved would be printed.
>
> This approach has much to recommend it. First, many databases can be searched, since the approach used in each database is a briefsearch, taking little connect time. Second, the client can use material retrieved as background material. Third, material of interest is likely to be peripherally treated in papers in which the central focus is another aspect of Sandburg's work. The only way to find such references is, presumably, to at least skim *all* papers discussing Sandburg, looking for pertinent comments relating to his work as a journalist. Finally, although there will be many false drops with this approach (in fact, every record retrieved may fall into this category), if there are pertinent records, the strategy will retrieve them. It is important to note that any strategy combining a journalism facet with the Sandburg facet takes the risk of missing a pertinent record if the terminology in the record does not coincide with that used in the journalism facet, i.e., words like 'journalism,' 'newspaper,' and 'reporter.'

The search was conducted in ten databases and retrieved about 150 records. Only one was likely to be directly on the problem requested. Client was, however, very pleased with the output, as it appeared to confirm his belief (and hope) that no work had been done. Also, it provided him with much useful background material on Sandburg.

Ideally, the multiple briefsearch strategy would be conducted by searching more than one database simultaneously. While no search system software except Wilsonline currently permits the simultaneous searching of several databases, this will surely be a future development to anticipate.

Citation Pearl Growing

All the strategies discussed so far have proceeded from an initial *high recall* formulation and moved toward increasing the precision of the search. Citation pearl growing moves in the opposite direction. It begins with a high precision formulation (100% precision) and moves toward increasing the recall of the search.

Citation pearl growing begins with a few documents known to be relevant (or pertinent) to the information need. Ideally, bibliographic information for such articles can be provided by the client. The records can then be quickly retrieved by a briefsearch based on the author, journal, words used in the title of the article, etc. Alternatively, a briefsearch based on the subject of the search problem can be constructed and a few records identified that appear to be on target. These can then be treated as known relevant documents.

The basic idea behind citation pearl growing is that descriptors, identifiers, and words from natural language fields are selected from documents *known to be relevant* (or, if provided by the client, pertinent) to the search problem. Terms are selected from these documents (the *pearl*) and are used to build facets in such a way that the known relevant documents will be retrieved, in addition to many others. A sample of retrieved titles is then printed in a short format and new relevant documents are then identified. The index terms associated with these documents are then examined and new search terms are added to each facet. The procedure can be cycled as many times as desired.

To facilitate the thinking process, logging off from the search system after each iteration is recommended (but the searcher should be certain that sets of postings already created will not be erased in the meantime). In each iteration, retrieved records are examined for relevancy and additional terms are selected from index records judged to be relevant. These terms are added to existing facets with Boolean OR. In this way the new formulation retrieves not only the documents already known to exist, but many others. Just as a pearl builds on itself, layer by layer, the search may proceed through several iterations, producing a larger retrieval set (and higher recall) at each stage. When the desired level of recall is reached or when no new terms can be found, the search is terminated.

Citation pearl growing is most useful if adequate database documentation such as word lists and thesauri are not available, or if a topic is so new that terminology has not become well established. Because of its iterative, interactive nature, citation pearl growing is more difficult than other approaches for novice searchers and is recommended for beginners only as a last resort. For best results, the client should be present during a citation pearl growing search.

Interactive Scanning

Suggested by Donald Hawkins and Robert Wagers [9], the *interactive scanning* strategy is perhaps the most time-consuming and iterative of all the approaches discussed. Like most of the other strategies discussed, it begins with a high recall formulation. The initial object is, using terms, classification codes, natural language, etc., to define a broad concept that should retrieve the bulk of the literature on the search problem. This initial set might contain several hundred citations. The idea is to print and study a sample of these records to obtain a clear picture of the literature of the field, including principal authors, methodologies, and related research. Then,

> Using this wealth of subject information, alternative strategies are formulated and entered, more citations are printed and compared to those retrieved earlier to determine how well the search has covered the range of topics first identified. One then continues to alter the search, adding synonyms and excluding less valuable terms, until the result is reached [10].

Hawkins and Wagers recommend the interactive scanning approach as being especially useful when high recall is a goal. More than any other of the strategies introduced, interactive scanning requires heavy interaction between searcher and system. It is also the most time-consuming and expensive approach. Finally, it probably requires the most collegial relationship between searcher and client, as well as the most creative work by the searcher. Because of these characteristics, interactive scanning is not a recommended approach for the novice searcher.

Implied Concepts [11]

As was observed in Chapter 4, many databases are characterized by an implicit focus in addition to an overall subject content. Thus fresh water shrimp are treated mainly from a biological point of view in BIOSIS, from an economic point of view in TRADE OPPORTUNITIES, and from the perspectives of ecology, possible health hazards, law, and food production in ENVIROLINE, MEDLINE, LEXIS, and FOOD SCIENCE AND TECH-NOLOGY ABSTRACTS, respectively.

Searching in ENVIROLINE *already* suggests (implicitly) a focus on environmental issues; hence creating a search facet for this concept is redundant. But worse, creating an environmental facet in this database is also likely to eliminate many useful items, since an environmental descriptor may not have been selected by indexers precisely because of the redundancy. If a focus is implicit to a given database, the searcher should consider *not* forming a search facet to represent this focus.

Example 7.10. Find articles discussing possible health hazards from foods cooked using microwave ovens.

Discussion. Searched in a general database such as Magazine Index, there would be three facets to this search: food and cooking, microwave ovens, and health hazards or dangers. But searched in Food Science and Technology Abstracts, which has a focus on food, dropping the food and cooking facet will produce the best results. However, a search conducted in MEDLINE for this problem could be carried out effectively without the "health hazards" facet, but including a facet on "food and cooking."

A final set of useful strategies involves the use of citation indexing. The next section introduces these approaches.

7.4   CITATION INDEXING STRATEGIES

Citation indexing was discussed in Chapter 2. Based on the assumption that the act of citing a work signifies that a semantic relationship exists between the cited and citing works, citation indexes offer powerful new strategies for online information retrieval. Semantic problems arising from the difficulty in expressing concepts by vocabulary elements do not exist with citation indexes, since the approach is through cited references rather than words and phrases. Citation strategies also offer highly interdisciplinary and multidisciplinary approaches to online searching, approaches that are independent of one's choice of database.

The Institute for Scientific Information (ISI) publishes three citation indexes that are available for online information retrieval: *Science Citation Index, Arts and Humanities Citation Index,* and *Social Science Citation Index.* In machine-readable form, these are known as SCISEARCH, ARTS & HUMANITIES SEARCH, and SOCIAL SCISEARCH, respectively. Their online use is described at length in reference [12]. There are three citation strategies for online information retrieval that will be briefly introduced here: cited publication, cited author, and cocited authors.

Cited Publication

The simplest strategy for using a citation approach to online searching is first to identify a work known to be highly pertinent to the information need, and likely to be cited by others. Seminal, or "classic" papers in a narrow field work especially well. The searcher then simply retrieves all documents (published in journals indexed by ISI) that have cited this work.

Example 7.11. Client wants to pursue the idea of *relevance* in the information science literature.

> *Discussion.* There is no doubt that 'relevance' is a fuzzy concept in information science. In ERIC, a database indexing the library and information science literature, the term is used in several ways (see also the *Thesaurus of ERIC Descriptors*). However, as a supplement or even a replacement for an ERIC search one might conduct a citation search on Saracevic's classic 1975 review paper [13], as well as examining his bibliography. In this way an entry point into the literature is provided, both pre- and post-1975 (the publication date of Saracevic's paper).

If DIALOG is searched for papers citing Saracevic's paper, the formulation would be:

SELECT CR = SARACEVIC T, 1975, V26, P321

This formulation retrieves all documents appearing in journals covered by Social Scisearch citing the Saracevic paper. When the formulation was put to the SOCIAL SCISEARCH database on DIALOG, 28 records were retrieved.

The cited reference field is parsed by DIALOG as a single character string, or phrase. If an error was made by the author of a paper in the spelling of the cited author's last name, first or second initial, year of publication, volume number, or starting page number of the article, or if a clerical error were made by ISI in keying one of these data, the citation will appear out of place, and will not be retrieved by the above formulation. This is a disadvantage, albeit probably not a serious one, of citation indexing approaches to online searching.

Cited Author

On search systems that parse the cited reference field as a long character string (phrase-indexed field), one can easily conduct a search for all works citing a given author, using truncation. On DIALOG, for example, the formulation would be:

SELECT CR = SARACEVIC T?

Unfortunately, if the last name plus the first initial (or if used, first and second initials) of the cited author is a combination belonging to other cited authors, these will be retrieved by the formulation as well. There are no easy solutions to this problem. One should be wary of false drops produced by this strategy, and should use it only when the possibility of false drops is considered to be minimal. Another problem with this formulation is that all cited Saracevic papers are retrieved, regardless of their subject. Particularly in the softer sciences and social sciences, areas of specialization and interest for researchers and writers frequently shift. In such a case this formulation may not be what is wanted.

One must also be very careful when searching on phrase-indexed fields. Since such fields are parsed as a single long character string, each comma and space must be entered exactly, following the syntax required by the search system. If a comma or space is inadvertently omitted or inserted, the search will result in zero postings. As with other phrase-indexed fields, one should probably view the postings file online to verify that the syntax is correct before creating retrieval sets.

Since the search system parses the cited reference as a phrase, one can truncate at any point in the string. On DIALOG

SELECT CR = SARACEVIC T, 1975?

retrieves all papers citing 1975 publications by T. Saracevic, again, of course, with the same caveats mentioned above.

Cocited Authors

An approach that solves virtually all the problems of cited author searches is the *cocitation* search strategy. Cocited author searches are performed by searching on *two* cited authors and finding the intersection of the two sets. Even if the last names are common, the probability that two authors with the same last names are working in the same narrow field is exceedingly small. The following DIALOG formulation is intended to retrieve all papers citing *both* Tefko Saracevic and Don R. Swanson:

SELECT CR = SARACEVIC T? AND CR = SWANSON D?

Clearly there will be few false drops from this formulation, since the probability is very small that more than one T. Saracevic and D. Swanson are working in the same field, regardless of what this field may be. The results of putting this formulation to DIALOG is given in Figure 7.5. Seventeen records were retrieved that cited both authors.

It has been found in experiments that the cocitation strategy retrieves a significant number of documents not found in a subject search conducted on the same search problem [14], and that it can effectively divide a literature into subliteratures [15]. The cocitation strategy is usefully extended by Knapp to cases in which three or more authors are known and the searcher wants to retrieve all papers citing any two of these authors, among other useful elaborations of the basic model [16].

Cited reference search strategies are approaches toward conducting *subject* searches, without the semantic problems attending the representation of concepts by words and phrases. They can be extremely valuable supplements to vocabulary approaches to online information retrieval and may even function very effectively as the primary or even the sole retrieval strategy.

7.5 NON-SUBJECT, FACT, AND MULTIPLE DATABASE SEARCHING

In addition to the classes of bibliographic search problems discussed in previous sections of the chapter, three additional types of search problems arise with sufficient frequency to deserve introduction. They are

1. Non-subject searching—in which sets of postings are created representing non-semantic characteristics of documents
2. Fact searching—in which bibliographic databases are searched, not to create a bibliography of references, but to discover a fact
3. Multiple database searching—in which a search is constructed so that it can be executed on more than one database.

Non-Subject Searching

Frequently an information seeker wishes to have non-semantic criteria applied to a retrieval set, so that only documents meeting the criteria are included, and all documents not meeting the criteria are excluded. There are many fields in bibliographic databases that do not report information related to the *subjects* of documents (see, for example, the summary of the ERIC database listed in Chapter 3). Among the most commonly searched of these fields are:

```
? ss cr=saracevic t? and cr=swanson d?
        10    180  CR=SARACEVIC T?
        11    456  CR=SWANSON D?
        12     17  10 AND 11
? t 12/6/1-17
12/6/1
1674466  ARTICLE  OATS ORDER#: RG559  15 REFS
  FAILURE IN THE LIBRARY - A CASE-STUDY  (EN)


12/6/2
1664400  REV OR BIB  OATS ORDER#: RC863  187 REFS
  EDUCATION FOR LIBRARIANSHIP AND INFORMATION-SCIENCE - A
RETROSPECT AND A REVALUATION  (EN)


12/6/3
1166075  ARTICLE  OATS ORDER#: LL229  32 REFS
  INFORMATION-SEEKING  BEHAVIOR  OF  CATALOG  USERS  IN  THE
LIBRARY  OF  INTERNATIONAL-CHRISTIAN-UNIVERSITY  -  A  STUDY  OF
THE  CATALOG  USE  BY  INTERVIEW  (JA)


12/6/4
1092968  ARTICLE  OATS ORDER#: JX119  18 REFS
  PERFORMANCE  TESTING  OF A BOOK AND ITS INDEX AS AN INFORMATION-
RETRIEVAL SYSTEM  (EN)


12/6/5
1024354  REV OR BIB  OATS ORDER#: JT807  256 REFS
  SYSTEM-DESIGN - PRINCIPLES AND TECHNIQUES  (EN)


12/6/6
997747  ARTICLE  OATS ORDER#: HU938  42 REFS
  ESSENTIALS  OR  DESIDERATA  OF  THE  BIBLIOGRAPHIC RECORD AS
DISCOVERED BY RESEARCH  (EN)


12/6/7
969503  ARTICLE  OATS ORDER#: HJ012  13 REFS
  RELEVANCE  (EN)


12/6/8
913825  ARTICLE  OATS ORDER#: GM172  43 REFS
  WRONG WAY TO GO  (EN)


12/6/9
763627  ARTICLE  OATS ORDER#: DQ612  54 REFS
  CONTEMPORARY ISSUES IN BIBLIOGRAPHIC-CONTROL  (EN)


12/6/10
736709  ARTICLE  OATS ORDER#: DG238  61 REFS
  MR DEWEYS CLASSIFICATION, MR CUTTERS CATALOG,  AND DR HITCHCOCKS
CHICKENS (EN)


12/6/11
727748  ARTICLE  OATS ORDER#: DC890  18 REFS
  INFORMATION-RETRIEVAL AS A TRIAL-AND-ERROR PROCESS  (EN)


12/6/12
684976  ARTICLE  OATS ORDER#: CH552  24 REFS
  IMMATERIALITY OF INFORMATION  (EN)


12/6/13
651654  ARTICLE  OATS ORDER#: BX202  14 REFS
  LIBRARY  AS AN INFORMATION UTILITY IN UNIVERSITY CONTEXT -
EVOLUTION AND MEASUREMENT OF SERVICE  (EN)


12/6/14
582089  REV OR BIB  OATS ORDER#: AZ129  133 REFS
  LIBRARY-AUTOMATION  (EN)


12/6/15
354359  ARTICLE  OATS ORDER#: R2946  111 REFS
  DOCUMENT DESCRIPTION AND REPRESENTATION  (EN)


12/6/16
224662  ARTICLE  OATS ORDER#: O0298  271 REFS
  DOCUMENT RETRIEVAL AND DISSEMINATION SYSTEMS  (EN)


12/6/17
074325  ARTICLE  OATS ORDER#: GC388  78 REFS
  10 YEARS PROGRESS IN QUANTITATIVE RESEARCH ON LIBRARIES  (EN)
```

Figure 7.5   Cocitation search on DIALOG. Search performed via the DIALOG* Information Retrieval Services, Inc. (*Servicemark Reg. U.S. Patent and Trademark Office). Search performed on Social SCISEARCH® (File 7). Copied with the permission of the Institute for Scientific Information © 1985.

* *document type*. What type of documents are wanted? Journal articles? Bibliographies? Speeches or conference papers? Technical reports?
* *year of publication*. When were the documents published?
* *language*. In what language was the document published?
* *author*. Who wrote the document?
* *corporate source*. With what organization is the author affiliated?

There are several reasons for wanting to employ a non-subject approach to a search. First, the search may be a *fact* search, in which such information as author or corporate source are characteristics of the fact to be retrieved. This class of searches is examined later.

Second, a non-subject search may be conducted to *disambiguate*, or make unambiguous, certain other semantic or non-semantic information. For example, if an author has a commonly occurring name, producing potential ambiguity, it can be disambiguated by creating a set of postings for the corporate source associated with the author, and intersecting it with the author set. Some words are homographs across languages, such as 'carbon,' which means coal in Spanish. In a large, multilanguage database such words can be disambiguated by specifying a language or by using NOT so that documents written in the language in question are not retrieved.

A final example of disambiguation again comes from the information science concept of relevance. This word has been used in other senses in many databases, e.g., ERIC. Thus searching for 'relevance' in natural language fields in ERIC can be expected to retrieve many false drops. One way to disambiguate the various meanings of 'relevance' in ERIC is to search on the origin of the documents in question. Documents entering the ERIC system from the Clearinghouse on Information Resources (see Chapter 3) can be assumed to be about relevance in the information science sense; documents coming from one of the other fifteen ERIC Clearinghouses can be assumed to be about another kind of relevance. Again, false drops and missed relevant documents are possible with this approach, but in general it should work well. Exceptions would occur with highly interdisciplinary problem areas.

A third reason to conduct a non-subject search is that a non-subject field may serve to uniquely identify a document. Accession numbers, grant or contract numbers, ISSN, or ISBN are examples of such fields. If known, such information can be used to retrieve a given document and no others.

Finally, a non-subject search is often conducted to reduce the output of a subject search by eliminating less desirable documents. If a solution set meets desired recall and precision goals but is too expensive (that is, contains too many postings) to print in full, additional conditions such as language, document type, and year of publication can be imposed on the output. Figure 7.6 illustrates an interesting elaboration of this approach [17]. The approach, called *doublelimiting*, involves limiting search output twice.

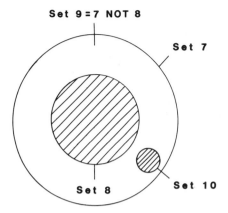

Figure 7.6 Doublelimiting.

In Figure 7.6, set 7 is a large set of postings that meets recall and precision criteria but is considered too expensive to print in full. Set 7 is moderately limited (for example, by limiting by publication date or language) to produce set 8 , and set 8 is printed in full. Now set 9 = 7 NOT 8 is created using Boolean NOT. Set 9 is then severely limited (for example, by restricting retrieved documents to bibliographies and literature reviews) to produce set 10. Set 10 is printed in full. In some databases, the accession numbers associated with documents can be used with the hard copy version of the database to permit the information seeker to examine retrieved records offline. Since accession numbers can usually be printed very inexpensively, set 9 can be printed in this format. Note that this last action will *not* be useful in a database in which accession numbers cannot be used to locate records in printed indexes.

Hence the client has three output sets. Set 8 consists of records meeting certain language, publication date, or other criteria, and printed in an ordinary bibliographic format. Set 10 consists of documents of more than usual value, meeting stringent conditions such as themselves being bibliographies. This set is also printed in an ordinary bibliographic format. Finally, set 9, consisting of the remaining records, are generally of lesser value but are still potentially useful. In some databases, these records can be printed in an inexpensive format, to be examined in depth later in a hard copy version of the database.

There are many different approaches to non-subject searching, varying widely from database to database. The reader is urged to become familiar with these fields and approaches. There are many creative ways to employ non-subject fields in traditional subject searching, but these depend heavily on the database employed.

Fact Searching

Fact searching can be conducted on databases specifically designed for this purpose, or on full text databases (see Chapter 8). However, fact searching can also be conducted on bibliographic databases. A simple example of a fact search on a bibliographic database is for the verification of the information in a bibliographic citation. Such a search is for a *known item*. The concepts of recall and precision are not particularly helpful in such a search, because the searcher expects, and can usually obtain, both high recall and high precision. It would not be unusual for a bibliographic verification to retrieve one and only one record, the exact one that is wanted. Such a search would achieve perfect recall as well as precision.

A searcher's approach to fact searching in bibliographic (and full text) databases should be to always be as specific as possible. Generic terms should be avoided. Because of the subjectivity inherent in the indexing process, controlled vocabularies should also be avoided.

In general, the "most specific concept first" strategy should be employed for fact searching. The searcher should create simple facets based on reported factual information, beginning with the most specific term of which the information seeker is *certain*. Proper nouns can be especially useful search terms. Ordinarily, overspecification should not be a problem, unless some of the known 'facts" are not accurate. However, this is quite possible, even probable. A fact that is easy to remember incorrectly is the form of a word: adjective, adverb, singular or plural noun, etc. But other remembered characteristics of a wanted item can also be wrong: journal name, title, and even author.

Example 7.12. I am looking for a citation to a paper by a man named Maron, in which the meaning of "about" and its relationship to information storage and retrieval are discussed. The paper was published between 1975 and 1980 in one of the major journals in information science.

Discussion. This is a rather vague fact search, although it can be attacked effectively online. The suggested approach should follow approximately in the order discussed. The most specific term is the author's name, Maron. One solution that could be considered if the first name were known or if the last name were sufficiently unusual would be to simply type all publications by the named author, looking for the one wanted. Or, one could assume that the word "about" would be present in the title of the article wanted. In any system in which 'about' is not a stopword, this set could be created and intersected with author Maron. Or, the searcher might hypothesize that 'about' is likely to have been assigned to the desired article as an identifier. The concept of information storage and retrieval is probably too broad and general to be useful in this search, and should be avoided if possible. The date range probably should also be ignored, at least initially. The journal information may be too vague to be useful, although it does suggest a way to disambiguate 'about' in ERIC; that is, by searching for documents coming out of the ERIC Clearinghouse for Information Resources and intersecting this with the Maron set. Sets for major journals in information science could also be created if necessary. Finally, one might infer that the meaning of about has to do with the notion of relevance, and that the latter word is probably mentioned in the record. This suggests creating a set for relevance, and intersecting it with the set of Maron postings.

Searching Multiple Databases

Some search systems permit creating, saving, and storing a search formulation, thus permitting its execution in more than one database. Similar capabilities are possible if a microcomputer is used to create and send formulations to one or more databases carried by a search service (see Chapter 9). In either case, precautions must be taken to ensure that searches prepared for one database will work properly on others.

First, care must be taken with parsing rules used in the databases to be searched. Parsing rules that apply to a given field in one database may not apply to the same field in another. Syntax and spacing rules may also differ. This is especially true of nonsubject fields such as author and corporate source.

Controlled vocabularies will also differ from one database to another. A phrase such as 'inventory models' may be a descriptor in one database but not in a second. In such a case, a formulation to be applied to both databases should be constructed to work on either. For example, if the descriptor field is both word-indexed and phrase-indexed in a given database, then the use of proximity features is recommended. Such a formulation will work on any database in which the field is word-indexed. Conversely, if descriptors are searched as phrases (with embedded blanks), they will not retrieve from natural language fields not parsed as full phrases. This latter approach, then, should be avoided in multiple database searching. Truncation can also be useful to employ, to retrieve two different word forms in two databases.

Vocabulary can be a major problem as well. British and American spellings differ for many words, and if one database producer is British, the spelling of such words as catalog, sulfur, and labor will be likely to be different in two databases. Even the spelling of proper names may differ, resulting from such decisions as how to treat umlauted O's. Truncation can be used in such cases, as can the simple use of OR, as in the expression:

catalog OR catalogue

Putting this formulation to two different databases, one English and one American, is likely to result in (expected) empty sets for one term or the other, depending on the database searched. But since A OR {} = A, for all A, the union of the two sets will be exactly what is wanted.

Finally, the omnipresent homograph and synonym problems will probably be worse for multiple database searching than for a single database. 'Lift' has a different meaning in British and American English, and 'charmed' means something different in physics than it does in literature. The searcher will need to construct solutions for these problems or suffer the consequences of false drops and missed relevant documents.

Conducting the same search in several files simultaneously is not the panacea it may first seem to be. In many ways it multiplies the problems present in searching a single database. However, if care is taken to construct formulations, having the capability of storing a search for several databases or for future searches can save time and money.

This capability can be especially useful for concepts that arise frequently in searches. Such formulations have been called *hedges*. A hedge is a collection of terms connected with Boolean OR that cover a topic for which no single term in the controlled vocabulary has sufficient extension [18]. Many hedges have been published in the professional literature [19].

Throughout this book, the importance of a heuristic, problem-solving approach to online searching has been stressed. The final section of this chapter brings together many of the most important heuristics for online searching that have been suggested in this text.

7.6 HEURISTICS FOR ONLINE SEARCHING

Regardless of the search problem or the overall strategy that has been selected initially to solve it, the ongoing *process* of online searching is best regarded as a heuristic, problem-solving activity, analogous to scientific inquiry. As one proceeds through a search, conducting the question negotiation session, establishing an overall strategy, selecting vocabulary elements, constructing specific search formulations, printing and evaluating samples of retrieved citations, and formulating and testing alternative hypotheses, one needs a rational basis on which to proceed. Unfortunately, current research can offer us little guidance in directions that ought to be taken in particular retrieval situations. There are few rules of conduct that can be offered that will guarantee success. Thus online information retrieval should be regarded as interactive and heuristic rather than algorithmic.

TABLE 7.5
Interactive Searching: Questions to Ask If Intermediate Output is Low Recall (including zero postings)

* Am I in the correct database?
* Have I overspecified the search problem?
* Is there anything done on the topic or problem? That is, is there a literature on this search problem?
* Have sufficient search terms been included to properly represent each concept of the search?
* Were the proximity specifications placed on the search terms too restrictive?
* Was Boolean logic used correctly?
* Did I make a technical error, e.g., in spelling or command syntax?
* Should I be searching in natural language fields?
* Have all word forms of search terms been used? Should truncation be employed?

While hard and fast rules for "how to do" an online search cannot be provided, numerous hints, rules of thumb, tactics and tricks—heuristics—have been offered by experts in the art of online information retrieval. These have appeared throughout this book as cautiously offered bits of general advice. There have been several excellent publications that have considered aspects of the online searching process and recommended appropriate heuristics [20]. An initial compilation and classification of general heuristics for online searching has been compiled by Harter and Peters [21]. In the following discussion, some of the most important heuristics for online searching discussed in earlier chapters are brought together and discussed briefly.

Heuristics are employed when the searcher's initial objectives have not been met by search formulations. In such cases, the searcher should ask several questions regarding the current state of the search. Examples of these questions are listed in Table 7.5 and 7.6. Based on an evaluation of search output, conclusions regarding these questions can be drawn, or hypotheses regarding the truth formulated. Heuristics aimed at correcting the situation can then be employed.

Table 7.5 lists examples of questions that should be asked if the output being evaluated is characterized by low recall, that is, if only a few relevant documents from those that exist in the database are being retrieved. This includes a result of zero postings as an extreme case. There are many possible explanations of low recall. First, the searcher may be searching the wrong database, either because of a typing error or an error in judgment. Or, too many facets may have been intersected, resulting in overspecification of the search problem.

A common mistake for beginning searchers is to become concerned if little can be found on a search problem if in fact little has been published on the problem. Certainly one cannot find what is not there!

TABLE 7.6

Interactive Searching: Questions to Ask if Intermediate Output is Low Precision (a high percentage of false drops)

---

* Am I in the correct database?
* Have I underspecified the search problem?
* Do I need to disambiguate a concept of the problem?
* Have I used Boolean logic correctly?
* Have I included vague or ambiguous terms, or terms that are too generic?
* Should I restrict search terms to elements of a controlled vocabulary?
* Were the proximity specifications too loosely placed on the search terms?
* Are false drops resulting from concepts having an unintended relationship with one another?
* Has a search term been truncated too severely?

Choice of language and omissions of plausible search terms are among common explanations of low recall searches. Frequently, many terms and word forms are required to adequately represent a given concept, especially in natural language.

Proximity specifications may have been too stringent as well. Requiring that a certain phrase appear *as a phrase* when the concept may be represented in many other forms can result in many lost relevant documents. Also, Boolean logic used carelessly will disrupt a search in a major way. Using Boolean AND instead of OR will have devastating effects. Is the order of Boolean operations carried out as the searcher desires? Was there an error in typing a set number to be combined or displayed?

Technical errors are possible as well. Simple typographical errors, or errors in command syntax, spacing, punctuation such as parentheses or hyphens may have been made. Or was an inappropriate parsing rule applied to a field?

Quite a different problem is to experience an unacceptably large percentage of non-relevant records, that is, a low precision search. There are many possible explanations of this result. Table 7.6 lists some of the questions that ought to be asked if this result is obtained.

Underspecification of the search problem probably occurs less frequently than overspecification, but is a possible explanation. Or, false drops may be resulting from concepts having an unintended relationship with one another, as with confusion between cause and effect.

Again, Boolean logic may be used incorrectly. Using Boolean OR instead of AND will flood the searcher with irrelevant records. A misunderstanding of the order of operations defined by a search system can explain this result.

Finally, the problem may be one of vocabulary. A homograph may be retrieving many false drops and require disambiguation. Perhaps some search terms are too vague or too generic, or proximity specifications placed on the terms are too loose. Or, a term may have been truncated too severely.

An online searcher seeking to remedy problems of low precision or low recall should try to correct one problem at a time and observe the results by printing a sample of citations. Heuristics for attacking each of the problems listed in Tables 7.5 and 7.6 are discussed in the paragraphs that follow.

Language Heuristics

That computers match symbols and not the concepts represented by those symbols implies a host of heuristics dealing with languages for problem representation. Especially important are differences between natural languages and controlled vocabularies, as discussed in Chapter 2. Search systems compare character strings, ultimately reducible to binary digits. The searcher has the responsibility of representing concepts in all possible forms, if complete retrieval is expected. Thus a searcher should consider such language variations as classification codes, descriptors, natural language expressions, abbreviations, usage and spelling differences, synonyms and near synonyms, antonyms, differences between English and other languages represented in the database searched, and acronyms.

One must especially take utmost care to identify all possible ways of representing a concept if a natural language field such as title, abstract, or full text is the object of search. Natural languages are extraordinarily rich in the variety of ways ideas can be expressed, although this is less so with highly technical, 'hard' sciences or disciplines. Many points of view can be represented with natural languages, which can represent new and complex concepts with ease. This richness carries with it problems, however, including those of semantic ambiguity caused by homographs, false drops resulting from contextual ambiguity, and the lack of ability to perform generic searches.

Artificial vocabularies control for homographs, synonyms, and other problems of natural language, but they have their own special difficulties. While the terms used in controlled vocabularies are relatively unambiguous, they have limited, rigid, and inflexible vocabularies, syntax, and structures. It may be difficult or impossible to represent new or complex concepts. It has been argued that controlled vocabularies, especially classification systems, are not representative of reality and represent only a single point of view. Finally, in most if not all databases, the level of exhaustivity of indexing is such that usually not all concepts of potential interest have been indexed.

Based on these differences between controlled vocabularies and natural language as used in title, abstract, and full text fields, the following language heuristics are suggested (see also Chapter 2). One should especially consider searching natural language fields if any of the following conditions seem especially characteristic of the information need:

* One or more of the concepts of interest involves a subtle nuance of meaning

* One or more of the concepts of interest is highly specific
* One or more of the concepts of interest is relatively new and appropriate terms in the controlled vocabulary do not exist
* A highly comprehensive search is desired (high recall)
* The literature to be searched is "soft."

Conversely, one should especially consider searching controlled vocabulary fields if any of the following conditions seem especially important to the information need:

* The concepts of interest can be expressed precisely and unambiguously in the controlled vocabulary
* A limited search retrieving a limited number of highly pertinent items is desired
* The literature to be searched is "hard."

In practice, most online searchers probably use a combination of approaches for most searches.

Command Language, Database and File Structure Heuristics

Care must be taken with the command language used in the search process, to ensure that the vocabulary, syntax, and meaning of the commands issued will accomplish what is intended. The search system will do what a searcher has commanded it to do, which does not necessarily correspond with what is wanted or intended. Logical, spelling, or even syntax errors do not always result in system error messages. As noted in Chapter 2, sometimes such errors result in output that is correct in appearance but is quite erroneous. The heuristics "know the syntax and vocabulary of the command language" and "know the actions produced by system commands" may seem almost too obvious to mention, but failure to observe them can result in subtle errors that the search system cannot detect, and therefore, that the search specialist must detect.

Chapter 3 examined concepts and principles of database structure, organization, and search. These led directly to the identification of several additional heuristics important for effective and efficient searching:

* Know the stop words used by the search system.
* Know the sort order associated with the binary coding system used by the host computer.
* Know which fields are searched by default, if search fields are not explicitly specified.

* Know the parsing rule used to index each field searched.
* Always question null sets.
* Understand Boolean operations with the null set and make use of this knowledge in reformulating search statements

Recall and Precision Heuristics

An information retrieval search is conducted for a client, who typically can state recall or precision *goals*. A client who wants a few documents exactly on the topic wants a high precision search; a university doctoral student or faculty member preparing a full-fledged literature review usually wants a comprehensive search, producing high recall. We assume that the searcher's purpose is to satisfy the information need of the client. It follows that:

* The searcher should be aware of, and try to move toward the recall/precision goal stated by the client.

There may be cost constraints as well. The recall and precision heuristics that should be followed in an online, interactive search are simply those most likely to lead the searcher to the fulfillment of these goals.

It may be that one day we will know, under general conditions, theoretical rules for moving rationally through the infinity of possible search formulations—to travel what might be called a *most rational path* for moving toward the achievement of recall/precision goals for a given cost. But for the present, online searchers must rely on common sense, experience, and on heuristics passed on by experts. Some of the most important heuristics frequently recommended for increasing the recall of a search formulation are listed below.

Heuristics for Increasing Recall

* Use additional synonyms and near synonyms combined with Boolean OR to represent search concepts.
* Use more generic terms in addition to specific terms to represent search concepts.
* Use natural language in addition to controlled vocabulary terms.
* Search additional subject fields.
* Delete AND and NOT facets from the formulation.
* Increase term truncation.
* Use less restrictive proximity operators, e.g., require that terms appear in the same paragraph rather than the same sentence.

* Remove any restrictions from the formulation, e.g., language, date of publication, type of publication

Heuristics for Increasing Precision

* Delete near synonyms and potentially ambiguous terms
* Use more specific terms to represent concepts.
* Use controlled vocabulary terms if a concept is precisely represented by them; delete controlled vocabulary terms that do not describe a concept precisely
* If multiple meaning does not appear to be a major problem, search natural language terms that represent the concepts of interest precisely.
* If none of the above conditions applies, search fewer subject fields, deleting fields in the approximate order: full text, abstract, title, identifier, and descriptor
* Add additional facets with AND or NOT
* Decrease term truncation.
* Use more restrictive proximity operators.
* Add restrictions to the formulation, e.g., by date of publication, type of publication, language, etc.

These heuristics should be used with caution. For example, underlying the suggestion to "search fewer subject fields" to increase precision is the assumption that the fields dropped from the search formulation are those least likely to produce relevant citations, as in the following example.

Example 7.13. Suppose that the searchable fields in a database are descriptor, title, and abstract, and that an initial search of these fields has produced far too many false drops, in the judgment of the searcher. How can the precision of the search rationally be increased?

> *Discussion.* As suggested by the heuristics listed above, there may be many possibilities. One approach is to search fewer data fields. In general (but not always) the field in this example most likely to be producing the highest percentage of false drops is the natural language full text or abstract field. (This common-sense assertion could be tested empirically by printing and evaluating a sample of retrieved citations, if the searcher feels that the cost of so doing is justified.) Hence one might hypothesize that dropping the abstract field from the next iteration will tend to increase precision of the search, as well as decreasing recall.

Example 7.14. Suppose that one interprets the heuristic "to increase precision, search fewer data fields" as a license to drop the descriptor field instead of the abstract. But one would expect that in general (but not always) the descriptor field ought to be the field most likely to produce hits and least likely to produce false drops. It follows that dropping this field from the search formulation will be likely to decrease precision *and* recall, and therefore is not a desirable action to take, in spite of its ostensible agreement with the stated heuristic.

This example shows that the sometimes stated "law" that recall and precision are inversely related is false in special cases (if 'common sense" is not followed). Indeed, the relation is true theoretically only under certain highly restrictive conditions [22].

There are other heuristics for increasing recall and precision that have been suggested in the literature. Unfortunately, by its nature, a heuristic cannot be provided with a set of unalterable rules governing its use. Several commonly recommended heuristics for increasing precision have been listed. But in a given retrieval situation, how is one to choose between them? Which of these (or of several others that might be mentioned) offers the best chance of success? Does it actually matter?

There are no easy answers to these questions. At the current rudimentary stage of knowledge, due at least in part to the extreme difficulty of conducting research in this area, one is left to one's own intuition, problem solving abilities and personal knowledge base in the choice of appropriate heuristics. Of course, as was suggested in Chapter 5, if such intuitive judgments are treated by the searcher as tentative hypotheses, with data being gathered to test each, one's initial choice of heuristic is not crucial. After evaluation of system feedback, a heuristic can easily be discarded in favor of other possibilities. Taking this idea further, one can identify several *personal* heuristics that have been recommended for success as an online information retrieval specialist. These were discussed in detail in Chapter 5.

Personal Heuristics

*   Be flexible; stay loose; be willing to look at a search in more than one way. Avoid rigidity in thought and action.
*   Browse samples of retrieved citations to assess relevancy.
*   Browse samples of retrieved citations to generate additional search terms.
*   Be heuristic, interactive. Don't do "fast batch" searching.
*   Evaluate one's own work critically.
*   Always be skeptical of search output.
*   A mindless faith in controlled vocabularies is not always justified. Be critical of the adequacy of artificial languages for the representation of concepts in documents.

The beginning searcher needs to build confidence and knowledge slowly and methodically by applying principles and concepts of information retrieval, problem solving skills, and a healthy attitude toward self-evaluation to the conduct of real searches. In this way a set of useful personal heuristics will slowly evolve, and the *art* of online searching on a personal level can begin to be developed.

PROBLEMS

1. Example 7.3 illustrates the usefulness of pre-coordinating concepts in a controlled vocabulary so that coordinating the concepts at the time of the search is not necessary, and false drops can be avoided. Such a device might be called a *precision* device, because it tends to increase the precision of the output. What effect do you think it would have on recall? How would you test your hypothesis?

2. Consider the following Briefsearch:

   (iran or iraq) and fundamentalism and (moslem or islam)

   a. Discuss approaches that you would take to increase the precision of this search. Try to identify approaches that are most likely to produce the desired results.

   b. Discuss approaches that you would take to increase the recall of the original Briefsearch. Try to identify approaches that are most likely to produce the desired results.

3. Describe the rationale for choosing and techniques for implementing each of the following overall approaches to online information retrieval:

   a. building blocks   d. pairwise facets
   b. citation pearl growing   e. multiple briefsearch
   c. most specific concept first f. cited references

4. A patron wants a few citations discussing members of minority groups working as police. Select an appropriate database and design a high precision search.

5. Answer the following questions for the search system of your choice:

   a. Will the system save your sets of postings when you logoff in the middle of strategies like citation pearl growing or interactive scanning? What do you need to do to ensure that this takes place, if anything?

   b. Can citation indexes be searched? If so, answer the following questions:

      i. What is the *exact* format required for searching for references that have cited a particular published paper?

      ii. How is the cited reference field parsed?

      iii. Is it possible to examine the postings file for the cited reference field online? Can sets for cited references be created by selecting a set directly from a display of the postings file? How would you recommend searching for cited references in this search system?

      iv. Design a small study to check for errors in listings for cited references (that is, errors in year of publication, pagination, etc., that would in turn cause searching errors). What proportion of entries are in error?

      v. How severe is the problem of different authors having the same last name and first initial(s), for cited author searching? How would one go about investigating this?

      vi. Do the system search *features* favor the use of particular strategies discussed in this chapter? How? Are some search systems better than others for some strategies?

6. I remember reading a paper that I think was published in *Library Trends* some years ago, establishing a parallel between hunting a submarine and browsing on a library shelf. I think that the paper made use of a technique of operations research, but I am not sure which technique was used. Find the complete bibliographic citation for me.

7. Construct an online search to find a few examples of teaching guides for classes in popular culture.

8. A client wants an article that he thinks is entitled "Cognitive Models for Reconstructive Memory and Rote Learning," but he cannot find it in any relevant print tool. Outline a plan for trying to find the citation online, as efficiently as possible.

NOTES AND REFERENCES

1. Bates, Marcia, "Information Search Tactics." *Journal of the American Society for Information Science* 30 (July 1979) 205-214; Bates, Marcia, "Idea Tactics." *Journal of the American Society for Information Science* 30 (September 1979) 280-289.

2. An outstanding early article addressing strategies and tactics of general reference work is Alexander, Carter. "Technique of library searching." *Special Libraries* 27 (7) (September 1936) 230-238. See also Bates, "Information Search Tactics," and Bates, "Idea Tactics."

3. Meadow, Charles T. and Pauline Cochrane. *Basics of Online Searching* (New York: John Wiley & Sons, 1981). pp. 136-141.

4. Lancaster, F. Wilfrid. *Information Retrieval Systems: Characteristics, Testing, and Evaluation.* (New York: Wiley, 1968); Lancaster, F. Wilfrid. *Information Retrieval Systems: Characteristics, Testing, and Evaluation.* Second edition. (New York: Wiley, 1979); Lancaster, F.W. "MEDLARS: Report on its Operating Efficiency." *American Documentation* 20 (April 1969) 119-142; Lancaster, F.W. and J. Mills. "Testing Indexes and Index Language Devices: The ASLIB Cranfield Project." *American Documentation* 15 (Jan 1964) 4-13; Lancaster, F. Wilfrid. *Vocabulary control for information retrieval.* (Washington, D.C.: Information Resources Press, 1972).

5. Many of the examples in this chapter were real search problems studied by students in the author's class, Information Storage and Retrieval, offered by the School of Library and Information Science, Indiana University. The work done by these students toward the solution of these problems is gratefully acknowledged.

6. This example was suggested by Meadow and Cochrane, p. 136.

7. Meadow and Cochrane, p. 140-141.

8. Hawkins, Donald T. and Robert Wagers. "Online Bibliographic Search Strategy Development." *Online* 6 (May 1982) 12-19.

9. Hawkins and Wagers, p. 13.

10. Hawkins and Wagers, p. 13.

11. *Search Strategy Seminar.* (DIALOG Information Retrieval Service, 1983). pp. 21-22.

12. Institute for Scientific Information, *User's Guide to Online Searching of Scisearch and Social Scisearch.* (Philadelphia, PA: Institute for Scientific Information, 1980).

13. Saracevic, Tefko, "Relevance: A Review of and a Framework for the Thinking on the Notion in Information Science." *Journal of the American Society for Information Science* (November-December 1975).

14. Chapman, Janet and K. Subramanyam. "Cocitation Search Strategy." In Williams, Martha E. and Thomas H. Hogan. *Proceedings of the National Online Meeting* (Medford, NJ: Learned Information, Inc., 1981) pp. 97–102.

15. White, Howard D. "Cocited Author Retrieval Online: An Experiment with the Social Indicators Literature." *Journal of the American Society for Information Science* 32 (No. 1) (January 1981) 16–21.

16. Knapp, Sara D. "Cocitation Searching: Some Useful Strategies." *Online* 8(July 1984) 43–48.

17. Suggested by Lisa Kennel in a private communication.

18. Sievert, Mary Ellen and Bert R. Boyce. "Hedge Trimming and the Resurrection of the Controlled Vocabulary." *Online Review* 7 (1983) 489–494.

19. For example, Atkinson, Stephen D. and D.R. Dolan. "In Search of Research Studies in Online Databases." *Online* 7 (March 1983) 51–63; Dolan, Donna. "A Guide to Locating Mini/Micro Information in Online Databases." *Online* 7 (March 1983) 78–81.

20. For example, Adams, Arthur L. "Planning search strategies for maximum retrieval from bibliographic databases." *Online Review* 3 (Dec. 1979) 373–379; Calkins, Mary L. "Free text or controlled vocabulary?" *Database* 3 (June 1980) 53–60; Donati, Robert. 'Spanning the social sciences: searching techniques when online." *Online* 2 (Jan. 1978) 41–52; Hawkins, Donald T. and Robert Wagers. "Online Bibliographic Search Strategy Development." *Online* 6 (May 1982) 12–19; Hawkins, Donald. "Multiple database searching: techniques and pitfalls." *Online* 2 (April 1978) 9–15; Knox, Douglas R. and Marjorie M. Hlava. "Effective search strategies." *Online Review* 3 (June 1979) 148–152; Marshall, Doris B. "To improve searching, check search results." *Online* 4 (July 1980) 32–47; Oldroyd, Betty K. and Charles L. Citroen. "Study of strategies used in on-line searching." *Online Review* 1 (1977) 295–310; Fidel, Raya. "Moves in online searching." *Online Review* 9 (1985) 61–74.

21. Harter, Stephen P. and Anne Rogers Peters. "Heuristics for Online Information Retrieval: A Typology and Preliminary Listing." *Online Review* 9 (1985) 407–424.

22. Harter, Stephen P. "A probabilistic approach to automatic keyword indexing." Part II. "An algorithm for probabilistic indexing." *JASIS* 26 (Sept./Oct. 1975) 280–289.

Chapter 8

Source Databases

8.1 INTRODUCTION

Borrowing from the classification developed by Cuadra Associates Inc.
[1], a 'reference database' is a collection of data referring a user to another,
more complete source of information. Records in reference databases are
surrogates of these primary sources, guiding the user to a published document or other information source. Until this chapter, the concentration in
this book has been on reference databases.

In contrast to reference databases, *source databases* are primary sources
of data or information. Source databases may be divided into three categories: numeric, textual-numeric, and full text. *Numeric databases* are defined
as machine-readable collections of primarily numeric data. *Textual-numeric
databases* contain records with both numeric and textual fields, and tend to
be designed as *fact* or *question-answering* in function. *Full-text* databases contain the complete text of a primary (document) source such as the text of
a court case, a piece in an encyclopedia, or a newspaper article. Although
these categories provide a convenient framework for discussing the similarities and differences between databases, the categories are neither mutually
exclusive, nor universally accepted.

Source databases are both more numerous and more varied than reference databases. Table 8.1 summarizes the percentages of source and reference databases listed in the Fall 1984 edition of Cuadra Associates' *Directory
of Online Databases* [2]. The preponderance of source databases should be
noted. Of the 2453 databases listed in this issue of the *Directory*, approximately 55% are source databases and more than half of these are numeric.

Source and referral databases together are sometimes called *nonbibliographic databases*. Several useful general survey articles have been published
that describe the entire spectrum of nonbibliographic databases [3], and nonbibliographic databases in the sciences [4].

TABLE 8.1
Percentages of Databases in Several Categories*

Type of database		Percentage of total
Source databases		
full text		16.0%
numeric		29.8
textual/numeric		9.0
software		0.5
	Total	55.3%
Reference databases		
referral		11.2%
bibliographic		23.4
	(total)	34.6%
Mixed types (more than one)		10.1%

*Percentages were computed on the basis of a random
sample of 188 databases drawn from the listings in Cuadra
Associates, Inc. *Directory of Online Databases* 6 (No. 1)
(Fall 1984).

The existence of nonbibliographic databases and systems poses serious questions for information specialists. Traditionally, the library and information science professions have worked most extensively with bibliographic databases, and the earliest search systems dealt exclusively with them. Even today, when nonbibliographic databases easily outnumber their bibliographic counterparts, many information specialists and librarians have never used numeric databases and probably have no intention of ever doing so. Perhaps artificial barriers separating bibliographic and nonbibliographic information sources have been erected by search specialists whose perspective is that of library and information science rather than a subject specialization.

The issues arise in part from differences of opinion regarding appropriate functions for an information specialist or librarian. Figure 8.1 shows several of these arranged in a continuum. The traditional reference librarian in an academic library, for example, operates mainly at the left end of the continuum, selecting, maintaining, and providing access to a document (print or non-print) collection. Services provided consist mainly of retrieving citations to documents through a catalog to the collection, printed indexes, or online bibliographic searching, supplying the full texts of documents, and answering simple questions. Databases used by such a librarian are mainly bibliographic, and to a lesser extent, referral and question answering.

Functions on the right half of the continuum in Figure 8.1 are commonly carried out by information specialists in business, industrial, government,

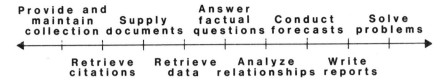

Figure 8.1 Functions of librarians and information specialists.

and other "special" environments. However, many "traditional" librarians consider analyzing relationships, forecasting, generating reports, and problem-solving as out of the scope of their profession. These services require the use of source databases, perhaps especially numeric databases. Indeed, while many users of bibliographic systems are trained information specialists, numeric, textual-numeric, and full text databases are probably used more by end-users than by information specialists. This is an unfortunate division, because from the perspective of satisfying the information needs of clients, the separation between bibliographic and nonbibliographic databases may often be artificial, irrelevant, unnecessary, and counter-productive.

However, because of the need for searchers to make complex judgments that must be based on subject knowledge, especially in the sciences, at least some nonbibliographic systems and databases may be unsuitable for effective use by searchers without subject expertise [5]. The chemical databases are probably the most obvious examples. The judgment of whether a given database can be used effectively by a searcher without subject expertise must be made on an individual basis. However, it seems clear that at least some information problems can be solved by search specialists with limited subject knowledge working with source databases, while others cannot. Although specialized subject knowledge is a prerequisite for many numeric databases and search systems, with study, enough knowledge can be gained by the nonspecialist to permit the effective use of such systems.

Traditional libraries have, by and large, ignored nonbibliographic databases and services. In part this may be because educational programs in library and information science have tended to ignore concepts of numeric data. In part it may be related to the fact that many librarians are neither mathematically inclined nor computer-literate. In part it arises from the 'fugitive" nature of numeric databases. Finally, it almost certainly is a function of the much greater diversity of nonbibliographic databases.

As a result, repositories for data files, especially numeric data, have arisen independently of libraries. The Institute for Research in the Social Sciences at the University of North Carolina, the Inter-university Consortium for Political and Social Research in Ann Arbor, and the Roper Center/Institute for Social Inquiry are outstanding examples of repositories for machine-readable data.

Numeric databases have also been made available on 'traditional'' search services such as DIALOG, perhaps playing a consciousness-raising role to librarians who previously had barely heard of them. Probably mainly for this reason, numeric databases have in recent years been the subject of greatly increased interest in the professional literature of library and information science.

8.2 NUMERIC AND TEXTUAL-NUMERIC DATABASES

In a comprehensive review of the literature on numeric databases and systems, Luedke defined a *numeric database* as "a computer-readable collection of data which are primarily numeric in nature" [6]. *Textual-numeric* databases also contain numeric data, as well as textual data. Because the division between these categories of databases is somewhat vague, and because their characteristics are similar in many respects, they will be discussed together.

An online numeric database *system* permits the retrieval of data (and any attributes of the data). Typically the system also permits further processing of the data. While DIALOG, BRS, and SDC offer access to a few numeric and textual-numeric databases, databases carried by these vendors are chiefly bibliographic. This may, of course, change in the future. Other, more specialized search services concentrate on numeric or textual-numeric databases. Examples include I.P. Sharp Associates, Ltd., Control Data Corporation/Business Information Services, Data Resources, Inc., Chemical Information Systems, Inc., and ADP Network Services, Inc. Numeric database systems can also be operated on in-house computers. Batelle's BASIS is a general purpose Database Management System that handles both numeric and textual data. BASIS is used in several numeric data information analysis centers [7].

Numeric database systems permit the online searcher to retrieve, display, manipulate, or otherwise "massage" a numeric database through statistical treatment. Examples of such functions include numeric lookup, range searching, computation of descriptive statistics, graphical presentation of data, sorting of output, and production of customized reports. More complex analyses may also be possible, including the construction of simulation models for complex phenomena, finding the "best fit" to numerical data using analytical techniques ranging from simple linear regression to multiple regression, forecasting, computing estimates of reliability, and hypothesis testing.

Examples of questions that might be directed to numeric or textual-numeric databases include What are fatigue properties of certain aluminum compounds under varying atmospheric conditions? What is the reliability of these estimates? What is the range of potential error? Do steel workers earn more money than construction workers? How much has the price of used automobiles increased during the past three years? How much beer do people currently drink in the U.S., and what is an analytical forecast for future consumption based on past trends? How have American opinions regarding Adolf Hitler and Nazi Germany changed since 1945? How likely is it that these recorded opinions represent "true" American opinion?

Questions can be seen to range from strictly factual inquiries to questions demanding an estimate of error that accompanies the fact, to questions regarding trends and projections, to questions regarding the statistical significance of empirical observations. Alice Robbin has identified six types of numeric data users, ranging from the *fact-finder, bottom-liner* and *trend-seeker* to the *high priest,* who makes "judgments about reliability, quality, and acceptable degree of error," and the *scientist-sage,* who evaluates statistical analyses of numerical data and engages in knowledge production [8].

Because of a lack of familiarity with concepts of scientific research and evaluation, most traditional librarians and information specialists may feel reasonably comfortable with the first two or three of these categories, but less so with the others. This is an unfortunate and deplorable result of a graduate educational process for library and information science that does not require familiarity with the *process* of research. Indeed, from 1956 to 1975 the percentage of accredited library schools requiring even one course in research methods declined from 57% to 37% [9].

For librarians and information specialists without a background in research methods and concepts, it is especially difficult to work with numeric databases and systems, because fundamentally, numeric and textual-numeric databases are the products of basic or applied research and measurement. Government is the largest producer of statistical data, with the largest federal distributors being the National Archives and Records Service, the National Technical Information Service, the Bureau of the Census, the National Center for Health Statistics, and the Bureau of Labor Statistics [10].

In the physical and biological sciences, textual-numeric databases may contain reference data relating to chemical or physical properties of compounds, including specific numeric values describing the property investigated (optical, thermophysical, transport, mechanical, electrical, etc.), laboratory animal data, crop production, and toxicity. Virtually all the fields of science and engineering are covered by one or more numeric or textual-numeric databases. The NIH/EPA Chemical Information System (CIS) alone contains 15 databases providing information on chemical and physical properties, toxicology data, structure and nomenclature, and mass spectra, for more than 500,000 chemicals [11].

In the social sciences, there are hundreds of publicly available numeric databases, ranging from census data and public opinion surveys (Roper, Gallop) to data on U.S. schools, criminal justice, health, and housing. Many of these are produced by agencies of the Federal Government, including the Departments of Agriculture, Education, Energy, Health and Human Services, Justice, Labor, Transportation, and other agencies [12]. A useful classification of major machine-readable databases in the social sciences by subject category has been compiled by McGee [13].

While there are far fewer numeric databases currently available in the humanities, there are more than might be expected. Many contemporary historical data such as census, medical, and educational records exist largely in machine-readable form. Moreover, there has been much retrospective conversion of printed historical materials to machine-readable form. The largest collection of historical databases is held by the Inter-university Consortium for Political and Social Research [14]. Examples of publicly available historical data files in machine-readable form include *United States Historical Election Returns, 1788-1979*; Warner, Sam Bass, Jr. *Nineteenth-Century Family History in Michigan*; Vinovskis, Maris, *Urban Composition of United States Counties, 1850; Social, Demographic and Educational Data for France, 1801-1897*; and Aarbrot, Frank and Kuhnle, Stein. *Norwegian Ecological Data, 1868-1903*. The existence of more and more historical material in machine-readable form calls for new techniques of historical analysis, and a new understanding of quantitative and analytical methods by historians. Judith S. Rowe comments in this connection: "Life for the historian of the future will be very different" [15].

There are probably more numeric databases in business and economics than in any other field. Data concerning national income, manufacturing, trade, employment, labor statistics, and industrial growth rates can be found in hundreds of publicly available numeric databases. These are produced by such government agencies as the Bureau of the Census and the Bureau of Labor Statistics as well as private commercial firms such as Predicasts, Inc. and I.P. Sharp Associates, Ltd.

Many numeric databases, especially in business and economics, are so-called *time series*. A time series is a set of historical, consecutive statistical observations evenly spaced over time and arranged in chronological order in a tabular format. Examples of time series data include a weekly series of end of the week U.S. bond prices for 1984, a monthly series of numbers of automobiles produced by Japanese manufacturers from 1980 to the present, or an annual series of amounts of coffee consumption by Europeans during the past twenty years. I.P. Sharp is perhaps the largest vendor of time series databases. I.P Sharp public databases now contain more than thirty-six million time series in over 90 databases in aviation, economics, energy, finance, and actuarial statistics [16].

Time series analysis involves the examination of past series to understand trends, cyclical fluctuations and other changes. Most important, time series analysis *forecasts* future movements through the extrapolation of *trend lines*.

The use of analytical techniques such as linear and non-linear curve fitting using regression analysis is an important part of time series analysis. Classical time series analysis is treated in most statistics textbooks [17].

Some numeric database systems can perform time series and other statistical analyses on numeric data automatically. However, an information specialist should understand underlying statistical concepts so that the results obtained by such analyses are properly applied and interpreted. This requires at least a passing familiarity with concepts of statistical analysis. It is beyond the scope of this book to address these concepts, except to point out their importance to the effective use of numeric database systems.

Data in textual-numeric and numeric databases contain empirical information representing some aspect of the physical world, whether this relates to chemistry, economics, mortality statistics, voting records, opinion surveys, or census data. As noted earlier, these numbers are the result of pure or applied research in some aspect of the physical, biological, or social universe. They are not arbitrary numerals such as classification codes (e.g., Dewey numbers or SIC codes) or accession numbers. Rather, they are the result of measurement. In science, they are derived from controlled experiment and subsequent measurement with calibrated instruments. An experimental approach to research is not likely to be used in most social science and humanities research resulting in numeric data, but the conditions underlying the research findings are no less important to document carefully and understand fully. Proper interpretation of results is impossible without a knowledge of such conditions.

In summary, as the products of pure or applied research, numeric and textual-numeric databases are subject to the criteria appropriate to the evaluation of research itself. These are even more important and rigorous than criteria for the evaluation of reference databases. An introduction to some of these criteria follows.

8.3 EVALUATION

The numbers that compose numeric and textual-numeric databases are empirical data—the results of counting or measuring something in the real world. As was observed earlier, the distinction between arbitrary numeric designations such as Dewey numbers and measured or counted quantities is crucial. To understand the latter, one must understand the conditions underlying the origins of the data—the procedures and methods that were used to generate the data and process it. This is the *research methodology*. Whether methodology consists of controlled experiments conducted using high precision instrumentation, or opinion surveys, or compilation of birth and death statistics, an understanding of methodology is central to an understanding of the data themselves. Data are most useful if these conditions are part of the database (that is, in machine-readable form) or at least, present in the documentation accompanying the database.

much . . . numeric data has meaning only in the context in which it was measured or derived. To be of use, each data value must be accompanied by enough descriptive information for it to be isolated and/or evaluated with comparable data. The logical data record format must completely characterize the environment surrounding each data point as well as any deviations and variations that may affect the data value [18].

Another writer puts it this way:

it is of utmost importance to ascertain the validity, accuracy, or reliability of the data, and to describe the conditions under which the data are valid or under which they were measured, including details of instrumentation, calibration, use of standards, and use of mathematical algorithms or statistical methods [19].

But because attention to quality control and peer review of data is "unglamorous" and is often professionally unrewarded, there is a paucity of evaluated or validated data. Thus there is much poor quality data, even in "hard" disciplines in the sciences and engineering [20]. The U.S. Congress established an Office of Standard Reference Data at the National Bureau of Standards to help with the problem of poor quality data, but lack of funding has prevented this office or others from producing large quantities of quality numeric data [21].

Information users and search specialists must make every effort to evaluate the data found in numeric or textual-numeric databases. To accept and use data uncritically can be the height of folly. The validity of the data as applied to a problem of interest depends completely on its quality and on the conditions under which it was gathered.

To understand the conditions prevailing during the collection of data from a research undertaking, such questions as the following might be asked: What was the population of interest? the sample design? What collection instruments were used? What uncertainty is associated with the data values? What quality control measures were used for the data collection? Such questions are questions of scientific method. Science (or more generally, a research-oriented approach to knowing) is always concerned with questions of reliability, validity, adequacy of operational definitions, characteristics of data gathering instruments, the environments of data values, and other methodological concerns. It follows that the information specialist working with numerical databases and systems must have a solid grounding in principles and methods of research, to be able to ask the right questions and to properly interpret the answers.

Table 8.2 lists general criteria for the evaluation of numeric and textual-numeric databases. Central to all the other criteria is the requirement that machine-readable data files be completely documented by a user's guide and a *data dictionary*, or *codebook*. Such documentation can be extensive, as it should contain detailed descriptive information regarding the remaining criteria listed in Table 8.2, at a minimum. References [22] and [23] are extremely useful tools for evaluating documentation for machine-readable data files.

Criterion groups two through four of Table 8.2 assess aspects of the methodology of the study that generated the data. A reader wishing to replicate such a study should be able to do so without ambiguity or uncertainty having been provided the information related to sampling procedures and data collection instruments. Moreover, from this information the interested user should be able to assess the validity of the data provided as well as its applicability to the information problem at hand. A detailed discussion of questions of research methodology is beyond the scope of this book. Interested readers are urged to pursue these questions with standard texts on research methods.

Criterion groups five through seven of Table 8.2 deal with procedures used to code the collected data and convert it to machine-readable form. Editing, proof-reading, error-checking, defining conventions for handling missing data, and creating new variables by recoding the data are important steps to review. A most important characteristic of the data is the level of aggregation provided the data elements (that is, whether and how data have been grouped into frequency classes) and whether data so treated can be disaggregated [24].

The evaluation of a numeric database *system* rests on what the system is able to do with the data, or how the data can be 'massaged.'' Table 8.3 summarizes some of the general capabilities of numeric database systems.

First are questions relating to how items in the database can be retrieved. Which data fields are searchable? Can Boolean operators be used? Can numeric ranges of data be specified? If so, is searching limited to predetermined ranges created by the database producer or search service or can the user define customized search ranges? Can searching using inequalities be conducted?

The next set of questions deals with the kinds of numerical analyses that are possible to conduct. Can measures of central tendency such as mean, median, and mode be computed? Other descriptive statistics such as range, standard deviation, and correlation coefficient? Can inferential testing such as error estimation and hypothesis testing be performed on retrieved data?

TABLE 8.2
Selected Criteria for the Evaluation of Numeric and Textual-Numeric
Databases*

1. *Documentation*
    a. user's guide
    b. data dictionary, or codebook with detailed descriptive information
2. *Summary Description*
    a. origin and availability of database
    b. project history
    c. nature of data included
    d. intended use of data
3. *Sampling/selection Design or Criteria*
    a. universe under consideration
    b. detailed sampling or selection procedures
    c. units of analysis
    d. weighting of responses
    e. response rates
    g. reliability/accuracy of data
    h. precision of data (error estimates)
    i. acceptability of operational definitions underlying data definitions
    j. overall assessment of validity
    k. age of data
    l. source of data
    m. completeness of data
4. *Collection Instruments*
    a. type
    b. time, place, and duration of data collection
    c. operation of collection instrumentation
    d. quality control
    e. correction and update procedures
    f. methodology or other design problems
    g. deviations and variations affecting data values
5. *Coding Procedures and Error Rates*
    a. manual editing procedures
    b. coding errors
6. *File Processing History*
    a. conversion of data to machine-readable form
    b. consistency checks on data
    c. recoding and creation of new variables
    d. conventions for handling missing data
7. *Variables and Data*
    a. units of measurement of variables
    b. range of possible values
    c. level of aggregation
    d. "adjustments" made to data

*The criteria listed draw heavily on two published lists of evaluative criteria
for machine-readable data files and their documentation by Roistacher and
Perry (references [22] and [23]. Criteria were selected from these lists and
augmented by others. For a more complete and detailed treatment of the
evaluation of machine-readable databases and their documentation the reader
should consult the listed sources.

TABLE 8.3
Some General Capabilities of Numeric Database Systems

1. *Retrieval*
   a. searchable fields
   b. Boolean operations AND, OR, and NOT
   c. range searching
   d. numerical lookup using operators $<$, $>$, $=$
2. *Analysis*
   a. descriptive statistics: measures of central tendency and variability
   b. inferential statistics: simple correlation and regression, multiple regression, hypothesis testing, computation of confidence intervals
   c. ability to create new variables from old variables
   d. ability to test functional relationships
   e. ability to run simulation models
   f. ability to aggregate and disaggregate data
3. *Display*
   a. sorting on specified fields
   b. formatting of output into customized reports
   c. types of graphics displays

Other characteristics important to some numeric database applications include the ability to combine variables to create new ones; to aggregate or disaggregate data, or to test simulation models or functional relationships among the data.

Finally, when data have been retrieved and analyzed, the results must be displayed. Characteristics that might be important in this regard include the capability of sorting data records on specified fields, printing the results into customized report formats, and displaying the results graphically, in histograms, pie charts, bivariate graphs, and other more sophisticated formats. Some specific applications, e.g., chemical substructures search and display, may require capabilities not listed here [25].

There are several important differences between reference databases and numeric and textual/numeric databases. The record structure associated with numeric databases varies much more widely than among reference databases. Strong subject expertise for searchers may be much more important for the effective use of numeric databases and search systems than for reference databases, although this depends heavily on the search problem, database, and search system.

The purpose for conducting a search is also often different. There is much more fact searching on numeric and textual-numeric databases and search systems, in which a single answer is wanted. In contrast, much bibliographic searching consists of an attempt to achieve high recall searches, in which everything written on a topic or related to a problem is wanted. Searching numeric and textual-numeric systems tends to be more straightforward with less need for complex search heuristics. The ability to perform numerical analyses and display of retrieved data can also be extremely important.

Moreover, a numeric or textual-numeric database is evaluated by different criteria than those applied to reference databases. The reliability, validity and accuracy of data are crucial, while currency may be much less important. Numeric data originate from counting, recording or measuring empirical phenomena. In the sciences, much data are generated under laboratory conditions, in which the experimental conditions, instrumentation, calibration, sampling procedures, statistical methods of data handling, and other concepts of research methodology are crucial. But especially to a naive searcher, "bad data can look quite as impressive and believable as good data" [26].

The most important similarity between reference and numeric databases and search systems must be stressed: each is carried out to satisfy a visceral need of an information seeker. It is difficult for this writer to understand the attitude of a librarian or information specialist who is anxious to conduct subject searches for clients but shrinks from the kinds of searches and analyses possible on numeric databases and search systems. Both are clearly satisfying an important need. Why must artificial lines be drawn?

Although we readily admit that some numeric databases and search systems require a degree of subject expertise (e.g., in chemistry), many are certainly usable by non-experts. It has been suggested that because of their diversity, nonbibliographic databases may have a greater long term impact on libraries than bibliographic databases [27]. In any case, how to integrate numeric and textual-numeric database services into traditional library service raises important questions. The next section of the chapter addresses these concerns.

8.4 NUMERIC DATABASE SERVICES IN LIBRARIES

Machine-readable "documents" are relatively new to libraries, and most librarians, especially in academic libraries, are unsure how to deal with them. Should they be treated like any other library resources and acquired and catalogued and indexed for future use in a separate collection of data archives? Should reference assistance be given in their use? Should librarians evaluate numeric databases for acquisition just as they apply evaluative criteria in the selection process for print and other non-print library materials? Should the use of numeric databases be limited to what can be done though online searching with systems like I.P. Sharp? Or should even this step be relegated to the end-users? Should the presence and increasingly heavy use of numeric databases by academic departments be ignored altogether, in the hope that the problem will eventually go away?

By and large, librarians have been slow to set up data archives within their organizations to systematically acquire and provide access to machine-readable data files. There are a few notable exceptions reported in the literature, at UCLA, Princeton and Rutgers [28], the Social Science Data Archive at Yale University [29], the Institute for Research in the Social Sciences at the University of North Carolina [30], the University of Wisconsin [31], the University of Florida Libraries [32], and Lawrence University Library in Wisconsin [33].

When a library has decided to commit itself to some level of support for numeric database use, it must then resolve several important policy questions. These have been discussed in detail in several papers [34]. Among the concerns identified in these papers are

1. What is the user community that is to be served? This decision will directly affect later decisions, especially those pertaining to selection policy, staff education and training, and location of the service and data.
2. Among the several levels of service possible, which will be provided? Will a full data archives program be established? Will the program be limited to providing online access to numeric databases through commercial search services?
3. Who will decide which data should be acquired? More generally, what will be the principal components of the selection policy governing the program?
4. Where should staff and data be housed?
5. What will be the source of funds supporting the program? This is an especially important consideration if a full level of service is provided.
6. Will there be user charges? This is another crucial consideration if a full level of service is to be provided.
7. What qualifications should library staff members possess? research skills? statistical skills? special subject expertise?
8. What level of bibliographic control will be implemented for the machine-readable files in the collection?

Among these questions, staff training and education are perhaps the principal source of potential difficulty. Most librarians are not particularly numerate, a major stumbling block in developing a level of competency with numeric databases. Knowledge can be developed in these areas by taking courses in research methods and statistics or by individual study of these subjects. In addition, we have noted that, as a generalization, specialized subject knowledge is more important for effective utilization of numeric databases than for reference databases. However, even in these cases, with study, some knowledge can be gained by the interested non-specialist. In this context, an excellent introduction to online chemical information is given by Palma and Hoover [35], and methods for searching for chemical substances online are introduced by Oppenheim [36].

If a library chooses to forego the data archive concept and instead to rely completely on online information retrieval using publicly available numeric databases and search systems, there are still important questions to be resolved. Most of those listed above still apply. In addition, one must select the search systems to which to subscribe, as well as the databases within these services that will be utilized.

Regardless of specific organizational patterns, librarians and information specialists who have instituted data archive programs or who are making use of numeric databases through commercial or public systems feel strongly that this kind of service is an integral part of library service. A sample of views follows:

> no library can completely abdicate its involvement in machine-readable data resources, unless it elects to abdicate part of its responsibility as an information center [37].

> Because people expect to be able to find information in a library, and because librarians are committed to responding to those expectations, a way must be found to access information that is held in data archives . . . [38].

> The challenge is quite clear. If librarians intend to continue to support the research of social scientists, *all types* of information—print and machine-readable—from *all types* of sources—industry, private research, and especially the federal government—must come under the control of the librarian or information specialist providing service to the social scientific clientele [39].

8.5 FULL TEXT DATABASES

The most recently introduced and fastest growing category of machine-readable databases publicly available for online searching consists of full text databases. In Wanger and Landau's 1980 discussion of nonbibliographic databases, only 17 full text databases, or approximately 4% of the 400 known databases listed in the *Directory of Online Databases* in 1980, were identified [40]. Only four years later, the *Directory* listed 2453 databases, of which approximately 16%, or about 390, were full text databases (see Table 8.1). This tremendous growth results from two main factors: the preponderant use of the computer for typesetting in the publishing industry, and the continued rapid decline in the cost of mass storage devices.

Several kinds of published materials are available for full text searching. These include, among others, newsletters and news digests, wire service summaries, classified advertisements, newspapers, encyclopedias, U.S. Government publications, scholarly and popular journals and magazines, and texts of legal decisions and statutes. Full text legal materials were the first to be introduced online, and Lexis and Westlaw continue to lead in the development of extensive and powerful full text systems [41].

Evaluative criteria for full text databases are chiefly those that would be applied to the printed version of the documents; of course, these vary as widely as the types of printed materials for which there are machine-readable equivalents. For example, an evaluation of the Academic American Encyclopedia would need to consider those criteria used by experts to evaluate encyclopedias [42]. An evaluation of the full text version of the *Harvard Business Review* would depend on judgmental criteria used by the scholars and practitioners in the business world for the evaluation of their scholarly and professional journals. Obviously discussion of such criteria is well beyond the scope of this book.

There are, however, other evaluative criteria and questions that deal with issues raised in Chapters 2–4. These are criteria dealing with vocabulary and database structure, content, and organization. Some of the most important are

* *Currency*. What is the time lapse between the appearance of the printed version of the text and the availability of the electronic version?

* *Indexing and cataloging practices*. Is a controlled vocabulary used? If so, what is the quality, depth of indexing, and specificity of the index language? What is the consistency of indexing and cataloging practices? Has authority control been used?

* *Free-text searching*. Is free-text searching (excepting stopwords) of the full text possible? That is, can every substantive word in the text be searched using the full power of the search system (proximity operators, truncation, etc.)? This question is not the same as asking if the full text is displayable.

* *Full text search capabilities*. Are search capabilities especially designed for lengthy texts available? The BRS Search System, for example, permits one to restrict retrieval to terms found within the same paragraph or within the same sentence. Lack of such features or their equivalent will produce many false drops.

* *Print capabilities*. Can selected portions of retrieved texts be printed, or must one print the entire retrieved document? In particular, is it possible

to print only those sentences or paragraphs or equivalent blocks of text containing the search terms of interest? Lack of such features will cause searchers to print much unwanted or unnecessary text.

  * *Field structure.* Have search fields been defined for particular kinds of data, as in bibliographic databases? In an encyclopedia, for example, the existence of predetermined fields of information would make it possible to answer a host of questions that would otherwise be impossible to consider, permitting the encyclopedia to take on many of the properties of an almanac or yearbook. And if arithmetic computations could be conducted on the values in numeric fields, the potential would be expanded even further [43].

  * *Searchable fields.* Are there searchable fields for the distinguishable parts of the text? For example, it can be useful to be able to restrict a search to specific parts of an article, such as title, section headings, tables, methodology, results, or cited references. These capabilities are currently available on some full test databases and search systems, for example, the International Research Communication System for medical and biomedical science on the BRS search system [44].

  * *Graphical information.* Is pictorial or graphical information important to the information problem? Is it possible to obtain such information online from the full text database?

Many of the criteria discussed in Chapters 2-4 also apply to the evaluation of full text databases.

Although publicly available full text databases are relatively new, several suggestions for searching them can be made. All the problems of using natural language for searching apply to full text databases, especially if controlled vocabularies do not exist or are not used for searching. Indeed, these problems are exacerbated in full texts because there are in general many more words available for searching. In particular, the probability of achieving a false drop by coordinating two terms with Boolean AND when in fact the two terms are not related to one another conceptually, is, presumably, much higher in full text files. For this reason, some vendors of full text databases recommend that search formulations should require that search terms be restricted to the same paragraph of text, or to use even more stringent proximity operators, and to avoid the use of Boolean AND altogether.

Other heuristics for working with full text databases have been suggested in the literature. Most are logical extensions of heuristics for searching using natural language terms. For example, Quint warns against false drops and recommends using specific search terms, proper names whenever possible. "To perform efficiently, searchers have to marshall every precision tool they can find" [45].

Fact searches can often be carried out on full text databases. The following are examples:

* Who wrote "From the Back of the Bus?"
* Are there any current job openings for indexers or abstractors in the Ohio, Indiana, Michigan, or Illinois area?
* Find me the recipe for cooking shrimp that appeared in the New York Times in 1983 [46].
* Have there been any court cases that have involved a librarian being sued for malpractice?
* Find movie reviews comparing "Star Wars" with "Close Encounters of the Third Kind."
* Who are the most noteworthy of modern, English-speaking poets [47]?

The more specific the fact wanted, the better. But sometimes careful analysis and verbal tricks must be played to cut retrieval down to manageable size. An interesting example of this was described in a letter by Lydia Jackson to *Online* magazine [48]. The search problem was to find an article confirming a rumor that the U.S. was about to pull its troops out of Lebanon through the Israeli lines. Terms to represent the important concepts of this problem that immediately came to the searcher's mind were too general, and would have resulted in many false drops: 'Lebanon', 'MNF', 'troops', 'military personnel', 'marines', 'Israel.' The search formulation eventually made, resulting in 11 references, all hits, was 'withdraw' truncated, and occurring in the same text paragraph as 'behind.'

Full text searches can also be conducted to achieve very high recall output, with precision being a function of the specificity of the term searched. A search on 'Hawthorne effect' in the Harvard Business Review full text file would retrieve all articles mentioning this phrase anywhere in the text of the article, and would probably achieve nearly perfect recall. Depending on the nature of the information need, the precision achieved by this formulation might also be reasonably high.

There has been little research directly conducted on large, full text files. Thus, although there are many conjectures regarding differences between full text searching and bibliographic searching, there is much to be learned. Two notable exceptions to this are doctoral dissertations, by Carol Tenopir and Jung Soon Ro [49]. Tenopir found, as she hypothesized, that full-text searches achieved higher recall but also higher per relevant document costs and lower precision than searches conducted in abstracts or using a controlled vocabulary. In another doctoral dissertation, Jung Soon Ro investigated methods intended to improve the precision of full text retrieval without degrading recall. Among other conclusions, Ro found that the use of ranking algorithms originally suggested for automatic indexing achieved significantly higher levels of precision than full text searching without the use of such algorithms. The relative performance of individual algorithms was found to depend on level of recall and search strategy. Carol Tenopir's review article

in the *Annual Review of Information Science and Technology* is an excellent
source for additional study of full text databases [50].

8.6 CONCLUSIONS

Although they will continue to grow in number, the relative importance
of reference databases (referral and bibliographic) will no doubt continue
to decline in comparison with source databases. Scientists and engineers are
likely to make heavier use of numeric and textual-numeric databases as these
proliferate and improve in quality. Social scientists, historians, lawyers, and
other scholars in the humanities will also make additional use of research
data in machine-readable form in their fields, as the number of databases
continues to grow. There seems no end in sight, as the computer is certain
to be used increasingly often to collect, analyze and manipulate research data
of all kinds.

As we have noted, the number of full text databases has increased twenty-
fold during the past four years, and will continue to increase. For many applications, it may not ever be necessary for a user to see the print version of
a database, if indeed one exists. Lancaster and others have predicted a future
of electronic libraries, in which print has all but disappeared [51]. One does
not need to agree completely with this assessment to see nevertheless the enormous potential and probable future use of full text databases in an online
mode.

Librarians and information specialists will need to adjust to this electronic
present and future or find their reference functions taken over by others.
Just as librarians of 1975 began learning about and using online searching
as a new reference tool, so must today's librarian be concerned with learning how to use numeric, textual-numeric, and full text databases effectively.
Future developments in online information retrieval are likely to occur largely
in these areas.

PROBLEMS

1. Examine the latest issue of Cuadra Associates *Directory of Online Databases*. If the number
of databases in each of the categories defined is not provided, select a random sample of two
hundred databases from the listing and compute the percentages in each category. Compare
to the percentages listed in Table 8.1. In which categories has there been the most growth since
Fall, 1984? In which has there been decline?

2. Examine the documentation of an online search service that provides access to numeric databases. For a particular numeric database offered, in what ways can the data be "massaged"
by the system? Can you suggest additional statistical treatments that would be useful but are
not provided by the search service?

3. Find and examine a codebook for a numeric database and evaluate it by the criteria in the Roistacher style manual for machine-readable data files and documentation (reference [22]).

4. Use the evaluative criteria for full text databases given in 8.5 to compare and contrast the Academic American Encyclopedia (a) as it can be searched on the BRS search system; (b) as it can be searched on DIALOG; (c) as it can be searched on Compuserve.

5. Conduct a literature search for material published during the past two years on the following topics:

   a. the establishment of machine-readable data archives in academic libraries
   b. online searching of source databases by end-users
   c. the role of the librarian or information specialist regarding the use of numeric and textual-numeric databases

NOTES AND REFERENCES

1. Cuadra Associates, Inc. *Directory of Online Databases* 5 (No. 1) (Fall, 1984).

2. Cuadra Associates, Inc., p. 5.

3. Wanger, Judith and Ruth N. Landau. "Nonbibliographic On-Line Data Base Services." *Journal of the American Society for Information Science* 31 (No. 3) (May 1980) 171–180; Berger, Mary C. and Judith Wanger. "Retrieval, analysis, and display of numeric data." *Drexel Library Quarterly* 18 (Nos. 3 and 4) (Summer–Fall, 1982) 11–26; White, Howard D. "Numeric data files: an introduction." *Drexel Library Quarterly* 13 (No. 1) (1977) 1–20.

4. Meschel, S.V. "Numeric databases in the sciences." *Online Review* 8 (No. 1) (1984) p. 99.

5. Wanger and Landau, p. 179.

6. Luedke, James A. Jr., et. al. "Numeric Data Bases and Systems." *Annual Review of Information Science and Technology* 12 (1977), p. 120.

7. Gubiotti, R., H. Pestel, and G. Kovacs. "Numeric Data Information Analysis Centers at Battelle." In: *Numeric Databases*, edited by Ching-chih Chen and Peter Hernon. (Norwood, NJ: Ablex Publishing Corp., 1984) pp. 71–104.

8. Robbin, Alice. *Strategies for increasing the use of statistical data.* Occasional papers. (Graduate School of Library and Information Science, University of Illinois, 1983) pp. 6–7.

9. Grotzinger, Laurel. "Characteristics of Research Courses in Masters' Level Curricula." *Journal of Education for Librarianship* 17(2) (Fall 1976) 85–97; Houser, Lloyd J.; Lazorick, George J. 'Introducing a Significant Statistics Component into a Library Science Research Methods Course." *Journal of Education for Librarianship* 18(3) (Winter 1978) 175–192.

10. Robbin, pp. 4–5.

11. Heller, Stephen R. "NIH/EPA Chemical Information System (CIS) Physical and Chemical Databases." *Drexel Library Quarterly* 18 (Summer–Fall 1982) 39–66.

12. Heim, Kathleen M. "Government-Produced Statistical Data for Social Science Inquiry: Scope, Problems, and Strategies." In: *Numeric Databases*, edited by Ching-chih Chen and Peter Hernon. (Norwood, NJ: Ablex Publishing Corp., 1984) 105–124.

13. McGee, Jacqueline M. and Donald P. Trees. "Major available social science machine-readable databases." *Drexel Library Quarterly* 18 (Summer–Fall 1982) 107–134.

14. Rowe, Judith S. "Primary Data for Historical Research: New Machine-Readable Resources." *RQ* 21 (Summer 1982), p. 352.

15. Rowe, p. 351.

16. I.P. Sharp Associates, *Public Data Bases Catalogue* (July 1983).

17. For example, Hamburg, Morris. *Statistical Analysis for Decision Making.* Second edition. (New York: Harcourt Brace Jovanovich, Inc., 1977). Chapter 10, "Time Series," pp. 443–490.

18. Gubiotti, pp 73–74.

19. Carter, Gesina C. "Numerical Databases for Science and Technology." In *Numeric Databases*, edited by Ching-chih Chen and Peter Hernon. (Norwood, NJ: Ablex Publishing Corp., 1984) p. 21.

20. Heller, p. 40.

21. Heller, p. 40.

22. Roistacher, Richard C., et. al. *A Style Manual for Machine-Readable Data Files and their Documentation.* Report Number SD-T-3, NCJ-62766. (Government Printing Office, Bureau of Justice Statistics, U.S. Department of Justice, 1980).

23. Perry, J. Chris and Dagobert Soergel. *Aids for the Planning and Implementation of Data Base Applications: Three Checklists.* Prepared for the Workshop on the Use and Management of Numeric Data Base Services, ASIS Annual Meeting in Minneapolis, MN: October 14, 1979.

24. McGee, p. 110.

25. See Meschel for a discussion of many of these.

26. Ewbank, W. Bruce. "Comparison guide to selection of databases and database services." *Drexel Library Quarterly* 18 (Summer–Fall, 1982) p. 189.

27. Meschel, p. 99.

28. Rowe, Judith S. and Mary Ryan. "Library Service from Numerical Data Bases: The 1970 Census as a Paradigm." *College and Research Libraries* 35 (1974) 7–15.

29. Dionne, JoAnn. "Why librarians need to know about numeric databases." In *Numeric Databases*, edited by Ching-chih Chen and Peter Hernon. (Norwood, NJ: Ablex Publishing Corp., 1984) pp. 237–246.

30. Adams, Margaret O'Neill. "Online Numeric Data-Base Systems: A Resource for the Traditional Library." *Library Trends* 30 (Winter 1982) p. 439.

31. Robbin, Alice. "The data and program library service: a case study in organizing special libraries for computer-readable statistical data." *Library Trends* 30 (Winter 1982) 407–434.

32. Jones, Ray and Barbara Wittkopf. "Computerized Census Data: Meeting Demands in an Academic Library." *RQ* 19 (Spring 1980) 246–251.

33. Isaacson, Kathy. "Machine-Readable Information in the Library." *RQ* 21 (Winter 1982) p. 167.

34. See the Rowe, Adams, Isaacson, and Dionne papers above. Also see Hernon, Peter, "Numeric databases and their relevance to library collections and services: A summary analysis." In *Numeric Databases*, edited by Ching-chih Chen and Peter Hernon. (Norwood, NJ: Ablex Publishing Corp., 1984) pp. 297–308.

35. Palma, Mary Ann and Ryan E. Hoover. "Chemical Information." In Hoover, *Online Search Strategies.* (White Plains, NY: Knowledge Industry Publications, 1982).

36. Oppenheim, Charles. "Methods for Chemical Substance Searching Online: I. The Basics." *Online Review* 3 (No. 4) (1979) 381–387.

37. Rowe and Ryan, p. 15.

38. Isaacson, p. 165.

39. Heim, p. 122.

40. Wanger and Landau, p. 172.

41. Tenopir, Carol, "Full Text Databases." *Annual Review of Information Science and Technology* 19 (1984) 215-246.

42. For example, those provided in detail in Kister, Kenneth F. *Encyclopedia Buying Guide: A Consumer Guide to General Encyclopedias in Print.* (New York: R.R. Bowker, 1981).

43. These ideas are discussed in detail in Harter, Stephen P. "Online Encyclopedias." To appear in the *Encyclopedia of Library and Information Science.*

44. Tenopir, p. 221.

45. Quint, Barbara. "Newsbanks and News Data Bases." In Hoover, Ryan E. *Online Search Strategies.* (White Plains, NY: Knowledge Industry Publications, 1982) p. 288.

46. The article could not be found by a library patron in the print version of the *New York Times Index.* It had been indexed under the term 'flavored butters.' Example is from Golomb, Katherine A. and Sydelle S. Reisman. "Using DIALOG for ready reference." *Library Journal* (April 15, 1984) 786-788.

47. This example is described in detail in Harter, Stephen P. "Online Encyclopedias."

48. Jackson, Lydia. "Pre-search interview even more useful in full-text searching." *Online* 8 (July, 1984) 5.

49. Tenopir, Carol. "Retrieval Performance in a Full Text Journal Article Database." Ph.D. dissertation, University of Illinois, 1984; Ro, Jung Soon. "An Evaluation of the Application of Ranking Algorithms to Improving the Effectiveness of Full Text Retrieval." Ph.D. dissertation, Indiana University, 1985.

50. Tenopir, "Full Text Databases."

51. Lancaster, F. W. "Whither Libraries? or, Wither Libraries." *College and Research Libraries* 39 (September 1978) 345-357.

Chapter 9
Trends, Problems, and Issues

Since the introduction of online information retrieval services, there have been many changes. There are now thousands of publicly available machine-readable databases instead of tens, and hundreds of search services instead of half a dozen. Computer terminals operating at 120 characters per second are commonplace, in contrast to the older machines operating at one-tenth this speed. Telecommunication systems and modems transmitting at 2400 baud and even higher speeds are being rapidly developed and implemented. The cost of computer hardware has dropped dramatically at the same time that its capabilities have increased. "Dumb" terminals, capable only of sending information through the terminal keyboard and displaying input on CRT screen or printed on paper, are being replaced by *intelligent terminals*. Such terminals can upload and download files to mass storage devices such as floppy disks, save and edit output in machine-readable form, and even carry out searches for clients. Databases are now being offered on CD-ROM and videodisk, for use on personal information retrieval systems.

In addition to these technological changes, the activity of online searching has changed as well. Not too long ago, the meaning of this phrase was clear. It referred to an activity practiced by information professionals. The usual sense of the term referred to searching large files of bibliographic records in machine-readable form, using a computer terminal, and printing selected subsets of these files, in response to information requests.

But today the phrase has taken on a cluster of much more general and ambiguous meanings. It is used equally to refer to what a middle management executive does when he or she retrieves a fact from Dow Jones using an IBM PC, the activity carried out by a high school student searching Wilsonline who has been taught the skill by a media specialist in a half-day workshop, the actions of a physician using BRS After Dark to search Medline on a portable TRS-80 Model 100 microcomputer and copying the output in machine-readable form for later printing, editing, and storage, the retrieval, capture, and analysis of numerical spectroscopic data by a chemist, and the efforts of a college undergraduate searching Knowledge Index following a half-hour instruction period.

The publishing industry has been affected as well. Full-text databases are common, and an increasing number of materials are available *only* in machine-readable form. While the cost of scholarly journals and printed abstracting and indexing journals has been increasing exponentially, the costs of accessing the same data electronically have increased far less quickly. The possibility of storing search output to one's own computer system for later processing (called *downloading*) also has pricing and legal implications for the publishing industry.

Online searching is no longer an activity practiced by electronically minded "computer types" who happen to be working in special libraries. It is now an accepted activity in virtually all academic libraries and many special, public, and even school libraries. It is commonly carried out not only by library and information professionals but also by interested end-users, professionals and amateurs alike. Newly developed *gateway* systems make it possible for anyone to carry out an online search, with little or no prior knowledge of the system or database being searched. How effective such searches may be is a different question.

This chapter will briefly introduce some of the changes currently taking place in online information retrieval. It will outline some of the major problems, trends, issues. It will especially attempt to ask hard questions. Specifically, this chapter focuses on gateway systems, microcomputers, downloading and in-house systems, end-user searching, copyright, and the ultimate effects of new technologies on the library and information professions.

9.2   USING A MICROCOMPUTER

One of the most significant technological developments affecting online information retrieval is the development of the microcomputer and its subsequent use in online searching. Some microcomputers come with the necessary hardware and software built-in, but even if it must be purchased, a 300 baud acoustical coupler and acceptable software can be purchased for under one hundred dollars.

The hardware and software required to convert (temporarily) a given microcomputer into a computer terminal depends on the particular microcomputer being discussed. First, the required circuitry must be present to convert the digital data used by the searcher's microcomputer to the analog signal carried by telecommunications networks and telephone lines, and conversely. This piece of hardware is called a *modem board* if it is built into the microcomputer, as is the case in many newer models such as the Radio Shack Model 100 and 200 portable computers. If modem hardware is not already present in the microcomputer, it must be purchased as a separate physical component and connected, usually by cable, to the serial port of the microcomputer. A third, now less used option, makes an *acoustical* connection between the microcomputer signals and the telephone line, by placing the receiver of the telephone into the rubber cups of an *acoustical coupler*. The conversion between analog and digital signals is also required at the search service end of the communication process.

In addition to the hardware required, one must also have software that, depending on its sophistication, lends a degree of 'intelligence'' to the microcomputer functioning as a terminal. *Communications software*, sometimes also called *modem programs*, may come ''built-in'' to the microcomputer, or they can be purchased for $100 or less, and excellent ones are available free, as public domain software. A common example of the latter is MODEM7 and its many descendants, available from microcomputer user's groups. Criteria for evaluating communications software and hardware are beyond the scope of this book. There have been several excellent published treatments of this important issue, especially in the microcomputer literature [1].

Many microcomputer owners originally became interested in information retrieval by accessing *bulletin board* systems operated by user's groups and private individuals. Such systems probably numbered in the thousands in 1985. They not only permit microcomputer users to post and receive messages, but also play games, chat, obtain information, and serve as a source of free public domain software [2].

Microcomputers functioning as intelligent terminals not only can send data typed on the keyboard of the microcomputer but also can send search formulations that have been prepared ahead of time, that is, offline, using a standard word processor. In this way the typing time and accompanying error-correction time associated with the use of a traditional computer terminal can be almost entirely eliminated. Even a fast typist can only type a word a second, or about five or six characters a second. Transmission of search formulations that have been previously prepared currently can take place at approximately 30, 120, or 240 characters per second, depending on the modem. The savings in connect time costs is obvious.

Microcomputers acting as intelligent terminals can also capture data in machine-readable form for later processing. Thus a search can be carried out by creating a machine-readable version of the searcher/search system dialog, which can be saved to floppy disk for later processing and printing. This process, called *downloading*, raises serious legal questions related to the ownership of the downloaded data. At the least, downloading the dialog of a search permits (and encourages) the use of a word processor to edit the output by adding headings, erasing errors, deleting non-relevant records, reformatting the output, and other cosmetic changes. However, a plethora of other actions are also possible, the most obvious of which is building an in-house database, capable of being searched later using the microcomputer or other, larger computers. Some of these copyright issues will be addressed later in the chapter.

A microcomputer owner considering the purchase of the necessary hardware and software to permit the machine to function as an intelligent terminal should make every effort to ascertain the degree of intelligence the software will permit, as well as the ease of use offered. Is downloading possible? Can pre-written commands be uploaded, one by one, to a command-driven search system that uses a prompt? How complicated are the steps that must be carried out before the connection, and how easy is it for the user to err? Can a printer be used simultaneously, so that if an error results in the loss of the machine-readable data, there will be at least a printed record of the transaction?

Probably the best way to answer these questions is through user's groups. Unfortunately, because of the multiplicity of possible combinations of search systems, microcomputers, modems, and modem software packages, one can offer general advice only. The user needs to decide what the requirements of the system are to be, including which systems are to be accessed. Then particular configurations can be examined with respect to these requirements. If it can be obtained, one could certainly do much worse than using a public domain package like MODEM7 initially, if only to provide a clearer basis for discussion and comparison of commercial alternatives.

Far simpler to use, but with their own associated problems, are the so-called *gateway* systems. These are discussed in the next section of the chapter.

9.3 GATEWAY SYSTEMS

If a modem, communications software, and a microcomputer are together termed an "intelligent terminal," then gateway systems might be called "super-intelligent interfaces." They carry the ideas expressed in the previous paragraphs even further.

Gateway software is microcomputer software that ideally removes many of the potential technical difficulties of using "simple" programs like MODEM7, and even permits online searches to be conducted by "naive" users who know little or nothing about information retrieval. Gateway systems can automatically connect to a requested search system, or even select an appropriate system automatically. The process of database selection may also be done by the system. Search formulations can be constructed by the system offline, by having the user respond to natural language questions. Even knowledge of Boolean logic may not be required. A sophisticated gateway system will make use of principles of artificial intelligence to use search heuristics to modify a search so that optimum results are achieved, based on user feedback. The system may also automatically store and reformat system output so that the building of an in-house database is facilitated. It may itself be able to function as a (local) search system for this database, permitting the same kind of searching as is possible on commercial search systems.

Many "first generation" gateway systems have been developed, among them Scimate [3] , CONIT [4] , IIDA [5] , Ol' Sam [6] , Search Helper, InSearch, PSI, and others [7] . Levy and Spigai have provided a useful comparison of several systems [8]. The functions carried out by specific systems will not be discussed here. However, an initial attempt will be made to identify some important criteria for the evaluation of gateway systems. These criteria are based on the assumption that online information retrieval can usefully be regarded as a heuristic, problem-solving process, in which hypotheses are formulated and tested, and in which heuristics are utilized to improve initial results. The adequacy of a gateway system must be based, then, at least in part, on the extent to which criteria for effective searching are met by the system. Most of this book has been devoted to discussions of such criteria. In summary, they are

* *Problems with the language for problem-representation.* To what extent does the gateway system recognize and deal with the characteristics of natural language versus controlled vocabularies? For example, is the system able to select terms from a controlled vocabulary from natural language terms provided by the user? How does the system deal with the problem of homographs? Synonyms? False drops? Hierarchical concepts? Can various fields for searching be specified by the searcher? Automatically by the system?

* *Problems of command language.* Does the gateway system use the full power of the search system to which it is connected? For example, can particular combinations of fields be searched? Can word proximity features be used in their full generality? Can all fields searchable on the host system be exploited on the gateway system? Can the language of the search system itself be used, should the searcher happen to know it? Are characteristics of the

database structure and organization—parsing rules, sort order, etc.,—recognized and used by the system?

* *Problems of Database Selection and Evaluation*. What criteria does the gateway system apply to the selection of databases for searching? In addition to subject content, is the particular focus of databases considered? The overall quality of indexing, exhaustivity of indexing, specificity of indexing language, and consistency of indexing? Other criteria identified in Chapter 4?

* *Problems Relating to the Online Search Process*. Does the gateway system appear to use reasonable overall search strategies? Does it attempt to improve search results by using heuristics? Are principles of artificial intelligence employed, so that the gateway system is truly an "expert system" in information retrieval? [9]

* *Problems Relating to the Question Negotiation and Search Effectiveness*. Several criteria were identified in Chapter 6 that relate to effective communication between information seekers and search systems. Does the gateway system attempt to establish a problem context so that this information can be used in the search formulation and reformulation process? For particular searches, to what extent does the system succeed in retrieving relevant documents? Pertinent documents? What are the recall and precision ratios, and what cost was required to achieve these? What would the approximate results and costs have been if the search had been carried out by a professional search specialist? Preliminary evidence with at least one gateway system suggests that users prefer the computer intermediary approach to that of the human intermediary [10].

* *Problems related to "user friendliness and ease of use."* To be effectively wielded by a naive end-user, the system must bypass the complex command structure presently used by systems such as DIALOG. However, achieving "ease of use" may require a loss of power and flexibility, and ultimately, the ability to carry out truly heuristic investigations. Thus the decision regarding the tradeoff between these design considerations is a delicate one, but also one that is vital to the success of the system.

In the final analysis, the success of gateway systems will depend on how well principles of artificial intelligence have been used to provide acceptable answers to these questions. But even if one day there are systems for which these questions can be answered positively, there is an underlying assumption that the host system remains unchanged. A microcomputer-based gateway system is fixed and cannot react to host system enhancements and other changes. A user must purchase updated versions of the gateway software to "keep up" with host system changes. And of course, the introduction of new host systems not currently addressed by the gateway system would not be dealt with at all.

A variation on the idea of the microcomputer-based gateway system is a gateway system loaded on a dial-up mainframe computer or minicomputer. Perhaps the first of these to appear was Easynet. A user connects to Easynet through its telephone number, 1-800-EASYNET. After establishing the adequacy of the user's credit rating (online), EASYNET conducts a search interview, logs onto the search system and database it feels are best suited for the inquiry, and then carries it out [11].

9.4 END-USER SEARCH SYSTEMS

Related to the question of gateway systems is the question of end-user search systems—systems that have been designed for 'naive" end-users, such as BRS After Dark and DIALOG'S Knowledge Index [12], as well as systems designed for a more popular audience, such as Dow Jones, Compuserve, the Source, and others [13]. In general, such systems use a much simplified command structure when compared to their counterparts that were developed for use by information professionals. Some are menu-driven with search languages not nearly as powerful or flexible as their 'professional" counterparts. Typically fewer fields are searchable, and it may not be possible to achieve the same specificity or variety of search technique that is possible on other systems. Nor in general do they offer as many databases or go back as far in time. Such systems are simply not able to accomplish as much, as effectively, as research-oriented systems such as DIALOG, BRS, and SDC. However, they often do not *need* to be as effective, because of their intended audience and the uses to which they are put.

Precisely the same questions can be posed for such systems as were asked for gateway systems. As with gateway systems, the final questions are To what extent do they meet their objectives effectively? Is a heuristic approach to online searching possible? Is it encouraged? Will naive end-users be pleased with the output provided? If so, are they justified by their pleasure? In at least one study, many end users reported achieving high precision in their searches [14]. Can this result be supported by other studies? What kind of recall are end users achieving on these systems? To what extent are underlying information needs met? For what kind and proportion of information problems? And if reasonably successful, to what extent will end-users want to conduct their own searches? The answers to many of these questions are still unknown. Both gateway systems and systems designed for end-user access are sufficiently novel that judgments cannot yet be made with any degree of confidence.

In two studies conducted with the use of BRS After Dark in college libraries, it was found that while end-users made many errors in logic, the syntax of search commands, and the overall search process, they were also generally pleased with their results [15]. Charles Meadow has argued that because of certain parallels between computer programming and online searching, that end–users will eventually do all their own searching [16].

To what extent reported positive reactions to end-user searching are the result of satisfied information needs and to what extent they result from other factors is difficult to say. Other possible explanations include the novelty associated with online searching, or ignorance regarding what really good search results might be like, or the prevalence of relatively simple searches, or the result of obvious strengths of online searching when compared to printed indexes: speed, Boolean logic, and the ability to search many fields. Thus, it would seem premature to conclude that end-user searches can succeed in satisfying the needs of information seekers to any appreciable extent.

Library and information professionals must ask themselves what professional posture to take regarding end-user searching with systems like BRS After Dark. Should they offer assistance to clients attempting to use such systems to solve information problems? Should *library instruction* in such systems be offered? The University of Ottawa encourages end-user searching of BRS/After Dark, even though many problems are reported, including failure to apply Boolean logic effectively, the need for extensive pre-search counseling, the lack of proper preparation, terminological problems in the social sciences, and other problems. In spite of this, the authors warn that libraries will ignore the spread of end-user searching at their peril, and encourage libraries to integrate assistance with end-user searching with traditional online searching services [17].

Online searching is a complex activity, depending on knowledge of principles, concepts, and techniques of information storage and retrieval. As a professional reference activity, online searching is at least as challenging and difficult, if not more so, as any other professional activity that library and information science has to offer. Can a librarian in good conscience offer a half-hour or even six-hour course in "how to do" online searching in these circumstances? More correctly, is it possible to achieve such a goal? Any competent searcher can teach a moderately intelligent novice to be a *bad* online searcher in 30 minutes, but is this desirable? What will be the long-term effect on the profession of training high school students and other end-users to become "bad" searchers? Indeed, how long does it take to become "good?" Even more fundamental, what does it mean to be "good?"

These are important questions for us to consider, and the answers are by no means obvious. This writer would argue the wisdom of leaving brain surgery to the brain surgeons, auto repair to the mechanics, and online searching to specialists in information storage and retrieval. Certainly a layperson at auto mechanics should feel free to dabble in a little auto repair work, even if not particularly skilled. Such a person might find the experience relaxing, or intellectually satisfying, or simply fun. It might even be possible to save money. But such a person will not be an expert, and will not in general be able to do a creditable job at general auto repair unless much time is spent with it, perhaps several hours per week. This is no less true for law, medicine, plumbing, or information retrieval.

It is characteristic of our specialized society that when we want a difficult job to be done properly, we call in an expert. With few exceptions, librarians and information specialists are the experts in online searching. Not that there are no information problems suitable for end-users to tackle. Some end-users can change sparkplugs and self-prescribe medication quite effectively. Others cannot. But ordinarily we expect to leave the more difficult and challenging problems to the experts in the appropriate fields. Why should this be different in library and information science?

9.5 PROLIFERATION OF SYSTEMS AND DATABASES

A major trend in online information services is the extraordinary growth in the number of search services and databases. More than 2450 databases and 350 vendors of online search services are described in the Fall, 1984 issue of Cuadra Associates' *Directory of Online Databases*. Each of these databases has a different field structure than the others. Most use different controlled vocabularies. They are produced by a variety of public, private, and commercial organizations with widely differing aims, goals, and objectives. How is the online searcher to cope with this extraordinary growth?

In addition, each of the 350 vendors that provide access to these databases uses a different command language. Even if the structures of two command languages were reasonably similar, the defaults used by the systems are likely to be different, as are the syntax rules for the command language, the keywords, stopwords, and other characteristics of the language.

What can be done to cope with this proliferation? One answer perhaps lies in specialization. Search services can be decentralized to take advantage of subject expertise possessed by searchers and to allow specialization in search services. Indeed, most writers suggest that subject expertise is perhaps the most important quality that should be possessed by a search specialist, although others have claimed that subject expertise is irrelevant, and that the only thing that is important is a disciplined approach to problem-solving. Another possible solution lies in the establishment of *standards*. Committee Z39 of the American National Standards Institute (ANSI) has been addressing this problem, but so far with little result. In a free entrepreneurial society such as ours, when anyone owning a microcomputer can create a database, it seems unlikely that standards can be made to have much of an impact.

A third solution is to develop gateway software that can translate statements made in a common, universal search language to search formulations that can be carried out in a multitude of databases and search systems. While offering at least temporary relief, such systems must be kept current with changes in search systems or databases or they will lose their effectiveness. Moreover, it seems likely that to make a single language serve the purposes of many search systems and databases, a certain loss of flexibility and power is inevitable. Much of the heuristic nature of the online search process that has been stressed in this book may be stifled as well in such systems.

What the future holds regarding the proliferation of databases and search systems is not clear. No doubt the marketplace will determine the nature of the eventual solutions to these problems.

9.6 LEGAL ISSUES

Downloading takes place when an online searcher copies machine-readable records from databases onto a digital storage device using a microcomputer. The ease with which downloading can be accomplished has raised many legal questions, most of which are still unanswered. These questions deal with the extent to which copyright laws apply to various forms of "copying" data belonging to another. Suppose that a librarian is using a microcomputer to conduct an online search, and that the output is stored on floppy disk as the search progresses. The search having been completed, the librarian might do any of the following. Which are legal and which are not?

1. The output is "dumped," that is, printed just as it was generated, using a printer attached to the microcomputer. The printed output is then utilized by the information seeker.

2. Certain data from the output are rekeyed on an electric typewriter, producing a typed bibliography of selected items.

3. The machine-readable data are edited to change the format of the bibliographic records somewhat and to eliminate non-relevant records. The bibliography is then printed.

4. Same as case #3, except that a copy of the bibliography is distributed to each scientist working within an academic or industrial department.

5. Same as case #3, except that the machine-readable record is used to set type for a printed manuscript that is offered for sale to the general public.

6. The citations are used to find the source documents, from which annotations are prepared by catalogers. The annotations are then keyed into machine-readable form and merged with the original data. The product is then printed and offered for sale to the general public.

7. The original output is marketed in machine-readable form to the general public.

8. The data are reformatted for use in a personal bibliographic information retrieval system. As such, the data are searched on a regular basis and are used to produce frequent customized bibliographies.

This list could go on almost indefinitely. The legal status of most of the above actions is in doubt. Indeed, as of July, 1982, no court had yet ruled whether downloading data for later use is a copyright infringement [18]. The National Commission on New Technological Uses of Copyrighted Works (CONTU) proposal for dealing with such issues has stated that the copyright owner has the exclusive right to store copyrighted works in machine-readable form [19], but the legal ramifications of this statement are not clear. A key issue may be whether financial advantage was gained through the copying [20]. Although the courts have not ruled on this specific issue as of this writing, at least one expert has predicted:

> The downloading of a large number of records but still less than the entire database is not likely to be found to be copyright infringement, especially where the use is non-commercial or where the data is in the public domain. Where the use is commercial, particularly where the user is believed to be one able to pay the full cost of using the database, or where the data itself is not in the public domain, a user is exposed to copyright infringement liability [21].

At least some database producers seem to have reacted to the 'threat'' of downloading by assuming that everyone requesting full format displays is downloading the data, and revised charges for online versus offline prints reflect this assumption [22]. This seems counter-productive, and even encourages downloading and misuse of copyrighted data by potential users. Similar to the copyright questions raised by video cassette recorders, photocopy machines, and other new devices that can be used to copy the intellectual property of others, the issues raised by the possibility of downloading data in machine-readable form promise to be with us for some time to come.

There is another legal issue associated with the provision of information services that has yet to be explored in much depth. The question has to do with ascertaining the liability of the librarian or information specialist for bad, "dirty," invalid, or erroneous data. Is there, or should there be, such a thing as information malpractice? Should information professionals be held legally responsible for high quality and ethical behavior in the service they provide, just as other professionals [23]?

9.7 LIBRARIANS AND ONLINE SEARCH SERVICES

This book has deliberately avoided questions of policy; these have been discussed extensively elsewhere. One issue must be discussed, however, since it directly affects the philosophy espoused in this book: that the act of information retrieval requires a careful and perhaps lengthy pre-search interview followed by thorough preparation and an interactive, problem-solving, evaluative approach to searching. Such an approach takes time, professional time, which translates into money. One to two hours or more of professional time are often expended in a comprehensive online search. How should online information retrieval be funded in a library or information center?

The controversy concerning whether user fees should be charged in academic or public libraries will not be addressed here. But what we want to emphasize is that online searching is *not* a different way of providing a service that has always been provided (except, possibly, in a few special libraries). Online searching is a *new* service. It goes far beyond the traditional use of printed indexing and abstracting tools. The act of online information retrieval is much more complex and challenging than manual searching, and an effective search can produce a product that is much superior as well as cheaper than anything possible with print tools. But it is also extremely labor-intensive.

How is this new service to be financed? Unfortunately, in many libraries, online searching is simply absorbed by the existing reference service, often without adding additional personnel. In such a library, other reference services will obviously suffer. Moreover, failure to recognize online searching as a new service and to fund it accordingly causes searchers to be extremely cost conscious and encourages "fast batch" searching. Furthermore, it raises real questions about whether and how the service should be promoted, for promotion can be expected to increase use, and increased use will increase costs, especially in professional time. Butler's law states that: "Libraries cannot tolerate substantial success" [24]. Sadly, this may be especially true when it is applied to the promotion of online searching.

In addition to regarding online information retrieval as a new service, it would also perhaps be helpful to consider looking at library service in a radically new way. Perhaps in this online age entirely too much attention is paid to *collecting* and not enough on *accessing* information and on *document delivery*. Shifting funds internally with this change in outlook could pay the entire cost of an online search service. Already there has been some indication that some libraries have cancelled subscriptions to printed publications in favor on online versions, although this appears to have had only a minor effect thus far [25].

Expectations of library clients are heightened with their new awareness of online services. It has been reported that interlibrary loan has increased by as much as 100% after introduction of online services, especially in smaller libraries. A professional librarian once suggested to this writer that perhaps libraries should avoid searching esoteric databases, as a means of avoiding so many requests for hard-to-find documents. If they aren't asked for, we can't say that we can't get them! This hardly coincides with the spirit of library service so often espoused in professional forums.

At the same time, many new approaches to document delivery are emerging, ranging from the use of "information entrepreneurs" to ordering one's own documents, directly online. Can librarians really afford to continue to view libraries as collections rather than as institutions providing access to data and information? In the latter case, the electronic revolution provides the opportunity not only to conduct searches electronically but also to retrieve needed documents and other information. If these capabilities represent a real need of end-users in a given library service group, a library's failure to provide them is likely to cause others to step in and fill the gap. This would be a major strategic error that will have eventual profound implications for future directions and opportunities in the information professions.

Related to this question is how library service should be viewed in an online world. Chapter 8 introduced source databases, especially numeric and textual-numeric databases. Should these databases and systems be regarded as legitimate tools of librarians and information specialists, or should we be content to search bibliographic and referral databases? Should librarians be content to provide *references* to documents that may or may not address the information need of a client? Or should fact and question-answering systems and databases also be considered appropriate sources? The increased use of online searching for ready reference is heartening in this regard [26].

Should librarians be able to evaluate methodological questions resulting in research findings? Is it the business of librarians to answer questions, provide analyses, write reports, or solve problems? Or should such matters be left to the end-user, along with the interrogation of numeric and textual-numeric databases and systems? Online information retrieval has been regarded in this book as a heuristic, problem-solving activity, in which the information need of a human being is addressed by consulting sources of data and information. There is nothing in this characterization that excludes numeric databases and systems. Indeed, such systems are ideal sources for many information needs. Our answer, then, is clear. Librarians *must* use whatever tools are at their disposal to attempt to satisfy the information needs of their clientele.

We see librarians and information specialists as professionals able to address complex information needs at many levels, from the provision of bibliographies and documents to the retrieval of facts to the analysis and solution of problems. Used efficiently and effectively, online information retrieval provides us with powerful tools to accomplish these objectives.

PROBLEMS

1. What makes a terminal "intelligent" as opposed to "dumb?" List as many characteristics as you can.

2. Expanding on the discussion in the text, try to find or construct a checklist of criteria for the evaluation of general purpose communications software for microcomputers. Use your checklist to evaluate a selected software package.

3. Expanding on the discussion in the text, try to find or construct a checklist of criteria for the evaluation of a gateway system. Use your checklist to evaluate a selected software package.

4. Discuss the question of menu-driven versus command driven systems for end-user access to information retrieval. What is the ideal configuration, in your opinion? Can you find research findings that support your views?

5. Find two or more recent research studies treating the efficacy of end-user searching. Evaluate this research critically. What are the findings? Are the findings valid, in your view? Why or why not? Pay special attention to the methodologies employed in the studies you examine.

6. Select a particular type of library: large or small academic, special, school media, or public. Try to think through the issues involved with the library's posture toward end-user searching. Write an essay stating your position on what you feel the purpose of a librarian or information specialist is, or should be, for this type of library, regarding end–user searching.

7. What is a "good" online search?

8. To the best of your ability to understand it, as a layperson, what is the current legal status of downloading machine-readable data from bibliographic databases? Other types of databases? You may need to conduct a literature search of sources published since 1984 to answer this question.

9. Discuss the article by Anne Mintz on information malpractice [23]. Do you think a librarian or information specialist should be held accountable for bad, dirty, or invalid data?

10. Select a particular type of library: large or small academic, special, school media, or public. Try to think through the issues involved with the library's posture toward financing the cost of online searching. Write an essay addressing these issues, based on your position on what you feel is the purpose of this type of library in the larger institutional or social setting.

11. Select a particular type of library: large or small academic, special, school media, or public. Discuss the appropriateness of Butler's law as applied to this type of library.

12. Databases are now being produced using compact disk read-only memory (CD-ROM) and videodisk technologies, e.g., by Digital Equipment Corporation [27]. These databases are intended for use on individual, personal information retrieval systems running on in-house microcomputers. For what markets and functions do you think such systems will replace large online systems like DIALOG? Discuss four different types of libraries and library users.

NOTES AND REFERENCES

1. See, for example, Barr, David and George Rogers. "Looking for the perfect [communications] program." *Byte* (Dec. 1984) 199–210; Fenichel, Carol H. and Thomas H. Hogan. *Online Searching: A Primer.* Second edition. (Marlton, NJ: Learned Information, 1984). "Using Microcomputers." 71–81; Mason, Robert M. "Communications Software: Linking your micro to other computers." *Library Journal* (October 1, 1983) 1855–1857; Kolner, Stuart J. "The IBM PC as an online search machine—Part I: Anatomy for searchers." *Online* 9 (January 1985) 37–42.

2. Hane, Paula. "Public domain software: A boon for libraries." *Online* 8 (5) (September, 1984) 8 (5) 31–34; Dewey, Patrick R. "A professional librarian looks at the consumer online services." Online 7(5) (Sept. 1983) 39–41.

3. Garfield, Eugene. "Introducing Sci-Mate—A Menu-Driven Microcomputer Software Package for Online and Offline Information Retrieval. Part 1. The Sci-Mate Personal Data Manager." *Current Contents* (March 21, 1983) 5–12; Garfield, Eugene. "Introducing Sci-Mate—A Menu-Driven Microcomputer Software Package for Online and Offline Information Retrieval. Part 2. The Sci-Mate Universal Online Searcher." *Current Contents* (April 4, 1983) 5–15.

4. Marcus, Richard S. and J. Francis Reintjes. "A translating computer interface for end-user operation of heterogeneous retrieval systems. I. Design." *Journal of the American Society for Information Science* 32 (July 1981) 287–317.

5. Meadow, Charles T., et. al. "A Computer intermediary for interactive database searching. I. Design." *Journal of the American Society for Information Science* 33 (Sept. 1982) 325–332.

6. Toliver, David E. "OL 'SAM: An intelligent front-end for bibliographic information retrieval." *Information Technology and Libraries* 1 (Dec. 1982) 317–326.

7. Shepherd, Michael A. and Carolyn Watters. "PSI: A portable self-contained intermediary for access to bibliographic database systems." *Online Review* 8(5) (1984) 451–463.

8. Levy, Louise R. "Gateway software: is it for you?" *Online* 8(6) (Nov. 1984) 67–79; Spigai, Fran. "Gateway Software: A Path to the End-User Market." *Information Today* 1 (February 1984) 6–7.

9. Smith, Linda C. "Artificial intelligence in information retrieval systems." *Information Processing and Management* 12 (1976) 189–222; Smith, Linda C. "Artificial intelligence in information retrieval systems." *Information Processing and Management* 12 (1976) 189–222; Smith, Linda C. "Implications of Artificial Intelligence for End User Use of Online Systems." *Online Review* 4(4) (December 1980) 383–391.

10. Marcus, Richard S. "Computers versus Humans as Search Intermediaries." *Proceedings of the ASIS Annual Meeting*, Vol. 19, 1982. pp. 182–185.

11. Howitt, Doran. "On-line Access is Simplified." *Infoworld* (Jan. 21, 1985) 32–33.

12. Trzebiatowski, Elaine. "End user study on BRS/After Dark." *RQ* 23(4) (Summer 1984) 446–450; Janke, Richard V. "Online after six: end user searching comes of age." *Online* 8(6) (November 1984) 15–29; Tenopir, Carol. "DIALOG's Knowledge Index and BRS/After Dark: Database Searching on Personal Computers." *Library Journal* (March 1, 1983) 471–474.

13. Falk, Howard. "The Source v. Compuserve." *Online Review* 8(3) (1984) 214–224.

14. Janke, pp. 23–24.

15. Trzebiatowski, Elaine. "End user study on BRS/After Dark." *RQ* 23(4) (Summer 1984) 446–450; Janke, "Online after six: end user searching comes of age."

16. Meadow, Charles T. "Online searching and computer programming: some behavioral similarities (or . . . why end users will eventually take over the terminal). *Online* 3 (Jan. 1979) 49–52.

17. Janke, "Online after six: end user searching comes of age."

18. Warrick, Thomas S. "Large databases, small computers and fast modems . . . an attorney looks at the legal ramifications of downloading." *Online* 8 (July 1984) 58–70.

19. Gasaway, Laura N. "Nonprint Works and Copyright in Special Libraries." *Special Libraries* 74 (April 1983) 156–170.

20. Warrick, p. 62.

21. Warrick, p. 66.

22. Tenopir, Carol. "Full Text, downloading, and other issues." *Library Journal* (June 1, 1983) 1111-1113.

23. Mintz, Anne P. "Information practice and malpractice . . . do we need malpractice insurance?" *Online* 8 (July 1984) 20-26.

24. Butler, Brett. "Online public access: the sleeping beast awakens." *American Society for Information Science Bulletin* (December 1983) 6-10.

25. Lancaster, F.W. and Herbert Goldhor. "The impact of online services on subscriptions to printed publications." *Online Review* 5 (4) (1981) 301-311.

26. Hitchingham, Eileen. "A survey of database use at the reference desk." *Online* 8 (July 1984) 20-26; Riechel, Rosemarie. 'The public library and the online news database experience: supplementing the ready-reference collection." 3rd National Online Meeting. *Proceedings*. New York, March 31-April 1, 1982.

27. Foster, Edward. "DEC Services Support CD-ROM Technology." *Infoworld* (Oct. 14, 1985) 19.

Glossary

accession number—a unique number assigned to an *entity* by a *database producer* or *search service*. In *document retrieval*, each accession number is associated with a *bibliographic record*, and thus, a document.

acoustical coupler—a hardware device that converts audible tones into digital signals, and conversely. See also *modem*.

algorithm—a well-defined procedure or set of rules for accomplishing a task.

AND—see *intersection*.

ASCII code—American Standard Code for Information Interchange. A standardized *binary code*, in which numerals, letters, and other characters are represented as seven binary digits.

assumption—a statement that is treated as if it were true, without proof.

attribute—a characteristic of an *entity*. For example, if entities are doctoral dissertations, an attribute of such entities is the degree-granting institution.

bibliographic database—a *database* containing *bibliographic records*.

bibliographic record—an *index record* standing for, or representing, a journal article, book, or other document.

binary code—a representation of a set of print and other characters as strings of *bits*. The *ASCII code* is an example of a commonly used binary code.

bit—a binary digit: 0 or 1.

Boolean logic—an algebra that permits operations on sets of elements. Principal Boolean operators are AND (*intersection*), OR (*union*), and NOT (*difference*).

bound descriptor—a multi-word *descriptor* for which an entry in the *inverted index* has been made as a *character string*, including any blank or other special characters. A bound descriptor is an example of a *phrase-indexed field*.

briefsearch—a single *search formulation*, intended to retrieve a few *relevant* or *pertinent* records. Normally there is little or no interaction between searcher and system in a briefsearch.

building blocks search strategy—the most commonly used *strategy* for online searching, in which major *facets* of the search problem are identified and terms are selected to represent each facet. These terms are combined with *Boolean* OR, for each facet. The facets themselves are then combined with Boolean operators, usually AND.

byte—the smallest addressable group of *bits* for a particular computer system. Usually, a byte represents a printable character, such as 'Q' or the space character.

character string—a group of contiguous characters. A character string may include letters, numerals, punctuation marks, spaces, or other special characters. See also *ASCII code*.

citation index—an index listing all publications appearing in a set of source publications (e.g., articles in journals) that cite a given publication in their bibliographies.

citation pearl growing—a search *strategy* that identifies vocabulary elements for the representation of *facets* by examining *index records* associated with documents that are known to be *relevant* or *pertinent* to a search problem and by selecting search terms from these records.

cited reference search—a search for all documents citing a given document in their bibliographies. See also *citation index*.

client—an *end-user* conducting a search through a *search specialist*.

cocited authors—a search *strategy* in which all papers citing a pair of authors are retrieved.

codebook—a codebook contains the complete documentation for a *numeric database*, including *research methodologies* employed, coding procedures used, file processing history, and other pertinent information.

command-driven system—an online interactive computer system in which the searcher communicates with the system using a *command language*. Commands can be entered when the system has displayed a *prompt*.

command language—a *formal language* for providing instructions to a computer system in an online, interactive mode. Command languages have a well-defined vocabulary, *syntax*, and logical structure.

communications software—software that permits a microcomputer to function as a computer terminal.

compromised need—a formalized information need that has been presented to an *information retrieval system*, in anticipation of what the files and system can deliver.

computer-readable—see *machine-readable form*.

concept—an abstract idea. Concepts are represented by *symbols*.

connect time—the amount of time the terminal of an online searcher has been directly connected to the host computer of an online *search service*. Connect time is a principal component of the cost of conducting an online search.

conscious need—the conscious understanding by an *end-user* of his or her *visceral need*.

contextual ambiguity—arising from cases in which two or more symbols appear in the same piece of text but are not semantically related, contrary to a common assumption in information retrieval. Such cases can result in the retrieval of documents not on the subject wanted. These are sometimes called *false drops* or false coordinations.

controlled vocabulary—an artificial language for the representation of *attributes* of *entities*, e.g., subjects of documents.

data dictionary—see *codebook*.

data retrieval—see *fact retrieval*.

database—a collection of data or information. As the term is usually employed in online information retrieval, it refers to a collection of *index records* in *machine-readable form*.

database producer—the publisher of a *database*. See also *search service*.

default—an action taken by a search system if a command is ambiguous and if no additional explanatory information is provided. An *assumption* made by the search system, invoked whenever necessary.

depth of indexing—see *exhaustivity* of indexing.

descriptor—an element of a *controlled vocabulary*, as listed in a *thesaurus*.

difference—the Boolean difference between two sets of elements (A NOT B) is the set of elements present in set A but not also present in set B.

digital signal—on/off two-state signals. Symbolized by the binary digits 0 and 1.

disambiguate—to make unambiguous. See also *homograph*.

document description language—a language used to represent an aspect of a document.

document retrieval—a search conducted to find citations to publications treating a topic or problem. Contrast to *fact retrieval*.

downloading—a process by which an *intelligent terminal* is used to capture output from an information retrieval system in *machine-readable form* for later processing and use by the searcher or end-user.

dumb terminal—a computer terminal capable of (a) as an input device, sending data that are keyed into the terminal keyboard; and (b) as an output device, displaying data on a screen or printing it on paper. Contrast to *intelligent terminal*.

effective communication—see *pragmatic communication*.

empty set—a set with no elements. Sometimes called the null set.

end-user—a person with an information need. End-users often employ information retrieval systems, either directly or through a *search specialist*.

entity—an object about which information will be stored. See also *attribute*.

exhaustivity of indexing—the number of concepts treated in a document or other entity that are indexed by a *database producer*.

facet—a concept group, consisting of terms that will be considered to be equivalent by a searcher for purposes of a given information need. Terms representing these concepts will be searched and the *union* of the resulting sets created using Boolean OR. See also *hedge*.

fact retrieval—a search conducted to find particular pieces of data or information. Contrast to *document retrieval*.

false coordination—see *false drop*.

false drop—a retrieved document that is not *relevant* to the question motivating the search. See also *contextual ambiguity*.

fast batch search mode—when searchers tend not to browse titles or descriptors, print samples of retrieved records, or otherwise use the interactive features of the information retrieval system.

fewest postings first strategy—see *successive facet strategies*.

field—the data value associated with a particular *attribute* of a set of *entities*. For example, *bibliographic records* invariably have a title field and an author field, among others.

file—see *database*.

formal language—an artificial, invented language of communication for application to a particular problem area. Examples are computer programming languages and *command languages* for information retrieval.

formalized need—the precise, qualified linguistic expression of a *visceral* information need.

free text searching—a search mode in which titles, abstracts, full texts, or other natural language fields of bibliographic or source databases are searched using *proximity operators.*

full text database—a database containing the complete text of a source document: e.g., a legal decision, a news story, a journal article, or other primary source.

full text searching—in which the full texts of source documents are searchable on a *free text* basis.

gateway system—a software interface between an online searcher and one or more search systems, facilitating the use of the system by searchers who are naive to it, or to online information retrieval in general.

generic search—a search on a general class of concepts.

hard discipline—a discipline in which fundamental concepts are relatively unambiguous, research-based, and well-defined. Contrast to *soft discipline.*

hedge—a collection of terms for representing a *facet* in a given database. Hedges are intended to be re-used for frequently needed facets, e.g., for the concept of "research."

heuristic—a mental operation, tactic, behavior, or attitude that tends to produce useful results in certain problem-solving situations; a move made to advance a particular search *strategy.*

hit—a retrieved document that is *relevant* to a search question posed.

homograph—two search terms are homographs if they are identical *character strings* but represent different *concepts.* The presence of homographs in text produces semantic ambiguity. In online searching, homographs may need to be *disambiguated.*

hypothesis—a statement of relationship between two or more concepts or variables, thought likely to be true. The truth or falsity of hypotheses is tested by gathering and evaluating empirical data.

identifier—a keyword, usually extracted from the text of a document, to represent an aspect of its contents.

implied facet—in which a database, through its overall orientation, already includes one of the *facets* of a search.

index record—a concise representation or surrogate of an *entity* from a particular point of view; the set of all values associated with the *attributes* of an entity. For example, a card in a library's catalog is an index record representing a book.

information retrieval problem—how to find a particular piece of information relating to an information need, from among the billions of bits of the accumulated human record that do not relate to that need.

information retrieval system—a device interposed between an *end-user* of an information collection and the collection itself. The purpose of the system is to capture wanted items and filter out unwanted items from the information collection.

information specialist—see *search specialist.*

information theory—Claude Shannon's mathematical theory of (*technical*) communication, referring to the transmission of data along a communication channel.

intelligent terminal—a computer terminal, or a microcomputer functioning as a terminal, that can process data files stored on mass storage devices, usually floppy disks. Such files can be output files received from the host computer, as well as input (command) files sent to the host computer. Contrast to *dumb terminal.*

interactive scanning—a high *recall*, interactive search *strategy* in which many records are examined to identify major authors, methodologies, and related research.

intermediary—see *search specialist*.

intersection—the *Boolean* intersection of two sets of elements (A AND B) is the set of elements common to A and B.

inverted index—a set of records created from a *linear file*. Each record consists of an *attribute* and a list of all *entities* that are associated with that attribute. Typically these are lists of *accession numbers*, where each accession number is associated with a different entity. A back of the book index is an example of an inverted index.

linear file—a set of *index records*, in which each record describes one item or *entity*, arranged in an order based on the values of one or more *attributes*.

literature search—a search intended to create a customized bibliography that treats aspects of a research, scholarly, or topical literature of interest.

logical operators—see *Boolean logic*. See also *proximity operators*.

machine-readable form—digital; readable by computer input devices. A database is in machine-readable form if it can be processed by a computer system.

menu-driven system—an online interactive computer system in which at each step the computer user makes forced choices of actions from among several options offered by the system.

miss—a document *relevant* or *pertinent* to a search question that is not retrieved by a *search formulation*.

modem—a hardware device that converts digital signals from a computer or computer terminal to and from analog signals for transmission along communication lines.

modem program—see *communications software*.

most rational path—the path through the infinity of possible *search formulations* that maximizes *recall* and *precision* for a given search problem and database.

most specific concept first—see *successive facet strategy*.

multiple briefsearch—a search *strategy* in which the same *briefsearch* is conducted on many databases

natural language—a language in active use by a community of human beings, such as English or Russian. Contrast to *formal language*.

noise—a source of distortion of data during a communications process. In online searching, noise can be caused by electrical disturbances in the atmosphere, a poor acoustical connection between the computer terminal and the communications line, ''bad'' telephone lines, and other causes.

nonbibliographic database—any database that is not bibliographic. The class includes *referral databases* and *source databases*.

NOT—see *difference*.

numeric database—a database that contains primarily numbers.

online information retrieval—the process of using an *information retrieval system* in an online mode to satisfy an information need.

online information retrieval system—an *information retrieval system* operating with a computer, terminals, communication lines and links, *modems*, disk drives, and *databases* in *machine-readable form* that are accessible in an online, interactive mode.

online searching—see *online information retrieval*.

operational definition—a method or procedure for measuring or representing a *concept* or variable for a specific purpose.

OR—see *union*.

order of operations—the *default* order in which *Boolean* operations are carried out by a search system, if disambiguating parentheses are omitted.

paradigm—a shared understanding among scientists or scholars working in a discipline regarding the important problems, structure, values, and assumptions determining that discipline. From Thomas Kuhn's *Structure of Scientific Revolutions*.

pairwise facets search strategy—a search *strategy* in which the *intersections* of three or more *facets* (usually three) are created, a pair at a time. The *union* of the (three) solution sets is then created to obtain the final solution.

parsing rule—The separating and sorting operations performed by a *search service* on a given data *field* when the *inverted index* is prepared from the *linear file*.

pertinence—a subjective, individual relation between an information need and a document, as judged by an end-user.

phrase-indexed field—a *field parsed* as a full phrase, including blank or other special characters. Phrase-indexed fields are entered into the inverted index as a single *character string*, and must be so searched.

post-coordination—the combination of *natural language* or *controlled vocabulary* terms at the time of retrieval, as opposed to *pre-coordination* of *concepts* in the indexing vocabulary.

postings—the set of *accession numbers* associated with a given *search formulation*; loosely, the set of retrieved documents.

pragmatic communication—referring to effective communication between the source and destination of information. Pragmatic communication in online information retrieval takes place if the actions of the online *searcher* effectively address the underlying (*visceral*) need of the *end-user*. From the Shannon/Weaver model of communication.

precision ratio—the proportion of documents retrieved by a given *search formulation* that are *relevant* or *pertinent* to the information problem or question posed.

pre-coordinated system—a *controlled vocabulary* in which specific, complex *concepts* involving the *intersection* of two or more concepts are themselves elements in the indexing vocabulary. For example, the term 'database producer' pre-coordinates the concepts of *database* and *publisher*.

print file—see *linear file*.

problem context—the environment of an information problem, considering such questions as the function and purpose of the information, its role in a larger setting, etc.

problem-description language—a language used to represent an aspect of an information problem. Problem-description languages are either *natural languages* or *controlled vocabularies*.

prompt—a special character or group of characters indicating that an online computer system is ready to receive a *command* or *menu*-response from a *searcher*.

proximity operator—an operator that makes it possible to search for two or more words in combination with one another, e.g., as a phrase, or to be present in the same field or paragraph. Proximity operators are used principally to conduct searches in *natural language* fields such as title, abstract, or full text.

question-negotiation session—see *reference interview*.

recall ratio—the proportion of documents *relevant* or *pertinent* to a search question that are retrieved by a given *search formulation*.

record—see *index record*.

reference database—a database containing surrogates or representations of data, information, or knowledge. Includes *bibliographic* and *referral* databases as subclasses.

reference interview—a conversation between an *end-user* and a *search specialist*, in which the latter attempts to understand the information need of the former.

referral database—a *reference database* that contains surrogates of *entities* other than documents: persons, organizations, research projects, and others.

relevance—an objective, *semantic* relation between a document and a question, as judged by a consensus of those practicing in a discipline. See also *paradigm*.

reliability—the extent to which an *operational definition* consistently measures that which is measured.

research methodology—the specific methods and procedures used during the collection of qualitative or quantitative data in a given research study.

retrieval effectiveness—the extent to which an information retrieval search has succeeded in retrieving all relevant documents in a collection and suppressing the retrieval of all non-relevant documents.

search formulation—a command or menu-response put to an information retrieval system that results in the creating of one or more sets of *postings*.

search service—an organization providing access to *databases* in *machine-readable* form through an *online information retrieval system*.

search specialist—a librarian or other expert in *online information retrieval*.

search strategy—see *strategy*.

search system—see *online information retrieval system*.

searcher—one who uses an *online information retrieval system*, either as a *search specialist* or *end-user*.

semantic ambiguity—See *homograph*.

semantic communication—referring to the communication of meaning between an information source and destination. From the Shannon/Weaver model of communication.

soft discipline—a discipline or field of study in which fundamental concepts are vague, fuzzy, ill-defined and difficult to measure. Contrast to *hard discipline*.

source databases—a collection of records of primary sources of data or information. Source databases include *numeric, textual-numeric,* and *full text* databases as subclasses.

specificity—the precision with which concepts can be represented in a given *controlled vocabulary* or in *natural language*.

stop word—a word considered to have no value for indexing or retrieval purposes, and for which no entries are made in the *inverted index*.

strategy—an overall plan or approach to a search problem.

successive facet strategy—any search *strategy* that relies on the formation and combination of *facets* one at a time, usually with Boolean AND. The search normally terminates before all the facets of the problem have been represented and combined.

symbol—a means of representing a *concept*. The concept represented by a symbol is called its meaning. In online searching, symbols are *character strings*, or character strings combined using *Boolean logic* or *proximity operators*.

synonym—two *symbols* are synonyms if they both represent the same *concept*.

syntax—the rules governing how elements of the vocabulary of a language can be combined to form legal expressions in the language.

syntax error—a combination of vocabulary elements in a manner that is not legal in a given language.

technical communication—referring to the communication of data between an information source and destination. From the Shannon/Weaver model of communication. See also *information theory*.

textual-numeric database—a *database* that contains *numerical* data as well as textual data.

thesaurus—a *controlled vocabulary* showing relationships between terms and developed from a dynamic, growing document collection. See also *descriptor*.

time series—a set of numerical data providing several measurements of the same quantity but at different, evenly spaced, time intervals.

truncation—a search on a piece of a longer word or phrase, usually its leftmost portion.

union—the *Boolean* union of two sets of elements (A OR B) is the set of elements present in A or in B or in both A and B.

unit record—see *index record*.

validity—the extent to which *operational definitions* accurately represent the *concepts* of interest.

variable—a *concept* or factor bearing on a problem to be investigated.

visceral need—the underlying subconscious information need of an *end-user*.

word-indexed field—a *field parsed* in such a way that an entry is made in the *inverted index* for every non-*stopword* appearing in the field.

Index